The Analysis of
Judicial Reform

he Analysis of Judicial Reform

Edited by
Philip L. Dubois
University of California, Davis

LexingtonBooks
D.C. Heath and Company
Lexington, Massachusetts
Toronto

Library of Congress Cataloging in Publication Data

Main entry under title:

The analysis of judicial reform.

  Includes indexes.
  1. Courts—United States. 2. Justice, Administration of—United
States. I. Dubois, Philip L.
KF8700.A96   347.73′1   80–8947
ISBN 0–669–04480–6   347.3071   AACR2

Published simultaneously in Canada

Printed in the United States of America

International Standard Book Number: 0–669–04480–6

Library of Congress Catalog Card Number: 80–8947

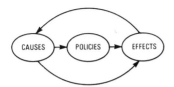

Policy Studies Organization Series

General Approaches to Policy Studies

Policy Studies in America and Elsewhere
  edited by Stuart S. Nagel
Policy Studies and the Social Studies
  edited by Stuart S. Nagel
Methodology for Analyzing Public Policies
  edited by Frank P. Scioli, Jr., and Thomas J. Cook
Urban Problems and Public Policy
  edited by Robert L. Lineberry and Louis H. Masoti
Problems of Theory in Policy Analysis
  edited by Philip M. Gregg
Using Social Research for Public Policy-Making
  edited by Carol H. Weiss
Public Administration and Public Policy
  edited by H. George Frederickson and Charles Wise
Policy Analysis and Deductive Reasoning
  edited by Gordon Tullock and Richard Wagner
Legislative Reform
  edited by Leroy N. Rieselbach
Teaching Policy Studies
  edited by William D. Coplin
Paths to Political Reform
  edited by William J. Crotty
Determinants of Public Policy
  edited by Thomas Dye and Virginia Gray
Effective Policy Implementation
  edited by Daniel Mazmanian and Paul Sabatier
Taxing and Spending Policy
  edited by Warren J. Samuels and Larry L. Wade
The Politics of Urban Public Services
  edited by Richard C. Rich
Analayzing Urban Service Distributions
  edited by Richard C. Rich
The Analysis of Policy Impact
  edited by John Grumm and Stephen Washby
Public Policies for Distressed Communities
  edited by F. Stevens Redburn and Terry F. Buss
Implementing Public Policy
  edited by Dennis J. Palumbo and Marvin A. Harder
Evaluating and Optimizing Public Policy
  edited by Dennis J. Palumbo, Stephen B. Fawcett, and Paula Wright
Representation and Redistricting Issues
  edited by Bernard Grofman, Arend Lijphart, Robert McKay, and
  Howard Scarrow
Administrative Reform Strategies
  edited by Gerald E. Caiden and Heinrich Siedentopf

Specific Policy Problems

Analyzing Poverty Policy
  edited by Dorothy Buckton James
Crime and Criminal Justice
  edited by John A. Gardiner and Michael Mulkey
Civil Liberties
  edited by Stephen L. Wasby
Foreign Policy Analysis
  edited by Richard L. Merritt
Economic Regulatory Policies
  edited by James E. Anderson
Political Science and School Politics
  edited by Samuel K. Gove and Frederick M. Wirt
Science and Technology Policy
  edited by Joseph Haberer
Population Policy Analysis
  edited by Michael E. Kraft and Mark Schneider
The New Politics of Food
  edited by Don F. Hadwiger and William P. Browne
New Dimensions to Energy Policy
  edited by Robert Lawrence
Race, Sex, and Policy Problems
  edited by Marian Lief Palley and Michael Preston
American Security Policy and Policy-Making
  edited by Robert Harkavy and Edward Kolodziej
Current Issues in Transportation Policy
  edited by Alan Altshuler
Security Policies of Developing Countries
  edited by Edward Kolodziej and Robert Harkavy
Determinants of Law-Enforcement Policies
  edited by Fred A. Meyer, Jr., and Ralph Baker
Evaluating Alternative Law-Enforcement Policies
  edited by Ralph Baker and Fred A. Meyer, Jr.
International Energy Policy
  edited by Robert M. Lawrence and Martin O. Heisler
Employment and Labor-Relations Policy
  edited by Charles Bulmer and John L. Carmichael, Jr.
Housing Policy for the 1980s
  edited by Roger Montgomery and Dale Rogers Marshall
Environmental Policy Formation
  edited by Dean E. Mann
Environmental Policy Implementation
  edited by Dean E. Mann
The Analysis of Judicial Reform
  edited by Philip L. Dubois
The Politics of Judicial Reform
  edited by Philip L. Dubois
Critical Issues in Health Policy
  edited by Ralph Straetz, Marvin Lieberman, and Alice Sardell
Rural Policy Problems
  edited by William P. Browne and Don F. Hadwiger

To the memory of my grandmother,
Sarah Asbury Goodrich

Contents

List of Figures and Tables   xi

Preface   xiii

Chapter 1   **Introduction**   *Philip L. Dubois*   1

Part I   *Perspectives on the Operation, Effectiveness, and Capacity of Courts*   15

Chapter 2   **The Twilight of Adversariness: Trends in Civil Justice**   *Kenneth M. Holland*   17

Chapter 3   **Judicial Capacity: Courts, Court Reform, and the Limits of the Judicial Process**   *Austin Sarat*   31

Chapter 4   **Data and Decisions: Judicial Reform and the Use of Social Science**   *Craig Haney*   43

Chapter 5   **Mediation and Arbitration: Their Promise and Performance as Alternatives to Court**   *Craig A. McEwen* and *Richard J. Maiman*   61

Part II   *Improving the Quality and Accountability of the Judiciary*   77

Chapter 6   **The Effects of Judicial-Selection Reform: What We Know and What We Do Not**   *Mary L. Volcansek*   79

Chapter 7   **Judicial Disciplinary Commissions: A New Approach to the Discipline and Removal of State Judges**   *Jolanta Juszkiewicz Perlstein* and *Nathan Goldman*   93

Chapter 8   **Judicial Discipline at the Federal Level: A New Response to an Old Problem**   *John H. Culver* and *Randal L. Cruikshanks*   107

Chapter 9   **Evaluating Judicial Performance: Problems of
                 Measurement and Politics**   *John Paul Ryan*   121

Part III   *The Effects of Changes in Court Structure*   135

Chapter 10   **A Tale of Two Reforms: On the Work of the
                 U.S. Supreme Court**   *Gregory A. Caldeira*   137

Chapter 11   **Creating an Intermediate Court of Appeals:
                 Work Load and Policymaking Consequences**
                 John A. Stookey   153

Part IV   *Theoretical and Empirical Perspectives on
                 Court Administration*   169

Chapter 12   **Justice-Impact Statements and Court
                 Management: And Never the Twain Shall
                 Meet**   *Cornelius M. Kerwin*   171

Chapter 13   **Alternative Models for the Organization of
                 State-Court Systems**   *Carl Baar* and
                 Thomas A. Henderson   183

Chapter 14   **Courts as Discrete Organizations and System
                 Components: The Case of the D.C. Circuit
                 Court of Appeals**   *Phillip J. Cooper*   195

                 Index   211

                 About the Contributors   219

                 About the Editor   223

List of Figures
and Tables

Figures

10–1	Increases in Cases Filed in the Supreme Court, 1880–1974	141
10–2	Four Results of an Intervention	142
10–3	State and Federal Statutes: The Number of Judicial Decisions Declaring a Law Unconstitutional	147
11–1	Level of Supreme Court Filings and Type of Access Method as Determinants of Supreme Court Work Load	160
11–2	Case Filings to the Arizona State Supreme Court, 1952–1979	163
11–3	Work Load of the Arizona State Supreme Court, 1954–1980	164
11–4	Dissent Rate for the Arizona State Supreme Court, 1962–1979	165

Tables

6–1	Studies Relating to Judicial Selection	81
7–1	Reported Cases of Misconduct Handled by Commissions, by Nature of Activity	96
7–2	Disciplinary Recommendations of Judges in Hypothetical Cases, by Composition of Commission	99
7–3	Reported Disciplinary Cases of State Supreme Courts, by Nature of Sanction	101
7–4	Effect of Commission Composition on State Supreme Courts' Disposition of Cases	102
8–1	Provisions of Three Congressional Judicial Disciplinary Bills	113

9–1   Trial Judges' Evaluations of Their Skills in Five
            Areas of Work   127

9–2   Interconnectedness of Trial Judges' Evaluations of
            Their Skills: Pearson Correlation Matrix   128

12–1   Percentage Change in Filings in Selected Districts,
            1963–1978   178

12–2   Change in Case-Load Composition in Selected
            Districts, 1963–1978   178

Preface

This book owes its origin to a symposium on judicial reform that was sponsored and funded by the National Institute of Justice and published by the *Policy Studies Journal*. Because the space limitations imposed by the journal were necessarily severe, this larger collection was created to allow a more-thorough coverage and analysis of judicial-reform issues. Some of the chapters in this book are revised and expanded versions of the contributions that first appeared in the journal, while others are presented here for the first time.

Like other collections of this kind, it was impossible to include articles touching on every topic that might be considered to fall under the rubric of judicial reform. The contributions included here are essentially directed toward the normative, methodological, and empirical issues surrounding the analysis and evaluation of policies aimed at improving the administration of the judiciary, defined broadly as the structure, staffing, and operation of the courts. Within that overall theme, the objective has been to feature works that address the major persisting issues of judicial reform, or those of particular contemporary interest, rather than the daily pragmatic concerns of those responsible for court operations. Moreover, current research efforts, investigating a wide range of reform policies such as those changing substantive legal rules (for example, those affecting judicial discretion in sentencing and juvenile-justice reform) or legal procedures, are necessarily not represented here, both because of space constraints and the desire to preserve the internal coherence of the collection.

Three distinct but interrelated types of chapters are included: (1) those that present or evaluate analyses of the effectiveness of major judicial-reform policies or that synthesize the results of prior research of this nature, (2) those that review the empirical techniques and methodological assumptions appropriate for evaluating specific judicial reforms, and (3) those that stress the importance of theoretical frameworks in the formulation and implementation of judicial reforms. Taken as a whole, the book seeks to present a broad representative sample of the work currently under way to analyze and evaluate either the results of past reforms or the prospects for future ones. A companion volume, *The Politics of Judicial Reform* (Lexington Books, 1982), focuses on the process of political change in the administration of the judiciary and on the political implications and consequences of alternative procedural, structural, and organizational arrangements of the courts.

In preparation of both the symposium issue and this book, Stuart Nagel of the Policy Studies Organization and the University of Illinois at Urbana-Champaign served as a wellspring of encouragement, advice, and information critical to the completion of these collections. My appreciation to the National Institute of Justice (NIJ) for its financial support of the symposium issue is gratefully acknowledged. Cheryl Martorana, director of the Adjudication Division of NIJ, was extremely helpful and personally supportive in the development of the symposium. Of course, no one other than the individual authors is responsible for the ideas advocated here.

During my year in Washington, D.C. (1979–1980), William B. Eldridge, director of research at the Federal Judicial Center, graciously allowed me the time and the valued staff assistance of Gloria Chamot to initiate this project. The lion's share of the work required to coordinate what now amounts to stacks of correspondence and material among publisher, editor, and contributors was magnificently performed by Brenda Petersen of the Department of Political Science at the University of California, Davis. Vickie Zinner of the University of California, Davis, was also extremely valued for keeping track of a mailing list that seemed to grow weekly.

I have dedicated this book to the memory of my grandmother because her dedication, by example, to a number of uncomplicated but essential values has left a lasting memory indeed. Her optimism in the face of life's occasional disappointments was perhaps unintentionally but unforgettably expressed to her grandsons one night during a thunderstorm that knocked down power lines and darkened the neighborhood: ''Oh well, we can always watch television.''

1 Introduction

Philip L. Dubois

In 1906, Roscoe Pound noted that popular dissatisfaction with the administration of justice "is as old as the law" (Pound 1906, p. 337). Often this dissatisfaction stems from the problem shared by all legal systems that law never seems sufficiently flexible, responsive, and adaptive to adjust to individual circumstances or to meet pressing social needs. At other times, popular criticism has been rooted in the peculiarities of the Anglo-American system of justice that has imposed substantive legal rules that many people would consider unjust or that has appeared to exalt adversarial procedures and legal advocacy at the expense of substantive justice and the discovery of truth (see Frank 1949).

Pound was equally aware of other causes of popular discontent with the judicial system, however. Although many defects in court systems are inherent in the nature of law and thus not easily remediable, Pound argued that "too much of the current dissatisfaction has a just origin in our judicial organization and procedure" (1906, p. 353). He criticized what he saw as archaic and outmoded judicial structures and processes that had produced a judicial system too often characterized by inefficiency, waste, delay, expense, and injustice.

Pound's address, delivered to the annual meeting of the American Bar Association, was not warmly received or embraced by what then was a conservative "gentlemen's club of very prosperous lawyers" (Levin and Wheeler 1979, p. 8). Over the next several decades, however, the legal profession assumed a leading role in addressing many of the problems Pound identified by proposing and seeing implemented "a remarkably consistent set of reform recommendations" concerning court organization, judicial procedure, and the recruitment and tenure of judges (see Gallas 1979, p. 29; Levin and Wheeler 1979, pp. 289–294; Berkson 1977; Volcansek 1977). In fact, so often and widely repeated were these reform recommendations that they first earned the coveted status as the "conventional wisdom" of court reform (Gallas 1976; Volcansek 1977) and then characterization as "the now dominant paradigm of judicial administration" (Gallas 1979, p. 29).

Almost precisely seventy years later, at the site of the 1906 speech, a national conference of leaders in the legal profession and the judiciary, along with distinguished legal scholars and social scientists, was held to review the reform efforts theretofore undertaken and to explore the strategies, yet untried, for dealing with courts that continued to be overloaded and slow, a judicial process growing more expensive to use and maintain, and judges found to be unqualified or otherwise unfit for office (see Levin and Wheeler 1979). Unfortunately, the efforts of those attending what was called the Pound Conference were hampered by what some participants (see Nader 1979, p. 115) recognized as the absence of available evidence to support either an adequate analysis of the causes of the major problems in court administration, an assessment of the effectiveness of the reforms attempted, or even an informed guess as to the probable effects of a proposed reform. As Wheeler (1979, p. 135) has observed, "because the field [of judicial administration] is so heavily influenced by lawyers—who are advocates by training—reform proposals have traditionally had much more advocacy than evaluation."

The decade of the 1970s, however, was an intense period of scholarly interest in uncovering the normative consequences, theoretical assumptions, and empirical evidence that might be collected to permit an evaluation of the various judicial-reform policies pursued in the shadow of Pound and other judicial-reform leaders. By 1979, critics began to openly question "the conventional understanding of the problems to be solved, the difficulties of implementation, possible negative consequences of reform measures, and the need for more explicit criteria of evaluation" (Gallas 1979, p. 29).

The chapters of this book continue in this young tradition of critical analyses of judicial-reform policies. "[T]he field of judicial administration is wide-open to evaluation and analysis, primarily because it has for so long been guided by horatory [sic] and rhetoric" (Wheeler 1979, p. 146). Moreover, as Gallas has shown, critical research can serve not just "as an antidote to naïve and overstated reformist claims" but also may "help define the areas which need further research, research that may ultimately result in more meaningful reform" (1979, p. 30).

Change in the Judicial System

In part I, Kenneth M. Holland examines the major forces causing, and the consequences of, two opposing trends in the U.S. judicial system.

On the one hand, the American system is becoming increasingly litigious—that is, individuals and groups are choosing more often than ever to resolve their differences within formal processes and structures rather than through informal and personal bargaining and compromise. As the increased case loads of the courts at least partially testify, adversariness is increasing. On the other hand, these disputes are more frequently being resolved in nonadversarial proceedings or in a nonadversarial manner within the judicial system. Many cases are diverted away from the courts by the availability and attractiveness of several nonadjudicative methods and forums for the resolution of disputes. Moreover, for various reasons related to protecting their own interests and those of their clients, lawyers now often attempt to direct clients toward negotiated settlements rather than to force resolution of disputes in the adversarial setting of the courts. When cases do reach the court system, Holland argues, the nature of adjudication has been transformed in such a way that the courts have become forums for negotiations to be conducted. Judges have become agents of conciliation and compromise rather than neutral arbiters of disputes between theoretically irreconcilable adversaries.

The courts have become less adversarial at least partially in response to criticism that the judicial process has been too slow, expensive, and inaccessible to large numbers of people. Many of the reforms promoting nonadjudicative dispute resolution, for instance, have been designed to make the judicial system work faster and at lower cost to litigants and to be available to a wider segment of the population than before. As Holland shows, however, adversariness has also been a victim of "inexorable social and political forces" that have changed the number, kinds, and complexity of disputes being brought to the courts. As Holland argues, courts today are being asked to perform a number of functions other than dispute resolution, including public policymaking and administration, which are not as easily managed within the rigidities of the traditional adversarial process (see Rifkind 1979).

The consequences of this decline in the adversarial mechanisms of justice are not yet clear. Holland suggests that the very legitimacy of the judicial system may be undermined to the extent that the public believes that justice and due process require adversarial proceedings. Increasing public awareness of the bureaucratization of the judicial process (a trend ironically accelerated by judicial reforms designed to make the process swifter, less costly, and more accessible) may undermine public support for the courts and, ultimately, popular obedience to the rule of law as expressed in judicial decisions (see Gambitta and May 1982).

The Effectiveness and Capacity of Courts

Holland's chapter casts a sharp focus on the increasing demands being pressed upon the courts and the ability or inability of the courts to process those demands within the traditional adversary framework of adjudication. In chapter 3, Austin Sarat considers a new debate that has accompanied the courts' involvement in resolving broad political, economic, and social-policy issues.

Professional discourse on courts continues to be concerned with the traditional question of whether courts should be engaging in such extensive policymaking activities in a democratic polity. There is now the additional concern, however, with whether courts are well equipped to perform such functions. Case-by-case adjudication is often viewed by critics as a process that is too rigid, inflexible, insular, incremental, and limited to rely on in designing and implementing public policies that will affect a wide spectrum of political, economic, and social interests. Other critics have questioned whether courts have "the manpower, the talent, the tools, or the authority" to be not just "dispute resolvers" but "problem solvers"—"the handymen of our society" (Rifkind 1979, pp. 58, 56, 53).

Sarat defends the capacity of the judicial process by reference to the flexibility demonstrated in the negotiation and settlement functions of courts, their historic adaptability to meet societal needs, the availability of enforcement mechanisms, and the important role courts have played in addressing policy issues that legislative and administrative institutions have been unwilling or unable to resolve.

The focus on judicial capacity will continue to be important. Only by an understanding of what courts can and cannot do well can sensible programs for court reform be designed. As Sarat shows, however, many of the strategies behind modern judicial reforms have been designed to help the courts solve conflicts that only reach the courts because other public (legislative and administrative) and private (family, church, workplace) institutions have failed. The crisis of the courts may be just one part of a larger crisis that reflects the inability of our institutions to adjust the competing interests that emerge during periods of rapid social change.

Another aspect of the current concern over judicial capacity revolves around criticisms aimed at the use by judges of scientific and social-science data to buttress the factual basis of judicial decision making. The debate is not a new one, of course, dating at least to the introduction by Louis Brandeis in 1908 of a legal brief asking the Supreme Court to take judicial recognition of certain social facts. More recently, a storm of controversy swirled around the Supreme Court's use in the case of *Brown* v. *Board of Education* (1954) of sociological and psychological data to justify its decision to desegregate the public schools. With the increasingly more complex nature of the disputes brought to the courts for resolution, and the rapid growth in the sophistication of social-science theories and empirical methodologies, the use of social-science evidence has found its way into a broader range of legal disputes than ever (see, for example, Sperlich 1980a).

In chapter 4, Craig Haney reviews the basic criticisms that have been leveled at the use of social science in judicial decision making. Social-science methods are alleged to be too imprecise and its results too probabilistic in nature to produce the degree of certainty required in the legal process. When social-science data are employed, the structure of adjudication of individual disputes is too narrow and limited to guarantee that all relevant information will be gathered and that the meaning of complex social-science findings will be fully comprehended.

Haney defends the use of social science in judicial decision making and reviews a number of proposals made to improve the courts' ability to deal competently with complex social-science information. These include better procedures to guarantee the compatibility of social-science data with the requisites of the adversary process (see also Sperlich 1980b); increased training for judges, attorneys, and law students; more assistance for judges in the form of court-appointed experts, special social-science masters, or specially trained law clerks; and formal structures or institutes to provide the courts with reliable syntheses and analyses of contemporary social-science findings.

Alternatives to Adjudication

In chapter 5, Craig McEwen and Richard J. Maiman explore some of the evidence now available on mediation and arbitration—two of the alternative processes explored in recent years to divert and resolve some of the disputes that would otherwise end up in court. Such non-adjudicative methods for resolving disputes have been advocated for a variety of reasons. For example, it is widely argued that diversion of some cases will help to relieve case-load pressures in the courts, lower court costs overall, and reduce delay in the adjudicative process (see Sander 1979). Additionally, however, such alternatives to court pre-

sumably offer disputants a less-expensive, less-intimidating, and potentially more-equitable way in which to resolve their competing claims
than full-dress court adjudication. Perceived by citizens as cheaper,
faster, and fairer, these alternatives to court are expected to make the
citizenry more willing to use the judicial system to resolve their disputes—an objective collected internationally under the rubric of access
to justice (see, for example, Cappelletti and Saulnier 1978, p. 231).

After an analysis of the rapidly growing body of literature on the
nation's experience with mediation and arbitration, McEwen and Maiman conclude that, although these alternatives are not as effective as
advocates have claimed, they nevertheless have proved to be of some
value as alternatives to courts. Mediation and arbitration do increase
court capacity by resolving some cases that would otherwise require
the attention of judges and perhaps juries. It is less certain, however,
that they lower the overall cost of the judicial system since these
processes must be supported by budgets of their own. It is also unclear
whether they expand access to justice; the judicial process is still
perceived by many citizens as formidable while others choose not to
resolve their grievances in any kind of public forum. Nevertheless, by
some measures, these methods (particularly mediation) have been
found by those who have chosen to utilize them to be highly satisfactory
in terms of cost, flexibility, and fairness—satisfaction that is reflected
in comparatively high rates of compliance with mediated judgments.

Improving the Quality and Accountability
of the Judiciary

Chapters 6 through 9 address different aspects of the problem of simultaneously assuring the quality of judicial performance, securing the
accountability of judges, and protecting the tradition of judicial independence.

A central debate in the arena of judicial reform has been over the
best way to select judges. This debate has cast the tensions among
judicial quality, accountability, and independence in high relief. As
Mary L. Volcansek shows in chapter 6, social scientists fortunately
have begun to evaluate with empirical evidence some of the claims and
counterclaims made concerning the major alternative ways in which
judges are selected in the United States—election, appointment, and
so-called merit selection and retention (see Berkson 1980). Although
this empirical evidence cannot resolve the tension among values, it can
contribute to an understanding of whether each alternative method of
selection actually achieves the objectives for which it was primarily

designed. Volcansek's analysis (and accompanying chronological table of the major studies on judicial selection) suggests that, although some of the more-extravagant claims made by supporters of the various selection systems have been undermined by empirical evidence, much remains to be known.

In no area is this assessment more appropriate than with respect to empirical studies concerning one of the leading items on the agenda of court reformers—namely, merit judicial selection. As Volcansek shows, research confirms that merit selection has been very successful in achieving its stated goal to lengthen the tenure of judicial office by increasing the security of judicial office. Conversely, analyses of the actual workings of merit retention elections and the behavior of judicial electorates have tempered what formerly was unqualified acceptance of reform claims that these elections will secure judicial accountability by providing a periodic public review of judicial performance. However, whether the merit plan has achieved its central objective of improving the quality of the judiciary through the selection process remains both unproved and only partially refuted. The many hazards associated with defining judicial quality, devising appropriate measures, and comparing results across states and selection systems have prevented a definitive answer and probably will continue to do so for the foreseeable future.

Although court reformers seek to insulate the judiciary in order to protect judicial independence and to make judicial tenure secure in order to attract well-qualified individuals to the bench, a potential problem attending these efforts is that judges may engage in unchecked abuses of power or, with years of service, develop physical or mental infirmities, thus preventing their efficient performance. Along with the adoption of mandatory-retirement laws and the shoring of judicial pension plans, all states have now adopted special structures to deal with problems of judicial misconduct and disability. These judicial-conduct commissions are responsible for reviewing complaints of judicial misbehavior or disability and for making recommendations to the state's supreme court for the discipline, removal, or retirement of judges (see ''Judicial Conduct Commissions'' 1979).

J.J. Perlstein and Nathan Goldman (chapter 7) have conducted some of the only research available on the operations of these commissions. Drawing from the results of their survey of the executive officers and members of these judicial-conduct commissions, Perlstein and Goldman offer important insights into how those responsible for checking judicial performance view their roles and the effectiveness of their efforts. Additionally, in asking their respondents to make decisions on several hypothetical complaints of judicial misconduct, the authors are able to analyze how the various kinds of individuals who serve on these commissions (judges, lawyers, and laypeople) react to different kinds of judicial misbehavior. Finally, by comparing the recommendations for discipline or removal made by judicial-conduct commissions with the sanctions ultimately imposed by state supreme courts, Perlstein and Goldman identify a relationship between commission composition and the ultimate outcome. These findings combine to allow a better understanding of the objectives of judicial disciplinary commissions, whether and how effectively they function as intended, and how different structural arrangements affect the outcome of judicial disciplinary proceedings.

Although the adoption of formal disciplinary mechanisms has proceeded rapidly in the states, the federal judicial system has only gradually (or, some would say, grudgingly) moved toward this kind of judicial reform. In chapter 8, John H. Culver and Randal L. Cruikshanks first review the nation's experience with the only disciplinary procedure provided by the federal constitution—the process of impeachment. As their chapter shows, not only has impeachment proved to be cumbersome and infrequently imposed but also inappropriate for judicial misbehavior that does not warrant removal from office. Although congressional attempts to create disciplinary methods other than impeachment date to the 1930s, the major debate over judicial discipline occurred in the decade of the 1970s. However, because of persisting questions about the constitutionality of these methods, and their potential for interfering with judicial independence, several proposals for federal disciplinary commissions were unable to secure congressional approval. Finally, however, in 1980 Congress approved the Judicial Conduct and Disability Act, which took effect in October 1981.

Rather than to establish judicial-conduct commissions modeled on the state experience, this Act designates the federal judicial councils as the primary disciplinary bodies for the federal courts, provides procedures for complaints against judges to be received, and sets disciplinary sanctions other than removal (for example, censure, reprimand) that can be imposed. In the event of judicial behavior that appears to warrant impeachment, the councils can file a report with the Judicial Conference of the United States for forwarding to the House of Representatives. In a very useful analysis, Culver and Cruikshanks examine and evaluate the composition, procedures, and potential impact of the new disciplinary mechanism. Although the authors do not expect these disciplinary methods to be much used, the public's support for, and confidence in, the courts may well depend upon the establishment and availability of methods by which judges may be called to account for their performances in office.

Chapter 9 concerns the widening debate over how best to evaluate judicial performance. The need for some way to evaluate the performance of judges is being felt or asserted more frequently in a wide variety of areas. Useful performance measures would presumably facilitate commission review of a judge alleged to be incompetent or incapacitated, provide voters with information relevant to deciding whether a sitting judge ought to be retained for another term, help citizen groups evaluate the administration of justice in their local courts, or inform legislative responses to asserted needs for additional judicial personnel and resources.

John Paul Ryan explores some of the key methodological and political issues associated with evaluating judicial performance—namely, what is to be measured, who is to conduct the evaluation, and how the evaluations are to be utilized (see Sterling, Stott, and Weller 1981). As Ryan shows, measuring judicial performance is difficult since much of what judges do is out of public view and is as often informal and administrative as it is formal and adjudicative. Additionally, the standards of quality against which judicial performance is to be compared are usually stated in terms that are vague, ill defined, value laden, and incapable of objective measurement. Moreover, Ryan's survey of nearly three thousand judges shows that judges perceive that they are not equally capable in the range of skills required by trial-court work—adjudication, administration, community relations, legal research, and negotiation. Unfortunately, few judicial-performance devices consider the fundamental diversity of the job of judging.

The political nature of judicial evaluation is revealed by Ryan's analysis of the basic models of such evaluation that are currently being used in some states. These different models reflect not so much differing perceptions as to what judges do or should be doing but rather widely divergent views as to who should be involved in the evaluative process, particularly the form and amount of citizen participation. For Ryan, the danger of citizen participation is that judicial quality will be defined in terms of judges' political compatibility with the preferences of those conducting the evaluation. Of course, that some commentators (Cohen 1982) see such political considerations as essential elements for holding judges accountable means that judicial evaluation will continue to be controversial.

The Effects of Change in Court Structure

Chapters 10 and 11 examine the anticipated effects and unintended consequences that changes in structure and jurisdiction can have upon court systems. Gregory A. Caldeira (chapter 10) considers the two major reforms, adopted by Congress, to alleviate what, on each of two separate occasions, was asserted to be an overload of cases demanding the attention of the U.S. Supreme Court. The Circuit Court of Appeals Act of 1891 was designed to provide a new level of appellate courts to handle some portion of the cases that would otherwise burden the Supreme Court. The Judges' Bill of 1925 relieved the Court of much of its obligatory jurisdiction and vested in the Court additional discretion in choosing cases for review.

Caldeira argues that most scholars have assumed uncritically that these reforms had the desired effect of reducing case filings in the Supreme Court without examining the other social, economic, and political factors that affect litigation rates generally and appellate filings in particular. Moreover, even if these reforms were the most likely cause of short-term decreases in the Court's work load, Caldeira points out that they had little long-term effect in stemming the flow of cases. Today the Court is faced once again with what many observers, including the chief justice, consider to be more demands for its attention than it can manage.

Caldeira also calls for future research to give more attention to the unintended impacts these reforms may have had upon the Court's role as a policymaking institution. Although empirical measures of judicial activism require refinement, most research suggests that granting the Supreme Court greater discretion in controlling its docket should increase its ability to become more involved in making public policy. As Caldeira shows, these research questions have a contemporary vitality and relevance to the discussions conducted over the last decade concerning whether a National Court of Appeals should be created to provide additional assistance to the Court. Chief Justice Burger has also advocated a further reduction in the Supreme Court's mandatory jurisdiction and an expansion of its discretionary powers (Cannon 1982). Although these proposed reforms may be justified as administrative measures to help the Court process its work load, Caldeira's analysis calls attention to the fact that these reforms also may have unintended effects upon the Court's policymaking potential that current research is ill equipped to predict.

Similar structural and jurisdictional reforms have been considered and adopted in many states to relieve overloaded state supreme courts. In chapter 11, John Stookey focuses his attention on research that has explored the impact of an intermediate court of appeals in a state court system upon the work load and policymaking of a state supreme court. Stookey's review of past research and his analysis of data from Arizona's reform experience show that the mere creation of an intermediate appellate court is not nearly as important as the granting of discretionary power to the state supreme court to control the size and composition of its docket. Stookey demonstrates the often overlooked point that granting discretionary control to the state's supreme court is not likely to stem the tide of filings. The case load of the supreme court will continue to increase as long as litigation rates also increase. However, the granting of discretionary power does reduce the court's work load (since fewer cases are accepted for full review on the merits) and simultaneously may expand the policymaking potential of the court by affording it more time to focus on specially selected controversial issues.

Theoretical and Empirical Perspectives on Court Administration

The last three chapters are concerned with the internal management and organization of court systems. Various changes in the ways in which courts are structured and administered are often advocated as essential to speeding the pace of litigation, reducing court costs, and improving the utilization of scarce resources (Wheeler 1979). Fortunately, in recent years, evaluation has followed upon advocacy, and "the complexity of designing sound judicial administration policies is becoming apparent" (Wheeler 1979, p. 135).

The complexity of court administration is highlighted by Cornelius Kerwin in chapter 12. Nearly a decade ago, Chief Justice Burger proposed that every new piece of congressional legislation that might create new cases for the federal courts be accompanied by a judicial-impact statement. Ideally, judicial-impact statements would sensitize Congress to the consequences of their actions for already understaffed and overburdened federal courts and would allow the courts to plan rationally for the future in anticipation of expected new kinds of litigation (see Boyum and Krislov 1980). As Kerwin shows, however, the methodological difficulties of predicting the effects of legislation on court case loads are formidable, not the least of which is the inability to predict litigant behavior. Additionally, impact statements would offer little to help individual courts since the complexities and idiosyncracies of federal district-court management mean that courts will respond quite differently to new case-load demands. Moreover, suggests Kerwin, the various political, economic, and social forces that produce litigation do not have uniform and thus easily predictable effects on the size and composition of the case loads of individual courts. Finally, because much litigation is generated from administrative and regulatory agencies, impact statements prepared only for new legislation may underestimate or even ignore what for some courts is a major source of their work load (see Davis and Nejelski 1978). Kerwin concludes hopefully but restrained; impact research can force legislators to give some attention to some of the general consequences new legislation is likely to have for the courts. However, impact research cannot yet estimate with any precision the magnitude or location of these effects—information that would be essential to make impact statements useful for improving court management.

A theoretical perspective on court administration is contributed by Carl Baar and Thomas A. Henderson in chapter 13. One of the leading assumptions of court reformers has been that the only rational administrative organization of a court system is one that is unified, with vertical lines of authority featuring centralized management, budgeting, and rule making vested in a central administrative office under the control of the state supreme court (see Wheeler 1979, p. 145; Gallas 1976). Baar and Henderson argue, however, that court reformers may want to consider a richer variety of organizational models. The authors discuss how franchise, corporate, and federal models of court organization provide a different mix of centralized and local authority. Elements of each might be appropriate in a particular court system, depending upon the available sources of court funding, the need for local flexibility and discretion, the pressures for standardization, and the strength of forces resistant to change and innovation.

Although unified court systems are often described with adjectives such as rational, advanced, and modern, Phillip J. Cooper (chapter 14) examines some of the management problems inherent in the prototype of unified court systems—the federal courts. Although centralized budget preparation, personnel administration, matériel control, and statistical analysis are useful for a variety of political and administrative reasons, Cooper argues that court management must also recognize that courts are discrete organizations that differ from one another in the size and mix of their case loads, their internal organizations, case-processing procedures, and so forth. In gauging the need for things such as additional judges or staff, systemwide administrators need to give attention to local peculiarities, problems, and circumstances.

Cooper applies this organizational perspective to the federal courts of appeals generally and the Court of Appeals for the District of Columbia Circuit in particular. Although the D.C. court shares many of the characteristics and problems of the other courts of appeals, it is distinguishable primarily by the number, complexity, and importance of the major administrative-law and national-policy questions it is asked to resolve. Gross statistical measures of court performance, such as number of cases disposed or average time from filing to disposition, are much too insensitive to the court's local peculiarities to allow either a meaningful comparison with other courts or a precise estimation of the court's needs for additional personnel and administrative support.

Cooper argues that other courts may also have organizational features that need to be considered by systemwide administrators in the preparation of budget estimates and in the allocation of personnel and matériel to the courts. Both the systemwide and organizational perspectives should be used when decisions are being made as to how resources should be used and when assessments are made as to how effectively they have been utilized.

References

Berkson, Larry C. 1977. "A Brief History of Court Reform." In L. Berkson, S. Hays, and S. Carbon (eds.). *Managing the State Courts*. St. Paul: West Publishing Co.

————. 1980. "Judicial Selection in the United States: A Special Report." 64 *Judicature* 176.

Berkson, Larry C., Steven W. Hays, and Susan J. Carbon. 1977. *Managing the State Courts: Text and Readings*. St. Paul: West Publishing Co.

Boyum, Keith, and Sam Krislov, eds. (1980). *Forecasting the Impact of Legislation on Courts*. Washington, D.C. National Academy Press.

Cannon, Mark W. 1982. "Innovation in the Administration of Justice, 1969–1981: An Overview." In Philip L. Dubois (ed.). *The Politics of Judicial Reform*. Lexington, Mass.: Lexington Books, D.C. Heath and Company.

Cappelletti, Mauro, and Julie Saulnier. 1978. "Access to Justice: Beyond the Traditional Adversary System." In T.J. Fetter (ed.). *State Courts: A Blueprint for the Future*. Williamsburg, Va.: National Center for State Courts.

Cohen, Larry C. 1982. "Assessing Judicial Competence: A Prolegomenon." In Philip L. Dubois (ed.). *The Politics of Judicial Reform*. Lexington, Mass.: Lexington Books, D.C. Heath and Company.

Davis, Robert P., and Paul Nejelski. 1978. "Justice Impact Statements: Determining How New Laws Will Affect the Courts." 62 *Judicature* 18.

Frank, Jerome. 1949. *Courts on Trial: Myth and Reality in American Justice*. Princeton, N.J.: Princeton University Press.

Gallas, Geoff. 1976. "The Conventional Wisdom of State Court

Administration: A Critical Assessment and an Alternative Approach." 2 *Justice System Journal* 35.

————. 1979. "Court Reform: Has It Been Built on an Adequate Foundation?" 63 *Judicature* 28.

Gambitta, Richard A.L., and Marlynn May. 1982. "Judicial Reform, the Myth of the Triad, and the Decline of Confidence in the Courts." In P.L. Dubois (ed.). *The Politics of Judicial Reform*. Lexington, Mass.: Lexington Books, D.C. Heath and Company.

"Judicial Conduct Commissions: The Process of Preserving Confidence in the Judiciary." 1979. 63 *Judicature* (Special Issue).

Levin, A. Leo, and Russell R. Wheeler, eds. 1979. *The Pound Conference: Perspectives on Justice in the Future*. St. Paul: West Publishing Co.

Nader, Laura. 1979. "Commentary: The Business of the Courts." In A.L. Levin and R.R. Wheeler (eds.). *The Pound Conference: Perspectives on Justice in the Future*. St. Paul: West Publishing Co.

Pound, Roscoe. 1906. "The Causes of Popular Dissatisfaction with the Administration of Justice." Reprinted in A.L. Levin and R.R. Wheeler, eds. 1979. *The Pound Conference: Perspectives on Justice in the Future*. St. Paul: West Publishing Co.

Rifkind, Simon H. 1979. "Are We Asking Too Much of Our Courts?." In A.L. Levin and R.R. Wheeler (eds.). *The Pound Conference: Perspectives on Justice in the Future*. St. Paul: West Publishing Co.

Sander, Frank E.A. 1979. "Varieties of Dispute Processing." In A.L. Levin and R.R. Wheeler (eds.). *The Pound Conference: Perspectives on Justice in the Future*. St. Paul: West Publishing Co.

Sperlich, Peter W. 1980a. "And Then There Were Six: The Decline of the American Jury." 63 *Judicature* 262.

————. 1980b. "Social Science Evidence and the Courts: Reaching Beyond the Adversary Process." 63 *Judicature* 280.

Sterling, Joyce, E. Keith Stott, Jr., and Steven Weller. 1981. "What Judges Think of Performance Evaluation: A Report on the Colorado Survey." 64 *Judicature* 414.

Volcansek, Mary L. 1977. "Conventional Wisdom of Court Reform." In L. Berkson, S. Hays, and S. Carbon (eds.). *Managing the State Courts*. St. Paul: West Publishing Co.

Wheeler, Russell. 1979. "Judicial Reform: Basic Issues and References." 8 *Policy Studies Journal* 134.

Wheeler, Russell, and Howard Whitcomb. 1977. *Judicial Administration: Test and Readings*. Englewood Cliffs: Prentice-Hall.

Part I
Perspectives on the Operation, Effectiveness, and Capacity of Courts

2 The Twilight of Adversariness: Trends in Civil Justice

Kenneth M. Holland

One of the issues on the judicial-reform agenda is whether the procedures presently available to the consumers of court services are adequate to secure the speedy, inexpensive, and just resolution of disputes. Some commentators vigorously defend the adequacy of the adversarial framework inherited from English law (see, for example, Fuller 1978); others contend that the traditional form of adjudication can no longer meet the needs of an increasingly complex society (see, for example, Fiss 1979). Complementing this normative debate is empirical disagreement on just how adversarial the present system is (see, for example, Grossman and Sarat 1979; Feeley 1975). Judging from the objects selected by researchers for analysis, most students of the judicial process assume that the system operates in an adversarial manner (Gallas 1979). This chapter seeks to answer the empirical question for the purposes of redirecting research and informing the public and professional debate over procedural reforms. The evidence is that, since 1938, there has been a substantial realignment in court activities and procedures and that the system of civil justice is, in fact, largely nonadversarial.

Evidence of an Increase in Adversariness

The Traditional Model

At the heart of the Anglo-American judicial process as it is traditionally understood lies the following conception of civil adjudication:

A lawsuit is a conflict about private rights between two individuals motivated by self-interest.

The dispute is about events that happened in the past—events that disturbed a preexisting social harmony.

A third party stands as a passive and impartial umpire who, after hearing arguments offered by each party in the presence of the other, resolves the dispute in accordance with preexisting legal rules.

The court must hear the plaintiff's claim, and the parties (the players in this game) initiate and control the definition of issues, the development of facts, and the presentation of law.

Stripped to its essentials, the adversary model requires a passive decision maker who permits each side in a conflict to present only those arguments most favorable to it (Lowi 1981, p. 360). The excellence of this mode of settling disputes is thought to lie in its accuracy in discovering facts (derived from its reliance on the principle of self-interest), its fairness (derived from the neutrality of the tribunal and the participation of both parties), and its support of individualism (the belief that each person is the best judge of his own interests and will voluntarily pursue them).

Adversariness and Litigiousness

One measure of the relevance of the traditional model is the frequency with which private disputes are adjudicated. There is evidence that in fact more conflicts exist in U.S. society than in the past and that a higher percentage of them is being translated into lawsuits than before. While from 1960 to 1978 the population of the United States increased 22 percent and the Gross National Product (GNP) increased 13 percent, the number of civil suits filed in federal trial courts grew by 134 percent and the average case load of federal trial judges increased 79 percent. Simultaneously, in Massachusetts the number of lawsuits filed more than tripled, and in Los Angeles County the number doubled (Marske and Vago 1980). Accompanying this increase in litigation from 1960 to 1978 was a substantial expansion in the size of the legal profession; the number of attorneys grew by 61 percent. How can we explain this explosion in legal activity?

In the first place, a number of developments has eased access to the courts, thus facilitating the transformation of disputes into lawsuits—for example, government-sponsored legal aid for the indigent; prepaid legal-service programs (judicare); lawyer advertising and competitive fee setting; the public-interest law movement and the practice of awarding provisional remedies, fees, and costs to so-called private attorneys general; and the class-action suit (Galanter 1974).

A second explanatory variable is the growing incapacity of nonjudicial institutions such as the local community, the church, the family, the workplace, the private association, and the cultural subgroup to resolve disputes between members. This atrophy of the ability of traditional institutions to resolve conflict is related to a decline in respect for authority, a rebellion against roles and rules, a disappearance of consensus on what constitutes proper and improper behavior, the replacement of personal relationships by episodic dealings among strangers, and an increasing focus on the primacy of personal rights over individual duties and obligations (see Nisbet 1975). It appears that, as U.S. society becomes more competitive and egalitarian, interpersonal relations become more adversarial, thereby increasing the importance of the state as an adjudicator of conflicts. Moreover, as disagreement on substantive rules has increased, procedural rules have become increasingly important. The Supreme Court's due-process revolution has greatly expanded the scope of the adversary system (Fleming 1974). Notable are the Court's attempts to transform juvenile-detention, misdemeanor, and civil-commitment hearings from paternalistic exertions of governmental power into trial-like proceedings.[1]

A third support for adversariness has been legislative activity. In the nineteenth century, legislatures abolished the practice of divorce by statute and converted the petition for dissolution of marriage into an adjudicative cause of action (Friedman 1973). Increased government regulation of the economy in the wake of the New Deal also generated substantial litigation. In the 1960s and 1970s, legislators burdened the courts by responding to a variety of social ills—pollution, sexual and racial discrimination, consumer fraud—by creating causes of action for aggrieved individuals (Macaulay 1979). A prolific source of legislatively generated adjudication has been growing government intrusion into domestic life through the creation of new legal rights such as bispousal alimony, child custody, and freedom from abuse (Grossman and Sarat 1979).

Fourth, adversariness has grown since the success of the National Association for the Advancement of Colored People (NAACP) in 1954 as interest groups who have failed to achieve their goals in the political process have increasingly sought and received satisfaction from the courts (Sorauf 1976). The courts, moreover, have responded to these organized demands on their policymaking capabilities and have created a variety of new rights and new causes of action—for example, a right to privacy and a right to humane institutional treatment. Thus, the adversary process has acquired a constituency (groups underrepresented in political forums) it did not have in the pre-Warren court period.

Finally, adversariness has in recent years acquired other new clientele in public and private institutions who increasingly turn to courtlike procedures to manage their conflicts. One finds the adversary method of dispute settlement increasingly employed by administrative agencies, universities, professional groups, and other private associations and organizations (Golding 1969; Aubert 1963). The unionization movement, of course, among both private and public employees, has generated substantial demand for formal dispute-resolution tribunals.

Evidence of a Decrease in Adversariness

The Inquisitorial Model

While England was developing its party-initiated and -controlled system for trying civil cases, a very different approach was evolving on the European continent. Whereas English courts sought to guarantee justice with procedures, European courts equated justice with particular substantive outcomes. The major features of this system (known as the inquisitorial) are as follows:

> The third party plays an active role and is seen not as a referee but as a key player in the determination of truth.
>
> The process is directed by the adjudicator—that is, it does not rely on aggressive action on the part of the claimant.
>
> The court uses its subpoena power to compel the production of evidence and to conduct its own independent investigation—that is, it calls its own witnesses and conducts its own questioning.
>
> The judge actively engages in suggesting to the parties possible settlements.
>
> The role of lawyers is restricted and their loyalty is to truth and justice rather than to their client's interests.
>
> Legal fees are set by law, and the loser must pay the fees and costs incurred by the winner. (see Kaplan, von Mehren, and Schaefer 1958)

The key element is that the judge investigates the situation for himself. The advantages of this method of trying cases are said to be accuracy (derived from the subordination of all considerations to the discovery of truth), speed, and low cost (benefits of judicial as opposed to party control).

Diversion from the Courts

The traditional adversary model is suffering both from the conceptual challenge of the European system and from nonuse. Countering the increases in legal activity and litigation rates is a trend toward diverting disputes from court and resolving them in noncourt forums employing nonadversarial procedures. Because most lawyers now prefer negotiating settlements to trying cases, the federal courts, with their broad pretrial-discovery rules, have become more attractive than their state counterparts, which have not departed as far from the adversarial model (Summers 1962). Costs, moreover, represented by delay in processing cases and by high and rapidly increasing legal fees, affect litigation decisions. Those who cannot afford formal justice are forced to resolve their grievances outside the judicial process. Even those disputants who can afford (either through their own resources or through legal aid) to seek the assistance of attorneys in vindicating their rights often find that their lawyer is unwilling to play an adversary role. The evidence is that many lawyers see themselves as problem solvers or attorneys for the situation rather than as hired guns or partisan advocates of their client's cause. Macaulay (1979) found that lawyers prefer to play a conciliatory role; they attempt to work out a solution that reflects a balance of all the competing interests. They regard themselves as therapists or counselors and will often try to persuade or coerce their clients to moderate their demands and to think in terms of the best interests of everyone involved.

This abandonment of the adversary posture by lawyers is due to a number of factors: the belief that adversariness impedes out-of-court settlements; ethically motivated demands for lawyers to assume responsibility for their clients' actions; the fact that client interests and attorney interests are never identical; the financial advantages of resolving large numbers of cases quickly; a reluctance to conduct legal research (a successful mediator need know little law); the need to develop cooperative relationships with other lawyers; and pressure from overburdened courts to regard adjudication as a last resort, as a sign of failure (see Kutak 1980; Yale Law Journal 1975). As a consequence in part of this reversal in role, "almost all civil cases are settled between the setting of the trial date and the trial itself" (Ball 1980, p. 148).[2]

Both the federal and state governments, moreover, alarmed at the perceived legalization of U.S. society, have consciously sought to divert civil disputes from the courts either by supporting existing, or by creating new, informal and personalized machinery for the nonadversary resolution of conflicts (Marske and Vago 1980). These nonadversarial alternatives include community courts, neighborhood-justice centers, small-claims courts, arbitration and mediation services, ombudsmen, newspaper action lines, and consumer-oriented attorneys general. The Law Enforcement Assistance Administration (LEAA) has sponsored instruction in the mediation of family squabbles and neighborhood conflicts, and the Ninety-Sixth Congress encouraged the development of nontraditional mechanisms by enacting the Dispute Resolution Act of 1980. Legislators have also eased the burden on the courts in some areas by eliminating causes of action, thereby avoiding the necessity for a formal means of dispute settlement; so-called no-fault-divorce and automobile-accident laws are prime examples (see Rubenstein 1976).

A final influence diverting disputes from formal adversary forums is the spreading bureaucratization of American life. The systematization and rationalization of private and public activity undermine procedural formalism by subordinating individual rights to organizational goals. Administrators manage conflicts so as to maximize the interests of the organization and to forestall grievance proceedings (Marske and Vago 1980). Courts, of course, are bureaucracies, and their organizational interests (such as speed and efficiency), as well as the interests of each participant (for example, minimizing time spent in court), work against the employment of adversarial procedures and in favor of negotiated outcomes (see Feeley 1979).

The Transformation of Adjudication

Adversariness is declining not only because many disputes that would have been adjudicated in the past are not finding their way into court but also because many of the disputes reaching courts are not being processed in the traditional manner. Even though court case loads in the aggregate indicate an increase in litigation, the number of contested cases has declined (Grossman and Sarat 1979). In major cities, 75 percent of landlord-tenant and creditor-debtor cases end in default judgments (Rubenstein 1976, pp. 66–67). Divorce cases, originally adversarial, are now almost entirely uncontested and are resolved by the manipulation of the parties' consent (Chayes 1976). The procedures followed are better described as bureaucratic and cooperative than adversarial. Juvenile and civil-commitment proceedings typically lack key adversarial features, Supreme Court decisions notwithstanding. The evidence is that trial courts have come to do fewer formal dispute resolutions and a larger proportion of routine, cut-and-dried administration (Friedman and Percival 1976). Trial judges are performing more clerical functions, simply validating plaintiff claims or outcomes negotiated by the parties. The rise in summary dispositions and the decline in formal opinions and findings also indicate that the overwhelming percentage of cases is routine and involves no real dispute (Friedman and Percival 1976).

Even when faced with real adversary parties, judges may take their cues from the inquisitorial rather than the adversarial model. Trial judges increasingly feel free to participate in examining witnesses and to summon witnesses whom neither litigant has called. Judges are especially likely to call scientific or technical experts or to investigate scientific literature on their own initiative (Sperlich 1980). Another indication of judicial abandonment of the passive, umpirelike role is the widespread belief that judges must actively manage cases to induce settlement and, thereby, to ensure efficiency. The National Center for State Courts and the Federal Judicial Center stress managerial skills in their judicial training programs, and managerial aptitude was one of President Carter's principal criteria for selecting judges. The replacement of the master by the individual calendar, the use of bifurcated trials, and the employment of pretrial conferences have amplified judicial control over litigation (Holland 1977). The Federal Rules of Civil Procedure (FRCP) have made a major contribution in transforming the judicial role in the inquisitorial direction: The rules authorize judges to manage the discovery phase of litigation and to sanction dilatory attorneys; judges may broaden the scope of litigation by joining all litigable issues between the parties; and because the FRCP abolished the distinction between actions at law and equity, judges may deny the right to trial by jury where it existed before. The adoption of the FRCP in 1938 represented a defeat for adversarial common-law procedure and a victory for inquisitorial equity procedure (see Holland 1981).

The European model was explicitly adopted by the leaders of the successful small-claims movement. Small-claims judges prefer to work out mutually satisfactory compromise solutions rather than to make decisions without the parties' concurrence; the parties' lawyers play a minor role and in fact are not welcomed; the judges actively elicit the facts surrounding the dispute and the feelings of the parties; and the emphasis is on preserving ongoing relationships rather than the vindication of rights (Sarat 1976).

The form of adjudication has changed in order to accommodate judges' administrative and inquisitorial roles. Courts have surrounded themselves with adjunct agencies and experts to facilitate fact determination and negotiation—for example, court-centered marriage-counseling agencies, magistrates, and special masters.

Complementing this increase in administrative activity has been a growth in the policymaking activity of judges. Instead of resolving narrowly drawn conflicts, judges are often called upon to decide broad issues of public policy—for example, school desegregation, employment discrimination, antitrust, reapportionment, and environmental management (Chayes 1976). In these public-law cases, the judge faces not two adversaries but an array of complexly related interest groups; the judge and not the lawyers guides the case and directs the factual inquiries. The FRCP, the Administrative Procedure Act of 1946, and a series of Warren Court decisions made possible this expansion in political activity by liberalizing the rules of jurisdiction and justiciability that had evolved from the adversary private-law model. Policy formulators need information, and judges are increasingly relying on amicus curiae briefs, ''the prime departure from the traditional system of justice'' (Barker 1967, p. 51), and outside experts. In these cases the assumption is no longer made that the victim is the best spokesperson for the plaintiff's interests or that the victim will be the beneficiary of the remedy. Also, the defendant is not necessarily seen as a wrongdoer or as the person who must provide the remedy (Fiss 1979).

Finally, dramatic change has occurred in judicial attitudes toward the scope of remedies to which plaintiffs are entitled. By exercising their equitable injunctive power, judges have reorganized and taken on the day-to-day management of mental institutions, police departments, schools, prisons, welfare agencies, and housing authorities in order to remedy threatened or abridged constitutional rights (Fiss 1979).

The cumulative effect of these changes has been to alter the way Americans conceptualize litigation. Some observers of recent legal history believe that the inquisitorial public-law model is quickly replacing the adversarial private-law conception of adjudication as the modern paradigm of legal action (see Nonet and Selznick 1978; Chayes 1976).

Reasons for the Waning of Adversariness

The significant alterations we are witnessing in the adversary system are in response to two pressures: (1) criticism of the system from both the Right and the Left and (2) underlying social forces. Business interests (other than creditors and landlords) have lost faith in the judicial system because it does not provide the climate of legal stability essential to business with speedy, inexpensive, and predictable decisions (Friedman 1973).[3] Corporations prefer to settle disputes, with each other, by means of commercial arbitration and, with consumers, by negotiation.

Most critical comment, however, has come from the Left. Those who thought in the 1960s that the expansion of legal services was a solution to the problems of the poor have become disillusioned. There is such a perceived disparity between the resources of rich plaintiffs and poor defendants that the adversary system (which assumes equality between the litigants) consistently generates unjust results (Fiss 1979; Hurst 1950). Not only does legalism benefit the haves at the expense of the have-nots, but also it erodes community cohesion and invites an excess of confrontation (see Galanter 1974). The Left favors alternative dispute-resolution mechanisms and cites the ability of undeveloped and socialist societies to resolve conflicts noncontentiously. These critics believe that the fact-finding capacities of adversary procedures are feeble and that they promote a mindless formalism at the expense of justice (Frank 1949).

Criticism, however, has not been the only source of procedural change. The adversary process has been the victim of a number of inexorable social and historical forces. As law became more sophisticated and lawyers more professional, the legal system became increasingly technical, slow, and costly, with the result that ordinary disputes simply drained out of the system, leaving mostly uncontested, routine cases (Friedman and Percival 1976). Nevertheless, since 1960, the absolute number of cases filed has dramatically increased, forcing procedural changes to facilitate efficiency, such as the informal pretrial conference and the use of summary, nonreasoned dispositions (Fiss 1979). The increased complexity of cases and interest-group pressure to tackle political issues have also forced important modifications in the traditional model (Read and McGough 1978). Courts simply cannot perform all the functions we assign to them—dispute resolution, norm enforcement, administration, policymaking, and social change—by staying within the adversary framework (Hurst 1950).

More profound, changes in adjudicatory forms reflect changes in U.S. society. The adversary system developed in the simplicity of the seventeenth and eighteenth centuries; contemporary society is marked, however, by the domination of large-scale organizations, the free market has been replaced by government and corporate control, and the individual is largely dependent on organizationally supplied benefits (Fiss 1979; Chayes 1976). In the welfare-bureaucratic state, the typical dispute is not between equals but between an individual and an organization (forcing judges to offset the imbalance), and it is of a kind that occurs repeatedly in enormous numbers—for example, termination of welfare benefits or employment (forcing summary procedures) (Rubenstein 1976).

The final force eroding adversariness is the rise of what Elliott (1974) calls the guardian ethic—the belief that a system based on economic freedom and laissez faire subjects the individual to too many risks. When Americans lost faith in the benefits of uncontrolled competition and unbridled individualism, one of the major props of the adversary form of adjudication collapsed (Frank 1949). A winner-takes-all judicial system is out of place in a political system that seeks to minimize risk. Judicial passivity is inappropriate in a society that aims to protect the weak against the strong and where the state performs a therapeutic as well as a regulatory role in social life (see Lasch 1977).

Implications

The forces undermining adversariness appear to be overpowering the forces supporting it. The resulting flight from the courts and the transformation in the form of adjudication have a number of implications. Researchers may alter the focus of their efforts from the dispute-resolution dimension of judicial activity to the administrative and policymaking functions of courts. The adoption of inquisitorial methods may be seen to interfere with the capacity of courts to resolve conflicts, thus making them even less attractive to disputants.

The great danger, however, is not loss of business but loss of public support. There appears to be a close relationship in the popular mind among adversariness, due process, and legitimacy (Cramton 1976; Sarat 1977). By maintaining the appearance of a neutral decision maker and equality between the contending parties, the adversary process generates an aura of fairness that inquisitorial proceedings do not (witness the negative connotation of the word *inquisition*). Moreover, if Lowi is correct that, in a democracy, passivity is the "key to the secret of judicial power and judicial legitimacy" (1981, p. 361), then a weakening of the adversary process may lead to popular demands to make the judiciary more accountable or to strip judges of their policymaking and other discretionary powers. A nonadversarial civil system is bound to influence criminal proceedings in such a way as to attenuate further the presumption of the accused's innocence, and the prevalence of equitable procedures and remedies in civil cases cannot but undermine the autonomy of the law. In short, the loss, no matter how inevitable, of adversariness (with its virtues as well as its vices) may well pose a threat to the legitimacy of judging.

Notes

1. See, for example, *In re Gault,* 387 U.S. 1 (1967); *Argersinger* v. *Hamlin,* 407 U.S. 25 (1972); and *Addington* v. Texas, 99 S.Ct. 1804 (1979).

2. The overwhelming majority of criminal cases is terminated by plea bargaining, where prosecutors and defense attorneys also act as counsel for the situation (Cole 1970; Feeley 1979).

3. Survey research supports this lack of confidence; those who have been involved in litigation (both winners and losers) are less satisfied with the legal system than those to whom it remains remote (Sarat 1977).

References

Aubert, Vilhelm. 1963. ''Competition and Dissensus: Two Types of Conflict and of Conflict Resolution.'' 7 *Journal of Conflict Resolution* 26.

Ball, Howard. 1980. *Courts and Politics: The Federal Judicial System.* Englewood Cliffs, N.J.: Prentice-Hall.

Barker, Lucius J. 1967. ''Third Parties in Litigation: A Systemic View of the Judicial Function.'' 29 *Journal of Politics* 41.

Chayes, Abram. 1976. ''The Role of the Judge in Public Law Litigation.'' 89 *Harvard Law Review* 1281.

Cole, George F. 1970. ''The Decision to Prosecute.'' 4 *Law and Society Review* 331.

Cramton, Roger C. 1976. ''Judicial Law Making and Administration.'' 36 *Public Administration Review* 551.

Elliott, Ward E.Y. 1974. *The Rise of Guardian Democracy: The Supreme Court's Role in Voting Rights Disputes, 1845—1969.* Cambridge: Harvard University Press.

Feeley, Malcolm M. 1975. ''The Effects of Heavy Caseloads.'' Presented at the Annual Meeting of the American Political Science Association.

———. 1979. *The Process Is the Punishment: Handling Cases in a Lower Criminal Court.* New York: Russell Sage Foundation.

Fiss, Owen M. 1979. ''Foreword: The Forms of Justice.'' 93 *Harvard Law Review* 1.

Fleming, Macklin. 1974. *The Price of Perfect Justice: The Adverse Consequences of Current Legal Doctrine on the American Courtroom*. New York: Basic Books.

Frank, Jerome. 1949. *Courts on Trial: Myth and Reality in American Justice*. Princeton: Princeton University Press.

Friedman, Lawrence M. 1973. *A History of American Law*. New York: Simon and Schuster.

Friedman, Lawrence M., and Robert Percival. 1976. "A Tale of Two Courts: Litigation in Alameda and San Benito Counties." 10 *Law and Society Review* 267.

Fuller, Lon L. 1978. "The Forms and Limits of Adjudication." 92 *Harvard Law Review* 353.

Galanter, Marc. 1974. "Why the 'Haves' Come Out Ahead: Speculations on the Limits of Legal Change." 9 *Law and Society Review* 95.

Gallas, Geoff. 1979. "Court Reform: Has It Been Built on an Adequate Foundation?" 63 *Judicature* 28.

Golding, Martin P. 1969. "Preliminaries to the Study of Procedural Justice." In G. Hughes (ed.). *Law, Reason, and Justice: Essays in Legal Philosophy*. New York: New York University Press.

Grossman, Joel B., and Austin Sarat. 1979. "Adversariness and Adjudication: Explaining the Legitimacy of Courts." Presented at the Eleventh World Congress of the International Political Science Association.

Holland, Kenneth M. 1977. "William J. Campbell: Case Study of an Activist U.S. District Judge." 3 *Justice System Journal* 143.

————. 1981. "The Federal Rules of Civil Procedure: A Policy Evaluation." 3 *Law and Policy Quarterly* 209.

Hurst, James W. 1950. *The Growth of American Law: The Law Makers*. Boston: Little, Brown & Co.

Kaplan, Benjamin, Arthur T. von Mehren, and Rudolf Schaefer. 1958. "Phases of German Civil Procedure I and II." 71 *Harvard Law Review* 1193, 1443.

Kutak, Robert J. 1980. "Coming: The New Model Rules of Professional Conduct." 66 *American Bar Association Journal* 47.

Lasch, Christopher. 1977. *Haven in a Heartless World: The Family Besieged*. New York: Basic Books.

Lowi, Theodore J. 1981. *Incomplete Conquest: Governing America*, 2d ed. New York: Holt, Rinehart & Winston.

Macaulay, Stewart. 1979. "Lawyers and Consumer Protection Laws: An Empirical Study." Working paper, Disputes Processing Research Program, University of Wisconsin—Madison.

Marske, Charles E., and Steven Vago. 1980. "Law and Dispute Processing in the Academic Community." 64 *Judicature* 165.

Nisbet, Robert. 1975. *Twilight of Authority*. New York: Oxford University Press.

Nonet, Phillipe, and Philip Selznick. 1978. *Law and Society in Transition: Toward Responsive Law*. New York: Harper & Row.

Read, Frank T., and Lucy S. McGough. 1978. *Let Them Be Judged: The Judicial Integration of the Deep South*. Metuchen, N.J.: Scarecrow Press.

Rubenstein, Leonard S. 1976. "Procedural Due Process and the Limits of the Adversary System." 11 *Harvard Civil Rights—Civil Liberties Law Review* 48.

Sarat, Austin. 1976. "Alternatives in Dispute Processing: Litigation in a Small Claims Court." 10 *Law and Society Review* 339.

———. 1977. "Studying American Legal Culture: An Assessment of Survey Evidence." 11 *Law and Society Review* 427.

Sorauf, Frank J. 1976. *The Wall of Separation: The Constitutional Politics of Church and State*. Princeton, N.J.: Princeton University Press.

Sperlich, Peter W. 1980. "Social Science Evidence in the Courts: Reaching Beyond the Adversary Process." 63 *Judicature* 280.

Summers, Marvin R. 1962. "Analysis of Factors That Influence Choice of Forum in Diversity Cases." 47 *Iowa Law Review* 933.

Yale Law Journal. 1975. "Note: The Role of Counsel in the Civil Commitment Process: A Theoretical Framework." 84 *Yale Law Journal* 1540.

3

Judicial Capacity: Courts, Court Reform, and the Limits of the Judicial Process

Austin Sarat

The 1970s were marked by a surge of interest in courts and the performance of the American judiciary. At one and the same time we were told of the rise of an "imperial judiciary" (Glazer 1975), of a movement toward "government by judiciary" (Berger 1978), that we were asking too much of our courts (Rifkind 1976), and that courts were losing their function as one of society's major dispute-resolution institutions (Friedman and Percival 1976). It appeared that, if trends were to continue, there would be a simultaneous dispersal and concentration of judicial functions with an ever greater investment of resources in a small number of major complex cases (see Galanter 1980). While some seemed to applaud this trend (Chayes 1976; Fiss 1978), an equally large and vocal group warned that it would damage both the courts and the society (see, for example, Rosenberg 1972; Cox 1976a, 1976b; Rehnquist 1978; Winter 1979).

Paralleling the evolution in judicial functions has been an evolution in the nature of our discourse about courts. Traditionally, that discourse was framed by an obsession with the undemocratic—that is, nonmajoritarian-character of judicial review and almost exclusive focus on the Supreme Court (see, for example, Thayer 1891; Commager 1950). Traditionally, the major preoccupation of critics of the courts was the question of judicial legitimacy. Do the courts have a right to interpose their judgments against the will of law-making institutions that, at least theoretically, are responsive to the expression of public preferences? Ingenious attempts to define judicial legitimacy and to identify indicators of its presence or absence did little, however, to put to rest the legitimacy debate (see Black 1960; Casper 1976). Indeed, even today questions of legitimacy still animate discussions of the role of courts in American society (compare Berns 1979 and Chayes 1976). I detect, however, a shift in emphasis, a shift away from an exclusive preoccupation with legitimacy and toward the issue of judicial capacity—that is, the ability of courts to effectively discharge their responsibility.

This neither means that considerations of legitimacy are no longer important in assessing the role of courts nor that the language of judicial capacity is entirely new in the literature on courts. Over twenty years ago, Bickel and Wellington warned

> The point is that the courts will draw from a body of experience not germane to the problem they will face. Given their limited means of informing themselves and the episodic nature of their efforts to do so, they will only dimly perceive the situations on which they impose their order. Even if they do perceive, they will necessarily come too late with a pound of "remedy" where a smaller measure of prevention was needed. Their rules, tailored to the last bit of trouble, will never catch up with the next and different dispute. They will allow or forbid and be wrong in either event. . . . All of this will not only, by its sheer volume, divert the energies of courts from their proper sphere but will also tend to bring the judicial process into disrepute by exposing it as inadequate to a task with which it should never have been entrusted. [1957, p. 25][1]

Their warning has most recently been echoed in Donald Horowitz's much-celebrated book, *The Courts and Social Policy* (1977). Judicial capacity as an issue has grown more important as the volume and range of judicial business has reached new peaks.

Unlike questions of legitimacy, the capacity issue is clearly linked to policy and reform concerns (Sarat 1980), concerns for altering the jurisdiction of federal courts and/or introducing procedural innovations and/or encouraging the development of nonjudicial alternatives to courts. There is demonstrable interest among judges, legislators, and others with responsibilities in and for the courts in identifying what courts can and cannot do well and in introducing reforms designed to eliminate trouble cases.

The discourse of judicial capacity has redirected attention among scholars and policymakers away from the traditional preoccupation with the Supreme Court toward trial courts. This is not to say that there is no longer a rich and important critical commentary on that court or its decisions. Such is surely not the case (see, for example, Ely 1980). However, as we have come to recognize the significance of trial courts, it has become evident that their major activities and responsibilities involve the evaluation of fact and the implementation of legal rights and remedies. The literature on judicial capacity is almost exclusively devoted to evaluating or commenting upon their performance in those activities (see Kolodner and Fishman 1978; Chayes 1976).

The development of interest in judicial capacity thus has important consequences for the way we study courts and the way we perceive and respond to their institutional problems. That interest may lead in one of two directions. It may frame and encourage those who wish to develop a focused agenda for court improvement (see Horowitz 1977), or it may lead to a recognition of a linkage between the performance of courts and the dilemmas and problems of liberal legalism and the liberal state (Unger 1976; Cavanagh and Sarat 1980). The direction chosen is very important both for courts and students of courts.

The Diagnosis and Its Limits

Despite its promise, the discourse on judicial capacity has, I think, failed, to this point, to accomplish a major redirection. This is largely a result of its own flaws and intrinsic limits. It is my purpose, in the remainder of this chapter, to identify those flaws and limits. I write in the guise of a sympathetic critic of an emerging research and policy concern. I am confident that, unless and until those flaws and limits are recognized, the literature on judicial capacity will not provide the kind of policy and practical payoff it seems to promise.

Defining and Appraising Judicial Capacity

I have already suggested that the phrase *judicial capacity* is simply one way of talking about the effectiveness of courts as institutions. It is, however, fair to suggest that neither judicial capacity nor *judicial effectiveness* is very precise in its meaning. One cannot readily point to a catalogue of definitions that have been self-consciously attached to either. The neglect of definition has had the effect of encouraging confusion in the employment of the concepts of judicial capacity and effectiveness. As one reads the literature, one frequently encounters statements that merge empirical or descriptive and evaluative or pre-scriptive elements. Horowitz (1977, p. 293), for example, argues that "where episodic intervention [by courts] would not be enough [to effectively resolve a problem], that is a sign that there is no judicial question presented." Courts' *cannot* statements merge with courts' *should not* statements. This is rather odd since Horowitz himself (1977, p. 18) suggests that the question of capacity refers "not to whether the courts *should* perform certain tasks but to whether they *can* perform them competently." Furthermore, Horowitz provides no clear and unambiguous indicators of capacity, no measures of performance. The problem does not belong to Horowitz alone, however. Measurement of judicial performance, as well as the performance of other legal institutions, has not, to this point, made dramatically impressive advances (see, for example, Wildhorn et al. 1977). It is, therefore, difficult to develop a literature around a concept that is neither clearly defined nor clearly operationalizable.

That difficulty has not, however, deterred Horowitz and others from making judgments about what courts can and cannot do well. Assessments of judicial capacity most often begin by positing a series of attributes that are typically associated with, or are essential to, adjudication (Fuller 1979). Notice the shift in language from courts to adjudication. What is assumed, if not argued, is that the most significant aspect of American courts is their role in deciding cases. Once the attributes of adjudication are set forth, analysis proceeds by examining the fit between what adjudication is and must be and the characteristics of cases decided by courts. It is then argued that courts should do only what they can do well and that what they can do well is fixed by the structure of adjudication (Horowitz 1977; for a contrary view, see Fiss 1979).

Most commentary on judicial capacity has focused on one of three relatively broad categories of cases: (1) cases arising out of ongoing personal relations (see Cratsley 1978); (2) cases involving complex factual or scientific issues (Boyer 1972); and (3) cases involving questions of social policy (Horowitz 1977). Of these, perhaps the most controversial are the last, which raise questions not only of the effectiveness of courts but also of their relation to executive and legislative institutions as well. Social-policy cases (which I understand to refer to litigation directly raising questions of a public nature with predictably widespread impact and consequences) seem to raise new issues for courts, to depart from traditional styles of litigation, and, therefore, to call for the kind of innovativeness and activism that excites critics of the courts (see Chayes 1976; Eisenberg and Yeazell 1980).

Critics usually argue that social-policy cases threaten the capacity of courts because they cannot be dealt with within the accepted framework of adjudication (Graglia 1976; Schaffer 1976). Because adjudication is an adversary process between two opposing parties, courts do not have adequate mechanisms for insuring that all who are affected by a particular social policy are before them. Absent a full representation of interests, courts will not be able to fully ascertain necessary facts. Furthermore, because adjudication involves case-by-case decision making, courts are said not to be able to understand the context and conditions out of which social-policy cases arise, nor to detect and respond to the underlying pattern of problems (Yeazell 1977; Mishkin 1978). As Horowitz argues, "the judicial process is prone to carve up related transactions and to treat as separate those events and relationships that are intertwined in social life" (1977, pp. 259–260).

Courts, we are told, must render decisions in cases properly before them, in accordance with preexisting legal rights, rights requiring a clear assignment of guilt or blame. As a result, judicial decision making is rigid, inflexible, and coercive—ill suited to social-policy issues in which flexibility and adaptability are necessary for optimum results. Finally, adjudication provides no mechanism for supervising and analyzing the consequences of court-policy decisions. In short, critics see courts as failing in the area of social policy because of built-in defects in the judicial decision-making process, defects of information, decisional style, and adaptability.

Limits of Perspective and Analysis

In my view, the critics have made several important errors that limit the utility of their analysis and prescription. First is the tip of the iceberg and the worst-case mistake. Critics of judicial capacity typically begin their work by narrowing the focus of inquiry from courts as institutions to adjudication as a decision-making process. Adjudication is not, however, coextensive with what courts do; indeed, adjudication is quite clearly the tip of the iceberg in all categories of cases, including those raising important social-policy issues (Galanter 1980). Judicial decision making on the merits of cases and on the details of remedies is one of the rarest of judicial activities. This is not to say that it is insignificant or to argue that it is not the most important thing that courts do (I am inclined, however, to disagree with this last proposition), but adjudication remains only one among many aspects of the work of courts.

More frequent than adjudication is the role of the courts in facilitating, encouraging, or promoting negotiated settlements. In many cases, there is no formal judge involvement, and in others there is no clear break between negotiation and adjudication (see Buckle and Buckle 1979; Diver 1979). In cases that do come to judges for decision, the continuity of the negotiation process may be interrupted only temporarily. Social-policy decisions may simply redirect the focus of that process to the remedial phase. Such decisions are often ''little more than judicial opinions blessing settlements negotiated by the parties. . . . [T]he intervention is initially mild, allowing defendants to devise programs that will square institutional conditions with constitutional requirements'' (Eisenberg and Yeazell 1980, p. 493). There is ample evidence that remedies and decrees produced in social-policy cases result from a judicially mandated process of consultation and bargaining between the parties.

Social-policy litigation does not displace negotiation and compromise; it is frequently an essential precondition to it. Many disadvantaged interests would never get to the bargaining table without filing lawsuits; our pluralistic society is not, for example, noted for the political clout it confers upon convicted felons and retarded children. Granting that altering the conditions that invade the rights of these groups should proceed by negotiations involving all affected parties, there remains the necessity of triggering such negotiations and ensuring that normally submerged interests are accorded the weight to which the law entitles them. This courts can do simply by threatening a judgment that may well be inferior to an alternative arrangement the parties can work out on their own. "The court's role . . . is to make sure that issues are addressed and choices made, not to make those choices itself" (Diver 1979, p. 92). The threat of a remedy fashioned by a judge on his own usually works to bring the parties together to work out a mutually agreeable course of remedial action. The argument that judges do not have the training or experience to devise appropriate solutions ignores the fact that "a large number of the institutional cases end in consent orders, and in most others agreement among the parties significantly reduces the scope of the dispute" (Diver 1979, p. 78).

What should most concern those interested in judicial capacity is whether courts can promote negotiation and settlements that would not otherwise occur or be attained. By the threat of adjudication that would limit party control over the outcome of disputes (Shapiro 1975), courts may stimulate genuine attempts at settlement. The capacity of the courts to promote such efforts is as much a function of their organization and procedures as their capacity to render effective decisions.

Finally, it seems quite odd that discussions of judicial capacity should proceed on a worst-case basis. For every failure of the judicial process in social policy, an equal number of successes could be cited. We learn little about judicial performance by concentrating on judicial failure. As in the study of policy impact, documenting individual instances of success or failure is less useful than uncovering the conditions that seem to influence the ability of courts to perform the full range of their activities.

The second error concerns the logic of form and function. Critics of judicial capacity seem to assume that the attributes of adjudication and the structure of courts have some fixed a priori status. The legitimacy of courts is thereby made a function of their fidelity to those attributes and that structure; what courts can do is determined by what courts are. Function follows form.

However, no empirical answer exists concerning the relationship of form and function. The assumption that the form of adjudication and the structure of courts is fixed is, I think, motivated by, or explicable in terms of, a particular political bias in favor of resisting access to, or reducing the work load of, courts. If one assumes that form is fixed or that the form of adjudication has some immutable moral value (Fuller 1979), then deficiencies in capacity can only be redressed by removing cases that produce such deficiencies from the courts.

In thinking about the logic of form and function, we should think about the basis upon which institutions like an independent judiciary are established. Such thought will reveal quickly that such institutions are established to accomplish some social task or to satisfy some social need, not to satisfy some aesthetic sense of precision in design. As needs change, we expect our political institutions to develop and adapt to meet them (see, for example, Huntington 1968). It may fairly be said that the legitimacy of political institutions is itself a function of their ability to satisfy social needs, whether those needs be for the maintenance of order or the relief of suffering. There is no reason why the courts should be any different. There are limitations, of course, on the extent to which institutions, especially our courts, can respond to changing social needs. In the case of judicial institutions, those limits are established by the requirements of due process of law (Cavanagh and Sarat 1980). However, unlike some axiomatic or a priori limitations, those derivable from due process are themselves both broad and flexible and are within the control of the courts.

The history of courts in the United States is, in fact, a history of adaptation (Shapiro 1975). The courts have evolved, or had imposed on them, numerous procedural innovations and structural changes designed to improve judicial performance or to update court processes. Such innovations and changes have not been as successful as they have been ubiquitous (Nimmer 1978), but they are clearly an important part of U.S. judicial history.

This is as much the case in the area of social policy as it is in other types of litigation. Consider, for example, the often noted inability of courts to implement, monitor, and supervise their decisions. It is true that courts do not have the kind of permanent bureaucratic structures that would appear necessary to insure implementation and evaluation in complex cases. It is true that they often rely on the initiative of one of the parties to bring failures of compliance to their attention. Nevertheless, courts have the ability to employ specialists, on an ad hoc basis, who can help design as well as monitor court decrees. The special master is the most prominent example (Project 1978).

Where a court seeks to become involved on a continuing basis with a complex institution like a prison or mental hospital, a special master may help compensate for the judge's lack of familiarity with details and procedures of the organization under supervision. Reliance on a special master violates none of the requisites of due process. In addition, a court can build a monitoring capacity into a decision by requiring regular reports or periodic hearings on the progress of implementation. Alternatively, the court may charge a special master "to report on the defendant's compliance with the decree and on the achievement of the decree's goals" (Project 1978, p. 828). These devices seem to be quite adequate for providing judges with the ability to oversee and to adjust the way in which decisions or consent decrees work. Their use demonstrates the adaptive capabilities of judicial institutions, capabilities that critics of judicial performance often neglect or ignore. In the end, such adaptability means that greater continuity exists in the functions of courts than in their forms and structures (Fiss 1979; Hurst 1950).

The significance of the form-and-function discussion is, as I suggested, to be found not so much in the annals of history as in the politics of judicial reform. Liberated from an axiomatic or a priori conception of judicial form, the very structure of courts becomes an object of attention. Policymakers are freed to assess the costs and benefits of altering jurisdiction, seeking nonjudicial alternatives, or upgrading judicial structures and procedures. The final choice may, of course, still be to limit jurisdiction, but at least it can be made with a clear sense of the priority of social need over institutional purity. Liberating discourse about capacity from the logic of its usual assumptions about form and function will increase its policy relevance, its historical accuracy, and its understanding of the context in which courts and other political institutions operate.

The third error of critics of judicial capacity is in not making comparison explicit. Courts have varying capacity to perform effectively in processing different kinds of cases. Pronouncing courts ineffective in social-policy matters is, however, the beginning, not the end, of the analysis. Capacity is a relative judgment that can only be made as the result of explicit comparisons between courts and legislative or executive institutions (Halpern 1978). Critics of judical capacity have, for the most part, assumed rather than proved the comparative ineffectiveness of courts. They participate in and encourage the normative degradation of judicial institutions. They do so partially out of a fear or dislike of the adversarial process and the spread of adversary norms in the culture (Rehnquist 1978), partially because they prefer the politics of administrative and legislative processes. Disappointed in the failure of the Burger Court to stem the tide at judicial activism, they seek to limit the opportunities for active judicial intervention by establishing the inadequacies of courts as institutions (Glazer 1979).

One may wonder, however, if administrative or legislative institutions perform much better than courts in social-policy activities. Empirical evidence is sparse. Judicial intervention is often sparked by legislative or administrative failure or inaction (Fiss 1979), and many people certainly believe that legislatures and administrative agencies have records of performance no better than courts (see, for example, Feeley and Sarat 1980; Pressman and Wildavsky 1976). What evidence there is suggests that the problems courts experience in handling social-policy matters are shared by legislatures and administrative agencies (see Rebell and Block 1979: pp. 578–579). This suggests that critics must be careful in making judgments about judicial capacity or judicial reform. Problems of judicial capacity may indeed be only symptomatic of more-fundamental problems of the state in dealing with and responding to social change and social disruption.

Conclusion

By concentrating on adjudication, working from a fixed, axiomatic perspective on judicial structure, and failing to undertake explicitly comparative assessments, those interested in judicial capacity have produced a biased picture of what courts can and cannot do well. As a result, the utility of their judgments about the role of the courts in American society has been diminished. The temptation to pick out sensational failures and to work from an established idea of what courts should do cautions against relying on these judgments as guides to policy and reform. Moreover, yet another tendency exists in the literature on judicial capacity that is equally important to inadequacies discussed thus far—namely, a tendency toward tunnel vision.

People who evaluate judicial performance and who identify problems in the courts and limits to their effectiveness rarely place those problems in a broader social and political context. They write as if the problems of the courts can be isolated and cured through limits on access or diversion of cases from the courts. Instead of establishing linkages with performance problems in legislatures and administrative agencies or connections with emerging social trends, they concentrate on judicial reform as a panacea. As I see them, problems of judicial capacity are merely symptomatic of more-basic social and political developments and dysfunctions, and they can only be treated effectively as part of a comprehensive program of social and political reform.

Note

1. Alexander Bickel and Harry Wellington. 1957. "Legislative
Purpose and Judicial Process." 71 *Harvard Law Review* 1, 25.
Copyright © 1957 by The Harvard Law Review Association. Reprinted
with permission.

References

Berger, Raoul. 1978 *Government by Judiciary*. Cambridge: Harvard
    University Press.
Berns, Walter. 1979. "The Least Dangerous Branch, But Only
    If. . . ." In L. Theberge (ed.). *The Judiciary in a Democratic
    Society*. Lexington, Mass.: Lexington Books, D.C. Heath and Co.
Bickel, Alexander, and Harry Wellington. 1957. "Legislative Purpose
    and Judicial Process." 71 *Harvard Law Review* 1.
Black, Charles. 1960. *The People and the Court*. New York: Mac-
    millan.
Boyer, Barry. 1972. "Alternatives to Administrative Trial-Type Hear-
    ings for Resolving Complex Scientific, Economic and Social Is-
    sues." 71 *Michigan Law Review* 811.
Buckle, Leonard, and Suzann Buckle. 1979. *Bargaining for Justice*.
    New York: Praeger.
Casper, Jonathan. 1976. "The Supreme Court and National Policy
    Making." 70 *American Political Science Review* 50.
Cavanagh, Ralph, and Austin Sarat. 1980. "Thinking About Courts."
    14 *Law and Society Review* 371.
Chayes, Abram. 1976. "The Role of the Judge in Public Law Liti-
    gation." 89 *Harvard Law Review* 1281.
Commager, Henry Steele. 1950. *Majority Rule and Minority Rights*.
    New York: Peter Smith.
Cox, Archibald. 1976a. *The Role of the United States Supreme Court
    in American Government*. New York: Oxford University Press.
————. 1976b. "The New Dimensions of Constitutional Adjudica-
    tion." 51 *Washington University Law Review* 791.
Cratsley, John C. 1978. "Community Courts: Offering Alternative
    Dispute Resolution within the Judicial System." 3 *Vermont Law
    Review* 1.
Diver, C. 1979. "The Judge as Political Powerbroker: Superintending

Structural Change in Public Institutions.'' 65 *Virginia Law Review* 43.

Eisenberg, Thomas, and Stephen Yeazell. 1980. ''The Ordinary and the Extraordinary in Institutional Litigation.'' 93 *Harvard Law Review* 465.

Ely, John. 1980. *Democracy and Distrust*. Cambridge: Harvard University Press.

Feeley, Malcolm, and Austin Sarat. 1980. *The Policy Dilemma*. Minneapolis: University Press.

Fiss, Owen. 1978. *The Civil Rights Injunction*. Bloomington: Indiana University Press.

———. 1979. ''The Forms of Justice.'' 93 *Harvard Law Review* 1.

Friedman, Lawrence M., and Robert V. Percival. 1976. ''A Tale of Two Courts: Litigation in Alameda and San Benito Counties.'' 10 *Law and Society Review* 267.

Fuller, Lon. 1979. ''The Forms and Limits of Adjudication.'' 92 *Harvard Law Review* 1.

Galanter, Marc. 1980. ''Adjudication, Litigation and Related Phenomena.'' Unpublished essay.

Glazer, Nathan. 1975. ''Toward an Imperial Judiciary.'' 41 *The Public Interest* 104.

———. 1979. ''The Judiciary and Social Policy. In L. Theberge (ed.). *The Judiciary in a Democratic Society*. Lexington, Mass.: Lexington Books, D.C. Heath and Company.

Graglia, Lino A. 1976. *Disaster by Decree: The Supreme Court Decisions on Race and the Schools*. Ithaca, N.Y.: Cornell University Press.

Halpern, Stephen. 1978. ''An Imperial Judiciary.'' Presented at the Annual Meeting of the American Political Science Association.

Horowitz, Donald. 1977. *The Courts and Social Policy*. Washington, D.C.: Brookings Institution.

Huntington, Samuel. 1968. *Political Order in Changing Societies*. New Haven: Yale University Press.

Hurst, W. 1950. *The Growth of American Law: The Law Makers*. Boston: Little, Brown & Co.

Kolodner, Howard, and James Fishman. 1978. *The Limits of Justice*. Cambridge, Mass.: Ballinger.

Mishkin, Paul. 1978. ''Federal Courts as State Reformers.'' 35 *Washington and Lee Law Review* 949.

Nimmer, Raymond. 1978. *The Nature of System Change*. Chicago: American Bar Foundation.

Pressman, Jeffrey, and Aaron Wildavsky. 1976. *Implementation.* Berkeley: University of California Press.

Project. 1978. "The Remedial Process in Institutional Reform Litigation." 1978 *Columbia Law Review* 788.

Rebell, Michael, and Arthur Block. 1979. "Educational Policy Making and the Courts." Unpublished essay.

Rehnquist, James. 1978. "The Adversary Society." Text of speech at University of Miami.

Rifkind, S.H. 1976. "Are We Asking Too Much of Our Courts?" 70 *Federal Rules Decisions* 96.

Rosenberg, Maurice. 1972. "Let's Everybody Litigate?" 50 *Texas Law Review* 1349.

Sarat, Austin. 1980. "The Role of Courts and the Logic of Court Reform." 64 *Judicature* 300.

Schaffer, Walter V. 1976. "Is the Adversary System Working in Optimal Fashion?" 70 *Federal Rules Decisions* 159.

Shapiro, Martin. 1975. "Courts." In N. Polsby and F.L. Greenstein. (eds.). *A Handbook of Political Science*. Reading, Mass.: Addison-Wesley.

Thayer, Ezra. 1891. "Judicial Legislation." 5 *Harvard Law Review* 172.

Unger, Roberto. 1976. *Law and Modern Society*. New York: Free Press.

Wildhorn, Sorrel, et al. 1977. *Indicators of Justice*. Lexington, Mass.: Lexington Books, D.C. Heath and Company.

Winter, Ralph K., Jr. 1979. "The Growth of Judicial Power," in L. Theberge (ed.). *The Judiciary in a Democratic Society*. Lexington, Mass.: Lexington Books, D.C. Heath and Company.

Yeazell, Stephen. 1977. "Intervention and the Idea of Litigation." 25 *U.C.L.A. Law Review* 244.

4

Data and Decisions: Judicial Reform and the Use of Social Science

Craig Haney

Discussions of judicial reform typically focus on questions of process and personnel. In other words, to improve the performance of the courts, most judicial reformers propose changes either in the procedures by which decisions are made or in the persons who make them. The crucial ingredients of legal decisions—rules and facts—are variously affected by these proposals. My concern here is with procedures and facts. In recent years, special attention has been devoted to the fact-finding mechanisms that are available to courts. More widespread judicial use of social-science facts, in particular, has precipitated a more-careful analysis of how courts use data. In this chapter, I briefly discuss the use of social science by the courts, review recent criticisms of judicial decision making that relies on social-science data, and examine several proposals to reform the manner in which social facts are determined in law.

Courts are arbiters of social reality. To resolve legal conflict, judges must do more than choose between competing legal theories or decide which of several legal precedents controls the instant case. Of course, trial courts must routinely reach conclusions about case-specific *historical* facts—what did and did not happen in a particular legal conflict or dispute. However, their interpretations of historical facts, as well as their decisions about which legal rule to apply to these facts, often are conditioned by a much broader factual context. *Social* facts give meaning and significance to specific events, and they provide a framework through which case-specific evidence is understood and weighed. Conflicts over the broad social facts that form the context of the legal dispute may well determine the outcome of a particular case.

In recent years, these social facts have been increasingly and explicitly contested. Broad factual matters that once went unchallenged as part of a legal ''commonsense'' or shared world view are now at the center of many legal conflicts. Social science is increasingly used as an authoritative tool for the resolution of such conflict. This development is, in part, a historical legacy of the Legal Realists, who

argued that courts should transcend the arid formalistic categories that
had dominated legal reasoning and urged lawmakers to employ the
insights of economics, psychology, and anthropology in fashioning
rules and rendering decisions. Not until *Brown* v. *Board of Education,*
347 U.S. 483 (1954), however, did it become apparent that social
science could be used effectively in raising social-fact issues in court.
The civil rights revolution of the last three decades has meant the
extension of legal representation and voice to persons traditionally
denied them. But these groups—the poor, minorities and women,
children, inmates—are especially unlikely to share the "commonsense" view of the world held by judges and incorporated into legal
decisions as implicit assumptions. Legal representation has given diverse and previously disenfranchised groups an opportunity to challenge legal common sense and to urge their own view of the world on
courts. Social science has become a vehicle with which certain social
facts can be contested.

The Reaction to Realism: Strict Constructionists and
Judicial Fact-Finding

Although opposition to the use of social science in law has always
existed, in recent years that opposition has become vocal and formidable. To be sure, some of the criticism is self-interested and comes
from persons whose legal and political positions have been threatened
by the recent influx of data into the law. Disagreements with specific
judicial decisions are thus transformed into a generic critique of jur-
isprudential proportions. Taken as a whole, however, criticism of the
use of social science by the courts is cogent enough to merit serious
consideration.

    One broad category of such criticism is directed at the very nature
of social-science data: Law should not use or rely on the social sciences
because of serious flaws in the data that these disciplines produce.
This criticism takes several different forms. Some critics contend that
the data are inherently biased, either because they are gathered by
researchers who are themselves political partisans or because certain
characteristics of the data work consistently to the advantage of only
one side in a legal or political dispute. Interestingly, however, the two
branches of the bias argument often lead in opposite directions. Specifically, some critics have suggested that the "pronounced 'liberal'
orientation of sociology, psychology, political science, and similar
fields is well established" (Moynihan 1979, p. 17). Thus, they argue,

social-science data are slanted in the direction of a liberal-radical world view, so much so that the data simply cannot withstand the "hard realities" of a tough-minded, presumably unbiased, conservative analysis (for example, Miller 1980).

Others suggest that social-science data are intrinsically inconclusive, or "soft," so that the legal import of the data will always be to counsel inaction. In the long run, of course, such inaction will work in favor of the status quo and produce consistently conservative results (for example, Horowitz 1977; O'Brien 1980). Because the law requires a high degree of certainty before mandating change, characteristically uncertain social-science data will be a conservative force in law. Daniels warns that "where social science is presented and cannot provide a clear and conclusive answer to a pertinent question, its inconclusiveness may be part of a justification for a status quo–oriented decision" (1979, p. 367).

A second kind of data-specific critique is less concerned with bias or softness in social-science data and more with its lack of generalizability. Important differences in the nature of the settings, persons, and procedures mean that the data and insights that are gleaned from the laboratory cannot be applied to legal realities outside the laboratory. For example, Meehl chastises law-related social scientists for their uncritical reliance on "shaky generalizations purporting to be rigorous deliverances of modern behavioral science" (1977, p. 11). What makes these deliverances rigorous—the researcher's ability to control, manipulate, and measure all potentially relevant variables—also may make them highly artificial and unrepresentative. Precision and rigor incur sacrifices in what methodologists term external validity (Campbell and Stanley 1966). Critics argue that these sacrifices seriously undermine the utility of social science for law.

Here, of course, it is important to distinguish bad data—poorly designed research, unknowledgeable researchers, and so on—from something that is endemic to the methodology itself. For example, when critics accuse psychology and law researchers of "sloppy scholarship" and even "legal naiveté" (Vidmar 1979), the criticism is not uniquely relevant to social science. Unsophisticated work can be done in any academic discipline or profession, including law. However, when critics go on to argue that the legal naiveté of researchers results from a persistent failure to include important legal variables in their simulations, and that some paradigms are incapable of incorporating the critical features, then the criticism becomes an external-validity argument of more-general proportions (compare Konecni and Ebbesen 1979 and Dillehay and Nietzel 1980). This criticism is made so often, and in such broad and sweeping fashion, that it is hard to avoid the inference that the critics believe certain social-science methods to be uniquely and perhaps incurably susceptible to this problem.

A separate but related line of criticism focuses less on alleged defects in the nature of social-science data and more on incompatibilities in the styles of thought, the operating assumptions, and the goals of law and social science (see Haney 1980). Here critics argue not that social science cannot match the presumed rigor or neutrality of law but rather that the tasks of both disciplines are simply very different. These differences make the judicial use of social-science data inappropriate.

For example, the observation is often made on the one hand that law is an essentially historical enterprise in which current decisions are controlled by past precedents. Most social science, on the other hand, is distinctly contemporaneous. Compared to lawyers and judges, social scientists are less influenced by the past in their interpretations of the present. Similarly, the law seeks certainty and not the inherently conditional truth characteristic of social science. Moreover, legal thinking often seeks to cover the last possible case, however unrepresentative, and so may have little use for the normative data of social sciences. Thus, the tension between the disciplines can be seen as arising from a pattern of cross-purposes, rather than from any inadequacy in either. Of course, this criticism is rarely couched in categorical terms. Most critics recognize that the friction between legal and social-scientific purposes and values is more important under some circumstances than others. For example, Tribe (1971) notes that in reaching decisions about guilt in criminal trials, the law requires a subjective state of certainty on the part of decision maker that is incompatible with the probabilistic quality of social-science data; but probabilistic data are tolerated in some legal contexts and even welcomed in a few others.

Criticism focusing on the incompatibility between the two disciplines is sometimes tied to the claim that the use of social science loosens the moral underpinnings of the law. Legal decisions, it is argued, should rest on moral absolutes, not mere data. Thus, this criticism posits a fundamental incompatibility between empiricism and moral strictures (for example, Cahn 1955; Robinson 1980). Since universals of right and wrong are not subject to social-scientific proof, courts that immerse themselves in social facts will lose sight of the universal principles that should guide them.

A final set of criticisms focuses upon the institutional limitations and inadequacies of courts as forums in which broad social facts can be presented and properly evaluated. The nature of courts—in terms of the occupational realities of judges and the vagaries of trial process and procedure—makes them inappropriate places for presenting and understanding complex social-science data. Horowitz (1977), for example, observes that the structure of adjudication tends to be focused and piecemeal rather than addressing a broad, or "total," picture. In addition, he suggests that courts are often forced to deal with unrepresentative litigants and problems that provide a distorted view of the social world and that judges are forced to become generalists who must rotate from one unrelated problem to another rather than becoming knowledgeable specialists in a single area. These critics suggest that courts will not be able to make use of social science because they will understand neither its data nor how to apply it in the context of the individual case. They also suggest that courts are especially ill situated to make declarations about social facts (see Chayes 1976).

Often, the institutional critique focuses upon the Supreme Court. For example, Miller and Barron (1975) have challenged use of social science by the Supreme Court on the grounds of insufficient rigor. Specifically, they are concerned with "independent research conducted sua sponte by the Justices," which escapes the test of contrary presentation and adversarial cross-examination. When the issue is not adequately addressed in the record of the court below or, at the very least, extensively briefed by both parties, appellate courts are in no position to find social facts on their own. Similarly, Davis is critical of Supreme Court decision making that is based on inadequate data or data known only to the Court. He is most concerned with those instances in which the Court goes beyond the record for facts that are crucial to the decision, only "casually acknowledging that it is doing so, and casually remaining silent about the possibility that fair procedure might require that the losing party be given a predecision chance to respond to the Court's extrarecord facts" (1980, p. 934).

Finally, Askin and Levin (1981) are equally critical of the Supreme Court's use of social science, but for different reasons. While their study suggests that the Court rarely cites social science not introduced by one or the other parties, they are concerned about the possibility that the quality of the advocacy, and not the amount or quality of the social-science data, will determine whether or not certain social facts will be used by the Court and with what effect.

In Defense of Social Science in Court

These widespread criticisms of judicial reliance upon social-science data can be reduced to three basic complaints: (1) flawed data,

(2) incompatibilities between the two disciplines, and (3) the institutional incompetencies of courts. The list is deceptively short. Although few in number, these are basic, fundamental objections that cut to the very heart of law and social science. At the same time, however, I believe that, despite many well-taken points, these criticisms do not justify a substantial reduction in the use of social science by the courts. In the following few pages, I elaborate on that belief and then examine a series of proposals that address many of the criticisms I discussed in the preceding section.

The first argument—that social-science data are imperfect—is in one sense incontrovertible. Some social scientists are biased, social-science data are sometimes equivocal, and some research designs do lack sufficient external validity to produce properly generalizable results. Despite these limitations, however, social-science data often constitute the very best evidence available to courts that grapple with critical social-fact issues. Purging the factual record of such data does not improve it. It is difficult to sustain the argument that less information is better.

Not even the staunchest advocates of social science propose that their data be exempted from the basic procedural mechanisms by which all legal evidence is tested, scrutinized, and weighed. Thus, there is every reason to believe that flawed social-science data will be recognized as such. To be sure, this assumes that there are perceptible differences between good and bad social science and that courts will be able to recognize them. Judges may vary in the ease and facility with which they can evaluate social science, but there are few examples of bad data having played a decisive role in judicial decisions. To argue that we should ignore social-science data is to suggest either that courts will have a better factual basis on which to premise a decision or that courts will not make factual assumptions at all. Neither suggestion seems viable.

Of course, courts never really escape the problem of unreliable evidence. Unlike other evidence admitted in legal proceedings, however, social-science evidence is first tested through separate procedures and independent criteria. In some ways, the social-science procedures are more rigorous than their legal counterparts; evidence that could not pass social-science review is presented regularly in court. In addition, concern over inevitable disagreements between social scientists needs to be placed in the context of typical legal cases in which evidentiary conflict is the rule rather than the exception. There will be many areas in which good social-science research will produce conflicting results. Yet, legal disputes are made of the stuff over which reasonable people—even reasonable social scientists—can disagree. Factual conflict is commonplace in law; it is not the occasion for the systematic exclusion of certain kinds of facts and information.

The second kind of criticism—that there are professional incompatibilities between law and social science—has diverse implications for the use of social science in court. Most of the incompatibilities act to hinder, but not to preclude, the effective use of data by courts. Moreover, the hindrances are not removed by proposals to further limit opportunities for the courts to consider and use such data. Some of these incompatibilities could be remedied by a fuller and more informed use of social-science data by the courts. Some legal accommodations may be necessitated by the increased use of social-science methodologies in law, and the parameters of legal conflicts may be altered somewhat by an influx of data. However, the legal conflicts will still proceed in traditional fashion, and their final resolution will be effected through familiar judicial procedures. Again, social-science data are tested and scrutinized by the same procedures as all other evidence. Moreover, to argue that the status and prestige of courts will be undermined by their use of social science is to bespeak a prejudice no longer widely held by the society at large. In large part, social science *is* the way our society now legitimates many social facts. A court that regularly ruled in the face of social-science data to the contrary might very well finds its legitimacy seriously eroded.

Perhaps the most peculiar argument against using social science in court is the final one, concerning institutional incompetence. This analysis seems at once too pessimistic about courts and too sanguine about their alternatives. There is little evidence that courts are actually incapable of effectively using social science, and there is even less evidence that they cannot get better at it. Moreover, the ostensible facts finding advantages of legislatures come at the expense of greater vulnerability to the kind of explicit political pressures that courts can avoid. Historically, legislatures have not been especially effective in establishing and protecting the legitimacy of minority world views or in defending social realities that contradict the majoritarian common sense.

Reforms in Legal Fact-Finding: New Mechanisms for Using Social Science

Even strident critics of social science like Moynihan now concede that "courts will learn to adapt to the changed conditions of evidence which social science imposes on contemporary [legal] argument" (1979, p. 30). The key issues thus become deciding when and how courts should adapt to social science to evaluate and employ its data more effectively. Numerous proposals have been made to upgrade the quality of the social-science data relied upon by courts and to improve the techniques by which they examine such data. The proposals range in focus and scale.

Procedural Safeguards

Several proposals are procedural rather than structural in nature. A number of them are designed to insure that already existing legal safeguards are applied with special care to social-science evidence. Often at issue here is the adequacy and completeness of the factual record on which courts base their decisions. Thus, critics who are concerned about one-sidedness in the presentation of social-science data or about the sua sponte discovery and use of such data by the courts have proposed maximizing the opportunities for all parties to contribute social-science evidence to the case. When social facts are in controversy, some have suggested the courts should at least require pretrial conferences in which ground rules for the handling of such data are established. Miller and Barron (1975) have proposed the compulsory exchange of all social-science data between parties beforehand, at pretrial conferences. Courts could also more routinely ask opposing counsel for further data on contested social-science points, and such requests could be entered either in the course of the trial itself or even after the trial had been completed. Davis (1980) has also suggested that when social facts are crucial to the case, and especially when they are either complex or doubtful, appellate courts might request factual briefs or remand the case to the trial court for further factual development. In addition, he has suggested that, for especially broad policy decisions, some form of notice-and-comment procedures be employed to elicit data from nonparties as well as parties.

Shifting Burdens of Proof

Several commentators have noted the crucial role played by burdens of proof in cases in which social-science data are employed. Under the conventional constitutional approach, evidence that suggests the mere existence of a social fact is usually sufficient to sustain a presumption of constitutionality. However, the burden of proving the validity of social facts is placed upon any party who would use such facts to challenge a statute's constitutionality. Daniels (1979) has suggested that this heavy burden is, in fact, insurmountable. The tentative and probabilistic nature of most social-science data means that the court will be reluctant to pronounce such facts ultimately valid and to rely upon them in sustaining a challenge to the constitutionality of a statute.

However, standards for allocating burdens of proof are applied inconsistently by the Supreme Court. Indeed, Davis has complained that the Court allocates burdens of proof "without guiding principle, without reasoned explanation, and without regard to its own precedents concerning the presumption of constitutionality" (1980, p. 938). Because social science is often employed in challenges to statutes that appear to violate civil rights guarantees, and given the ease with which questionable social-science studies can be generated and used to cast doubt upon the validity of certain social facts, new standards for allocating burdens of proof in social-science cases may well be warranted.

Increasing the Sophistication of Court Personnel

Another set of proposals concerns the training and sophistication of the persons who present and evaluate social-science data in legal proceedings. For example, Miller and Barron (1975) have proposed the licensure of a specialized Supreme Court bar as a corrective to perceived inadequacies in the flow of social-science information at that level. Presumably, skilled and experienced attorneys would be better able to present all relevant data to the Court and to uncover weaknesses in the social-science case of the opposing party. Of course, a sophisticated Supreme Court bar would have little direct effect on the nature and quality of social-science data introduced into lower-court proceedings, particularly at the trial-court level where the basic factual record is made. Greater attention to social-science methods and issues in the law-school curriculum, as well as the creation of formal specialization or certification in law and social science, might help minimize deficiencies and imbalances in the presentation of social facts. In fact, Moynihan (1979) predicts the emergence of a group of lawyers trained in both social science and law and suggests that such combined sophistication would have a salutary effect on courtroom fact-finding, especially in improving standards of cross-examination.

Others have suggested that the ultimate responsibility for gaining expertise and sophistication in social science resides with the judges themselves. Only when the judge has learned the social-fact context of pending litigation will he be able to "fashion his own opinions with the aid, but not the domination, of experts'' (Loh 1979, p. 36). However, there is some deep-seated resistance toward social science that persists among many members of the U.S. judiciary. If the judiciary is to master social science, it must at least become familiar with its methods and assumptions.

Court-Appointed Experts

Typically, social-science data are presented to trial courts by expert witnesses. Courts consider the credentials of proferred witnesses, estimate the potential relevance of their testimony, and decide whether or not to qualify them as experts and to permit them to testify. Widespread use of experts is a relatively recent phenomenon. Less than fifty years ago, Sheldon Glueck (1933) could observe that the use of experts was "not sufficiently cultivated" to evaluate or recommend. Even then, however, Glueck and others were concerned that experts "be truly *neutral*" (1933, p. 117, emphasis in original). To insure neutrality, he proposed that experts be chosen by the court rather than the parties and that the experts be selected from a panel that was screened and approved by the relevant "scientific association."

Glueck's proposal has been often repeated. Court-appointed experts are thought by some to be free of the partisan pressures that might lead witnesses retained by one or the other party to overstate their positions or to delete information that might be damaging to their side. However, there is no unanimity on this point. Diamond, for example, has discussed the institutional sources of partiality that can influence even court-appointed experts and concludes that "there is no such thing as a neutral, impartial witness" (1968, p. 148). Indeed, court-appointed status may mask inevitable limitations beneath the appearance of impartiality. In fact, Rivlin has encouraged the development of "forensic social science" to reduce "the hypocrisy of pseudo-objectivity and hidden biases" of traditional social-science scholarship (1973, p. 62). Rather than striving for balanced objectivity, forensic social scientists would "take on the task of writing briefs for or against particular policy positions" (p. 61). Such experts would have to guard against misrepresentation and would be required to make their data available to opposing parties, but they would not seek or adopt the pretense of objectivity. Legal decision makers would be left to ferret valid social facts from this adversarial clash of opposing-expert views of the truth.

Social-Science Masters

Several proposals address the problem of partiality and bias in another way, by expanding and institutionalizing the role of court-appointed expert. In essence, they attempt to create an explicitly neutral role whose occupant could strive to impartially and objectively summarize and evaluate conflicting data for the court. For example, one proposal at the Supreme Court level would have an official and presumably neutral party regularly serve as amicus in social-science cases to provide the court with a balanced summary of the evidence. The amicus would function essentially as a servant of the court, one who "acts for no one, but simply seeks to give information to the court" [*Campbell* v. *Swasey,* 12 Ind. 70, 72 (1859)]. However, at least one notable attempt to implement this procedure proved quite unsuccessful. On several occasions the U.S. Solicitor General, then Robert Bork, entered death-penalty cases pending before the Supreme Court, summarizing and interpreting conflicting social-science data concerning the deterrent effect of the death penalty. In each instance, however, the presumably impartial party acted with much apparent partiality, presenting positions that were soundly condemned by the great majority of social-science experts who had studied the issue. The problem is not specific to any particular individual, or to any institutional role for that matter; although partisan roles may intensify bias, truly neutral and impartial roles are psychologically elusive and difficult to create and maintain.

Several other proposals would also empower presumably impartial officers to summarize and interpret social-science evidence. Askin and Levin have suggested that "social science clerks" be used by the appellate courts to provide them with "independent access to social-science expertise" when parties fail to provide sufficient data or "for advice or sorting out and interpreting the data that the parties do present" (1981, pp. 455–456); (see also Leventhal 1974).

A somewhat different model used in the Los Angeles school-desegregation case (*Crawford* v. *Board of Education,* Case no. 822, 854, Superior Court, County of Los Angeles) has been favorably described by one of the court-appointed experts, Thomas Pettigrew (1979). The trial-court judge selected eight experts from diverse disciplines who were then instructed to address a series of questions that the judge felt were crucial to the case. After an initial meeting, however, the experts had no continuing ex parte communication with the judge. Instead, they dealt directly with the parties and with a law professor who served as a court-appointed referee. They also conducted interviews and collected data jointly and individually and filed eight separate reports to the court. The model is unusual in the sense that, although several experts brought different perspectives to bear on the issue, their relationship to the problem was continuing and collective, rather than brief and adversarial.

In a related proposal, Miller and Barron suggest that the Supreme Court might appoint a panel of resident social scientists to assist them in investigating and understanding various social-fact questions. Their lingering concerns over the "inherent subjectivity that social science unavoidably involves, and the consequent lack of agreement among social scientists on the controversial issues presented to the Court for resolution" (1975, p. 1240), might well be addressed in a model that underscored the nonbinding, purely advisory capacity in which the panel might serve. A little-used provision of the FRCP (Federal Rules of Civil Procedure) permits a similar process on a potentially widespread basis. Rule 39(c) provides that an advisory jury may be impaneled in actions not triable before ordinary juries. The court may initiate this process itself or upon motion of the parties. Such advisory juries could be composed of social scientists and used by the courts to provide them with advisory interpretations of complicated social-fact evidence presented by the parties at trial.

A Social-Science Institute

One proposal that would formalize the legal advisory role of social scientists involves the creation of a social-science board or institute whose members would synthesize and codify existing data for use by the courts. Some time ago, Cardozo (1921) envisioned a "ministry of justice" in which social and economic expertise would be focused upon critical factual issues and questions. The agency would provide presumably accurate factual knowledge upon which the judiciary could fashion more-informed legal rules.

This suggestion was modified and extended somewhat by Glueck (1933) who proposed that the American Law Institute sponsor a clearinghouse where authoritative materials from law-related fields (organizational behavior, marriage and family, criminology) would be assembled. Glueck thought that "creative" law professors could analyze the assembled materials for possible legal application. Their analyses could be systematically disseminated to various legal communities (courts, legislatures, law schools, and so on).

On occasion, the National Academy of Sciences has served in an analogous capacity, albeit on an informal and ad hoc basis. As an organization of distinguished scientists, the Academy is in a position to present legitimated scientific analyses of contested factual questions as well as to issue summaries of the scientific consensus on various topics. The Academy itself, of course, has the stability and prestige that a social-science institute might attain, but it appoints committees or panels on a case-by-case basis. It does not perform the continuing function of evaluating and synthesizing law-related data that an institute devoted exclusively to the task could manage.

The Science Court

The final and most extreme proposal would create a separate court for the resolution of legally relevant scientific fact questions. First suggested by Arthur Kantrowitz (U.S. Congress 1967) to assist courts that are "forced to deal with disputes between experts about scientific facts that are clearly beyond the law's competence" (Kantrowitz 1975, p. 48), the science court would incorporate elements of both legal and scientific fact-findings. There have been numerous variations and modifications of the science-court proposal, but the basic procedure involves the adversarial presentation of conflicting points of view to expert scientist-judges. Presentations would be made by "devoted advocates," while judges would be selected from among members of the scientific community "who have no involvement in the field in question" (Kantrowitz 1977, p. 49).

The science court would then issue a series of statements to be published and disseminated to the relevant legal audience. The court's statements would describe and characterize factual conclusions, both in terms of the level of agreement between court participants themselves and the degree of tentativeness or finality that the court perceives in the factual issues. This proposal envisions the separate, independent resolution of law and fact questions. Although the science court would use quasi-legal procedures to resolve factual disputes, the findings of the court would not be legally binding. The relevance and impact of science-court findings in any specific legal case would be a matter for the traditional court to determine through traditional processes of adjudication. As Kantrowitz sees it, "the sole authority for the resultant factual output will reside in the credibility of the procedure with the public" (1977, p. 54).

Conclusion: The Context of Reform
in Social Fact-Finding

Like most reforms, these proposals to change the manner in which social-science data are used in court have qualities that recommend both for and against them. Rather than evaluating the specific virtues and limitations of each proposal, however, I offer some observations about the context in which these reforms will be implemented and evaluated.

1. Judicial use of social science must be justified ultimately in the name of accurate and complete fact-finding. Thus, reforms that require the full disclosure of social-science evidence and that provide opportunities for parties to challenge such data should represent procedural minima in complex social-fact cases.

2. The legal credibility of social-science evidence derives as much from the adversarial forum in which it is tested as the presumed truth value of the data. Reforms that seek to circumvent this process also ignore the procedural definitions of truth and justice on which our present system is based.

3. Courts remain reluctant to yield fact-finding power to social-science experts, especially to ones whose perspectives on social facts challenge or threaten legal common sense. The ability of reforms in social fact-finding to effect meaningful legal change is drastically limited by this fact.

4. Despite an unrealistic distinction between facts and values that plagues the application of social science to law, social-science reformers must learn that data need not be value free to be valuable. Many social facts are value laden, as is the judicial process that evaluates them.

5. Much social science is beset with conflicting facts and diverse opinion. Yet, such conflict and diversity does not preclude courts from distinguishing good data from bad or from deciding what constitutes the best evidence in a particular case.

6. Legal doctrines allocating burdens of proof define the comparative superiority of evidence that one party must establish to prevail over another. In constitutional litigation, these doctrines should balance inherent difficulties in establishing certain social facts against the nature of the constitutional interest at stake.

7. Reforms in social fact-finding are legal experiments that should be proposed, implemented, and evaluated as such. The legal quest for certainty and finality should not dictate the form or outcome of new models for using social science in law.

8. One final point requires some elaboration. Courts serve two

separate but related basic functions: (1) they solve problems and (2) they legitimate values. They do not always do both at once, and they do not always do either well. Use of social science by the courts is commonly related to the first of these functions. Since judges who would solve problems must first understand them, courts should have access to the best available data. Yet, many critics contend that the use of social science by the courts actually undermines their moralizing and legitimating function. This claim should be understood in terms of the typical coincidence between legal common sense and majoritarian views of the world and the degree to which social science may interject a dissonant perspective. Thus, one critic argues that whether judges can find and use reliable social-science data in their decisions is far less critical than whether the public agrees with them: "Factual premises may be either incorrect or, *more importantly,* perceived by the public to be so, and, thus, provide an occasion for political conflict" (O'Brien 1980, p. 19, emphasis added).

Yet, legal common sense may provide a highly biased and imperfect picture of the social world in which conflicts arise and decisions are rendered. Justice Cardozo, who sometimes wrote quite perceptively about various influences on the judicial world view, once noted that "the spirit of the age, as it is revealed to each of us, is too often only the spirit of the group in which the accidents of birth or education or occupation or fellowship have given us a place" (1921, p. 174). Increased use of social science by the courts promises a different perspective on the social facts and the "spirit of the age" that influences judicial decision making. Despite real limitations, court adjudication can act to reduce the impact of certain social and political inequalities on dispute resolution and social science can assist in this process. At the same time, however, this potential should not be compromised in the transfer of fact-finding power to experts who could impose elitist visions of their own or by legal attempts to make essentially political decisions in the name of science.

References

Askin, Frank, and Hannah Levin. 1981. "Final Report to the National Science Foundation on Social Science in the Courts." Washington, D.C.

Cahn, Edward. 1955. "Jurisprudence." 30 *New York University Law Review* 150.

Campbell, Donald, and Julian Stanley. 1966. *Experimental and Quasi-Experimental Designs for Research.* Chicago: Rand McNally.

Cardozo, Benjamin. 1921. *The Nature of the Judicial Process.* New Haven: Yale University Press.

Chayes, Abram. 1976. "The Role of the Judge in Public Law Litigation." 89 *Harvard Law Review* 1281.

Clark, Kenneth. 1960. "The Desegregation Cases: Criticism of the Social Scientist's Role." 5 *Villanova Law Review* 224.

Daniels, Steven. 1979. "Social Science and the Death Penalty Cases." 1 *Law and Policy Quarterly* 336.

Davis, Kenneth. 1980. "Facts in Lawmaking." 80 *Columbia Law Review* 931.

Diamond, Bernard. 1968. "The Fallacy of the Impartial Expert." In R. Allen, E. Ferster, and J. Rubin (eds.). *Readings in Psychiatry and Law.* Baltimore: Johns Hopkins University Press.

Dillehay, Ronald, and Michael Nietzel. 1980. "Conceptualizing Mock Juror/Jury Research: Critique and Illustrations." In K. Larsen (ed.). *Social Psychology: Crisis or Failure.* Monmouth, Or.: Institute for Theoretical History.

Glueck, Sheldon. 1933. "The Social Sciences and Scientific Method in the Administration of Justice." 167 *The Annals* 106.

Haney, Craig. 1980. "Psychology and Legal Change: On the Limits of a Factual Jurisprudence." 4 *Law and Human Behavior* 147.

Horowitz, Donald. 1977. *The Courts and Social Policy.* Washington, D.C.: The Brookings Institution.

Kantrowitz, Arthur. 1975. "Controlling Technology Democratically." *American Scientist* 505.

———. 1977. "The Science Court Experiment." 1977. *Trial* 48.

Konecni, Vladimir, and Ebbe Ebbesen. 1979. "External Validity of Research in Legal Psychology." 3 *Law and Human Behavior* 39.

Leventhal, Harold. 1974. "Environmental Decisionmaking and the Role of the Courts." 122 *University of Pennsylvania Law Review.*

Loh, Wallace. 1979. "Some Uses and Limits of Statistics and Social Science in the Judicial Process." In L. Abt and I. Stuart (eds.). *Social Psychology and Discretionary Law.* New York: Van Nostrand.

Meehl, Paul. 1977. "Law and the Fireside Inductions: Some Reflections of a Clinical Psychologist." In J. Tapp and F. Levine (eds.). *Law, Justice, and the Individual in Society: Psychological and Legal Issues.* New York: Holt, Rinehart & Winston.

Miller, Arthur, and Jerome Barron. 1975. "The Supreme Court, the Adversary System, and the Flow of Information to the Justices: A Preliminary Inquiry." 61 *Virginia Law Review* 1187.

Miller, H. 1980. "Hard Realities and Soft Social Science." 59 *The Public Interest* 67.

Moynihan, Daniel. 1979. "Social Science and the Court." 54 *The Public Interest* 12.
O'Brien, David. 1980. "The Seduction of the Judiciary: Social Science and the Courts." 64 *Judicature* 8.
Pettigrew, Thomas. 1979. "Tension Between the Law and Social Science: An Expert Witness' View." In J. Greenberg et al. (eds.). *Schools and the Courts*. Volume I—Desegregation. Eugene, Or.: ERIC Clearinghouse.
Rivlin, Alice. 1973. "Forensic Social Science." 43 *Harvard Educational Review* 61.
Robinson, Daniel. 1980. *Psychology and Law: Can Justice Survive the Social Sciences?* New York: Oxford University Press.
Rosen, Paul. 1972. *The Supreme Court and Social Science*. Urbana, Ill.: University of Illinois Press.
Tribe, Lawrence. 1971. "Trial by Mathematics: Precision and Ritual in the Legal Process." 84 *Harvard Law Review* 1329.
U.S. Congress. 1967. Senate Testimony of Arthur Kantrowitz before the Subcommittee on Government Research of the Committee on Government Operations. 90th Congress, 1st Session (March 16). 113 *Congressional Record* 15256.
Vidmar, Neil. 1979. "The Other Issues in Jury Simulation Research: A Commentary with Particular Reference to Defendant Character Studies." 3 *Law and Human Behavior* 95.
White, Edward. 1972. "From Sociological Jurisprudence to Realism: Jurisprudence and Social Change in Early Twentieth Century America." 58 *Virginia Law Review* 999.

Mediation and Arbitration: Their Promise and Performance as Alternatives to Court

Craig A. McEwen and
Richard J. Maiman

In the decade of the 1970s, strong momentum developed for one of the most radical and promising of judicial-reform efforts—the alternatives-to-court movement. The litany of criticisms directed at courts by Roscoe Pound in 1906 had altered little by the opening in 1976 of the commemorative conference on the "Causes of Popular Dissatisfaction with the Administration of Justice." Among Pound's concerns were the limited access to justice caused by the delay, high costs, and intimidating character of courts; the failure to achieve substantive justice caused by the nature of the adversary process and overriding concern with the etiquette of law; and the inevitable inability of courts, guided by general legal principles, to make decisions responsive to the subtle variations among cases (Pound 1906). These same problems still plagued the justice system seventy years later, but prominent among the new solutions advocated for them in the 1976 Pound Conference was increased reliance on nonadjudicative-dispute forums, particularly arbitration and mediation (Sander 1976a; 1976b). Such advocacy had its greatest symbolic victory in 1979 when Congress unanimously passed (but did not fund) the Dispute Resolution Act, authorizing, among other things, a program within the Justice Department supporting local development of alternative dispute-resolution mechanisms.

Proponents of arbitration and mediation contended that these procedures could aid courts and the justice system by relieving some of the backlog, saving money, removing inappropriate cases, decreasing barriers to access, and arriving at fairer, more-flexible resolutions to disputes (Heher 1978; Cratsley 1978). Such advocacy was echoed

Work on this chapter has been supported in part by a grant from the Law and Social Sciences Program of the National Science Foundation (SES-7908872). The opinions and points of view expressed in this publication are the authors' alone and do not necessarily reflect the position of the National Science Foundation.

61

internationally in what Cappelletti and his colleagues call the access-to-justice movement (Cappelletti and Garth 1978). Until recently, little more than faith and theory have guided the introduction of alternatives to court. As we enter the 1980s, however, it is possible to employ evidence from the accumulated experience with mediation and arbitration in order to assess more systematically their potential for resolving some of the recurring problems of the judicial system.

Arbitration and Mediation as Distinctive Processes

Arbitration and mediation both differ from adjudication, but equally important, they are quite different from each other. These substantial distinctions sometimes are obscured by inappropriate nomenclature such as in Florida's short-lived medical-malpractice mediation act, or Michigan's so-called mediation of some automobile-accident cases— situations in fact, where arbitration was apparently employed (Ehrhardt 1980; Miller 1973). The use of both mediation and arbitration in pioneering arbitration-as-an-alternative programs such as in Philadelphia and elsewhere may add to the confusion (Stulberg 1975; Sarat 1976).

Arbitration closely resembles adjudication in that a third party hears evidence (often, in the United States, using rules of civil procedure) and either makes a binding decision or presents an advisory opinion to resolve the dispute. The differences from adjudication— when they exist—are subtle, having to do, in labor arbitration, largely with the ability of the parties to select the arbitrator and to formulate through collective bargaining the rules that govern the arbitration (Getman 1979; Heher 1978). These distinguishing characteristics result from the special collective-bargaining relationships of labor and management and rarely hold in other settings, making nonlabor arbitration "almost indistinguishable from agency adjudication" (Getman 1979, p. 938; see also Fuller 1978). In many settings, however, the arbitration process is bound less by procedural rules than adjudication, and an arbitrator's decisions reflect an attempt at equity, broadly tailored to the parties' priorities, needs, responsibilities, and liabilities. In contrast, the judicial process is tightly constrained by procedure, and the judge's or jury's win-lose decision presumably rests on the law and evidence germane only to the official charge or suit.

Mediation involves a third party's encouragement of negotiation and settlement by two (or more) disputing parties (Gulliver 1979). Unlike an arbitrator, the mediator possesses no authority to impose a settlement and in practice often avoids even suggesting one. By its very nature, mediation is much less formal than either adjudication or arbitration and leaves the decision-making responsibility to the disputing parties rather than to a third party. In these ways, mediation departs more radically from adjudication than arbitration. In other ways, mediation does not differ much from current practice; it simply extends the negotiation process that in fact now serves as the backbone of the civil- and criminal-justice systems.

Arbitration and Mediation in the United States Today

Arbitration has a long history in the United States, but its applications have broadened dramatically in the last twenty years (Alper and Nichols 1981). Today people arbitrate all manner of issues such as prison grievances, some juvenile criminal offenses, medical-malpractice claims, taxation appeals, small civil disputes, investor-broker disagreements, landlord-tenant conflicts, consumer complaints, and divorce/custody disagreements, among others. Lawyer volunteers, receiving little more than token remuneration for their work, frequently serves as arbitrators. Cases reach arbitration in a variety of ways, although mandatory hearings appear increasingly common. States such as Pennsylvania and Washington have made arbitration of some civil disputes compulsory while preserving the right to a trial de novo on appeal (Steelman 1980; Tegland and Blair 1980).

Although the use of mediation outside of labor disputes is considered innovative in the United States today, techniques of conciliation and mediation have long played a central role in dispute resolution in other societies including Germany (Bierbrauer, Falke, and Koch 1978), the People's Republic of China (Cohen 1966), Japan (Kojima and Taniguchi 1978), and many small-scale societies such as the Kpelle (Gibbs 1963) and the Ndendeuli (Gulliver 1963) in Africa. In the United States, mediation as an alternative to court has spread almost as widely as arbitration. Mediation programs have been established to resolve many criminal matters between related persons (Stulberg 1975; McGillis and Mullen 1977), child-custody disputes (Pearson 1981), and small-claims matters and consumer complaints (McEwen and Maiman 1981). Mediators have also undertaken broader community disputes and environmental disputes, but these are beyond the scope of this review (Ford Foundation 1978).

Measuring the Success of Alternatives to Court

Policy decisions about devoting resources to the development of mediation or arbitration programs should rest on careful and far-ranging assessments of many dimensions of performance, and these must in turn be ranked and weighed in policymaking. All too often, however, program evaluations are narrowly conceived (Merry 1981). Mediation centers, for example, typically claim success in terms of their high rates of settlement. Because it does not require the consent of the parties, arbitration leads to awards in all cases, but as a consequence of appeals, from 1 percent to 9 percent of these actually end in a trial de novo (Heher 1978; Lind and Shapard 1981). However, brief reflection should convince even the most ardent advocates of mediation and arbitration that success should not be measured solely by the percentage of resolutions achieved; by that standard, courts are always better than their alternatives because they successfully dispose of 100 percent of the cases they receive. We should not assume too readily that because alternatives to court work—in whatever sense we mean that—they work better than courts. The critical rhetoric about courts disguises a real absence of systematic evidence of their successes and shortcomings, save for the extensive literature on the delays courts suffer in hearing cases (Zeisel, Kalven, and Buchholz 1959; Church et al. 1978). Far-reaching comparisons between courts and their alternatives are critical in order to make informed judgments about other approaches to resolving the problems of the courts.

Unfortunately, comprehensive evidence comparing courts and mediation or arbitration alternatives is relatively rare for it is difficult and expensive to collect. With one notable exception (Lind and Shapard 1981), evidence concerning the effects of arbitration has been limited almost exclusively to statistics about case loads, time between filing and award, proportion of awards appealed to courts, and the relief of docket pressures in the courts. These measures indicate the fundamental purpose of arbitration as a court alternative—namely, to relieve congested courts and thus to reduce delays. The richer evidence concerning some mediation efforts reflects in turn the greater expectations of mediation advocates that the quality of mediated settlements will be better than judgments reached by courts. Thus, systematic evaluation efforts including interviews with litigants accompanied the implementation of Neighborhood Justice Centers in Atlanta, Kansas City, and Venice MarVista, California (Cook, Roehl, and Sheppard 1980), and true experimental design (random assignment of litigants to mediation or adjudication) has been employed in evaluating the Vera Institute's Brooklyn Dispute Resolution Center (Davis, Tichane, and Grayson 1980) and the Denver Custody Mediation Project (Pearson 1981). Other studies such as our own of Maine's small-claims mediation have not involved true experimental design but do include thorough follow-up interviews with plaintiffs and defendants in both mediated and adjudicated cases. It is upon this varied research tradition that we now may draw to assess—relative to adjudication—the effectiveness of arbitration and mediation in achieving the major policy objectives of the alternatives-to-court movement: reduced court case loads, delays, and costs; increased access to justice; and improved quality of justice.

Impact on the Courts

In theory, mediation and arbitration programs should remove cases from crowded courts, handle them at lower costs to taxpayers than the more-formal and -elaborate courts, and resolve them finally. By reducing backlog and delay and saving the court system money, these alternatives might be considered cost-effective.

Exactly what impact do mediation and arbitration have on the court case loads and backlogs they were presumably created to relieve? The minor criminal cases among nonstrangers that occupy much of the time of Neighborhood Justice Centers (Cook, Roehl, and Sheppard 1980) or similar programs (Stulberg 1975; Felstiner and Williams 1980) subtract only a small proportion of cases from the heavy case loads of the courts they supplement. This is also true of experimental court-annexed arbitration in limited civil cases described by the Federal Judicial Center (Lind and Shapard 1981). Thus, narrow restrictions on the cases eligible for alternatives to court necessarily limit their impact on case loads.

In more-specialized courts (for example, small-claims or family courts) where mediation and arbitration are applied less selectively or are mandatory for certain classes of cases, these alternatives may absorb a far higher percentage of the case load and reduce the backlog considerably (for example, see Heher 1978).

Unfortunately, diverting case loads to mediation or arbitration may not have a parallel direct effect in reducing delay in the courts. In the first place, evidence suggests that court delays result largely from local legal culture and attorney expectations rather than the volume of cases awaiting adjudication (Church et al. 1978). Reductions in the volume of cases awaiting trial may affect delay, but mainly through their uncertain impact on attorney expectations and behavior (Lind and Shapard 1981). Second, many of the cases absorbed by mediation or arbitration might never have been tried at all (Cook, Roehl, and Sheppard 1980; Felstiner and Williams 1980); the vast majority of civil and criminal complaints end in dismissal, default, or negotiated settlement rather than trial. The major impact of some arbitration and mediation programs thus may be to speed the pretrial-settlement process or to provide a third-party hearing in cases in which none would otherwise have occurred. In contrast, programs that take cases on the day of trial run little risk of absorbing cases that would have settled on their own. Under these circumstances, mediation and arbitration can substantially reduce the number of trials. Thus, the impact on delay of alternatives that accept cases earlier and that schedule them independently remains unclear (Lind and Shapard 1981; McEwen and Maiman 1981). Third, given the fact that disputants may refuse to settle in mediation or may appeal an arbitration award, some cases actually end in a trial anyway and these trials may be time consuming. For example, in the Brooklyn Dispute Resolution Center's field experiment, the large number of court appearances required for felony arrestees whose mediations failed elevated the average number of court appearances for the mediation group so that it was actually greater than for the group assigned directly to adjudication.

The attractiveness of mediation and arbitration to courts and legal professionals may ultimately depend less on the volume than on the character of the cases they remove from judicial hearing. In particular, recurring disputes among relatives, friends, or acquaintances often cannot be satisfactorily handled by courts (Cook, Roehl, and Sheppard 1980). In addition, our observations of small-claims mediation suggest that many civil cases among strangers turn on misunderstandings and poor communication rather than on clearly adjudicable issues. Judges typically find such cases frustrating and frequently face the risk of imposing an arbitrary or an inappropriate judgment. Attorneys may find also that the pressures of mediation proceedings and of arbitration awards or recommendations help bring unreasonable clients into line and thus aid the negotiation process on which they rely to help them avoid costly and unnecessary trials (Miller 1973).

When these difficulties are compounded by uncertainty about what proportions of mediated or arbitrated cases would actually have gone to trial, analyses of costs and savings are risky indeed, although claims of savings through alternatives abound (for example, Conner and Surette 1977; Alper and Nichols 1981). As a corrective to these claims, one estimate of a community mediation program running at full capacity gauged its costs at roughly twice that of formal judicial processing, largely because it hears cases that would otherwise never have been tried in court (Felstiner and Williams 1980).

Ultimately, the addition of mediation or arbitration services probably never saves money in the sense that other court costs are reduced. Even if mediation, for example, is cheaper per resolution than adjudication (Cook, Roehl, and Sheppard 1980), it will not save much money in actual practice. These mediated cases would have been processed by the courts as presently staffed had no mediation alternative been available. Instead of reducing costs, mediation and arbitration services add costs to the legal system that are roughly equal to their operating budgets. The real issue is whether these costs are lower than those that would have been incurred by allocating funds to support additional judicial personnel and resources. Thus, perhaps the major practical advantage of these alternatives to court is that the freshness of their approach has justified the injection of new money and personnel into a judicial system that has seen its resources increase far less quickly than its case load. Spending more money on these new alternatives rather than on more of the old suggests that their attractiveness may rest more heavily on their anticipated beneficial effects on improving access to the courts and raising the quality of justice than on their capacity to relieve pressures on courts.

Impact on Access to Justice

A second major policy issue is the extent to which alternatives to court increase citizens' access to justice. Pound set forth the argument in 1906: Courts are intimidating to the citizenry because of their formal rules and language, discouraging because of the inappropriateness of their solutions to disputes, and inaccessible because of the high costs in time. More recently scholars have debated the relative social costs of "lumping it" compared to "litigating it" (Felstiner 1974; Danzig and Lowy 1975). Today, alternatives to court are promoted in part for their ability to provide a middle ground between lumping and litigating and for their promise in increasing access to justice by decreasing costs and delays and by making legal procedures more understandable.

By and large, mediation and arbitration speed the process of hearing the cases they take in, if for no other reason than that they are the work of specialized agencies that often have flexible resources (for example, volunteer-attorney arbitrators) that can expand or contract to meet case load demands. There is clearly a trade-off, however, between the speed of hearing and the chance of absorbing cases that would have dropped out of the court queue because of negotiated settlement or some other reason. Alternatives made available to litigants near or on the trial date (for example, Maine's small-claims mediation) neither reduce delay for individual litigants nor affect cases that would otherwise have been settled or dropped prior to trial. Alternatives made available to litigants soon after cases are filed will process many disputes that would otherwise never have reached adjudication.

Little evidence exists concerning the relative costs to litigants of arbitration or mediation compared to adjudication. Because the likelihood of lower costs to those who settle early in mediation or arbitration may be balanced by the greater costs of a failed mediation or appealed arbitration, there may be on average little, if any, savings to litigants (Lind and Shapard 1981).

The most striking difference between adjudication and mediation appears in litigant perceptions of the processes. People feel more comfortable in and satisfied with mediation than adjudication, even the less-formal version of the latter commonly found in small-claims courts. In mediation, citizens usually are more likely to believe they were not rushed and that they were understood by the mediator (for example, McEwen and Maiman 1981; Davis, Tichane, and Grayson 1980).

The significance of these positive perceptions for access to justice is not clear, however. These perceptions are retrospective and, though they might influence future use, have done little to encourage people to choose to air their grievances in the first place. Neighborhood Justice Centers have typically found it very difficult to attract walk-ins and instead rely on police and court officials for most referrals (McGillis and Mullen 1977; Cook, Roehl, and Sheppard 1980). The Custody Mediation Project in Denver experienced similar difficulties in attracting clients until it began relying on attorneys for referrals (Pearson 1981). Some of the most significant barriers to access apparently have to do with a culturally supported reluctance to air grievances in public, especially interpersonal ones. Once that threshold is crossed, typically through calling a public agency or consulting a lawyer with the intent (however vague) of going to court, people may be willing to bring their grievances to mediation or arbitration.

Impact on Quality of Justice

The strongest of the claims for mediation has to do with its presumed superiority to adjudication—at least in some kinds of cases—in reaching settlements that both parties feel to be just. The informal and supportive mediation environment presumably allows each party to air a whole range of grievances and feelings and to hear and perhaps to understand the other party's position. Because they fashion and consent to the settlements themselves, litigants should find such resolutions fairer than those who have judgments imposed in court.

Weaker but somewhat similar claims may be made for arbitration, although the power of the arbitrator to impose an award, however flexible and evenhanded that may be, considerably softens the contrast to adjudication. Because very little is known about litigant perceptions of the fairness of arbitration awards, the available evidence draws almost exclusively upon litigant experience with mediation.[1]

This evidence supports the claims made for mediation. All mediation programs whose clients have been asked follow-up questions show high levels of satisfaction with the process and the outcome of their mediation. For example, one study of three Neighborhood Justice Centers found that from 77 percent to 90 percent of complainants and respondents were satisfied with the mediation process and that from 73 percent to 87 percent were satisfied with the terms of the mediated agreement. These results contrast with those from a small sample of complainants who went to court—from 33 percent to 42 percent were satisfied with the handling of their case in court and 33 percent believed the sentence was fair (Cook, Roehl, and Sheppard 1980). The stronger experimental design of research concerning felony mediation in Brooklyn lends support to these conclusions. In the mediated cases, 77 percent of the complainants and 79 percent of the defendants thought the outcome fair as opposed to 56 percent of the complainants and 58 percent of the defendants in the adjudicated cases (Davis, Tichane, and Grayson 1980). Similar results from our study of small-claims mediation and adjudication support a comparable, though less-pronounced, preference for mediation (McEwen and Maiman 1981).

A large part of the advantage claimed for mediation probably rests on the flexibility of the settlements available to parties and on the tendency to make mutual, even if one-sided, concessions that give each party the feeling that it has been taken into account. It is likely that arbitration with a similar range of awards may be appreciated in much the same way (Sarat 1976).

The quality of justice ultimately rests not only on the achievement of a fair court judgment, arbitrator's award, or mediated settlement but also on the implementation of the settlement. Does the process used to arrive at resolution affect the likelihood of its implementation? Although evaluations of Neighborhood Justice Centers and the Brooklyn Felony Mediation Project indicate high rates of reported compliance with mediated agreements, they also show little difference between adjudicated and mediated cases in the likelihood of recurring conflict among parties and of consequent police intervention (Cook, Roehl, and Sheppard 1980; Davis, Tichane, and Grayson 1980). By contrast, our small-claims data show striking differences in the rate of payment between mediated and adjudicated cases: 71 percent of the former were fully paid compared to only 34 percent of the latter, with roughly equal percentages partially paid in the two groups (McEwen and Maiman

1981). Divorce and custody mediation apparently hold a similar advantage over adjudication. Violation of mediated settlements and consequent relitigation are less likely than in court judgments in divorce and custody cases (Pearson 1981). These contrasting findings may highlight the important differences between criminal and civil cases and courts; the impact of mediation or arbitration will vary substantially depending on the kind of court it supplements (McEwen and Maiman 1981).

Not everyone agrees that the quality of justice should be measured primarily through the eyes of disputants or in rates of implementation (Abel 1981). Concern with social justice may point us to the contribution made by a style of dispute resolution to redressing imbalances of wealth and power within the society. Mediation and arbitration may effectively relax persons who feel aggrieved and prevent them from developing a consciousness that their grievances are widely shared and have broader political as opposed to narrower, self-serving personal implications. Although no systematic social research has addressed these issues directly, informal alternatives may differ little from courts with regard to these larger issues.

Other issues pertaining to the quality of justice also remain subject to debate. Critics of mediation in particular raise questions about the extent and propriety of coercion or pressure applied during mediation (Harrington 1980) and about the degree to which informal alternatives strip weaker parties of due-process protections and disadvantage them in protecting their interests (Singer 1979; Tomasic 1980).

The coercion issue is especially difficult since, in theory, mediation rests on the voluntary participation and agreement of parties. Nonetheless, coercion often enters the process. At times parties are required by law to attempt mediation (McEwen and Maiman 1981) just as arbitration is often mandated by statute (Heher 1978). Many disputants perceive even a recommendation to mediate by judges, prosecutors, or court officials as an order to do so, and as a consequence they usually appear for mediation (Felstiner and Williams 1980; Cook, Roehl, and Sheppard 1980).

The process of mediation also develops its own momentum and pressure. It is difficult for a party simply to depart if the mediator wishes to persist in seeking a settlement. Perhaps for that reason data on small-claims mediation show sharply declining levels of perceived fairness of outcome as the length of mediation sessions increases (McEwen and Maiman 1981). If the presentation of the dispute in all its nuances does not lead parties to recognize the fairness of compromise, mediators often push for a settlement on other grounds—in particular, the additional time a trial would take or the possible costs and uncertainty of a court decision. Parties often give in grudgingly to these warnings or to the intransigence of the other party. The fact that one-third to one-half of mediations fail in most programs, however, indicates that these pressures are not irresistible.

Although some evidence suggests that inequities in power and legal resources between parties will have less impact on mediated than adjudicated outcomes (Sarat 1976), critics remain concerned that informal proceedings deprive weaker parties of important due-process protections. They point out, for example, that many criminal defendants who accept obligations in mediation would most likely have had none imposed had they gone to court (Felstiner and Williams 1980; Davis, Tichane, and Grayson 1980).

Since few mediation programs have been reviewed on constitutional grounds, there is as yet no significant body of applicable case law. The author of a study of legal issues in pretrial diversion programs using mediation and arbitration identifies constitutional questions that should be raised at various stages of the process (Rice 1979). However, after an exhaustive analysis of legal precedents, he concludes that such problems are "insignificant in light of the potential benefit that these programs offer" (1979, p. 86). In arbitration or mediation of civil cases, the opportunity for a party to obtain a trial de novo by appealing an arbitration award or rejecting a mediated settlement seems to many observers to satisfy the requirements of due process. While others are not so sanguine, the due-process issue has not perceptibly slowed the momentum of the alternatives-to-court movement.

Implementation Issues

The sorts of consequences to be expected from adoption of an arbitration or mediation alternative depend as much on the specific character of implementation as on the distinctive features of these processes. Variations in implementation abound, and careful consideration must be given to these differences if the apparent successes of one program are to be replicated elsewhere. For example, one set of questions relates to the legal and organizational context of mediation or arbitration. How closely is the program to be associated with the courts (for example, in location and in providing judicial referral of cases and endorsement of settlements)? To what sorts of cases should the program be open? How free should parties be to choose the alternative initially and to reject or appeal its outcomes? Where in the period between the experience of a dispute and a hearing in court should the arbitration or mediation alternative become available?

Other implementation questions pertain to the style of mediation or arbitration employed. Should mediators or arbitrators work singly or in panels? How tight or loose should the procedural rules be that govern the process? What respective roles should be given to attorneys and to their clients in this process? How much should private caucuses between mediators and each party be relied upon as the major vehicle for negotiation? Should mediators render an arbitration award if the parties refuse to settle in mediation? How deeply should mediators probe the personal feelings and relationships among parties in trying to achieve a tangible settlement? Ultimately, these questions relate to the manner in which mediators and arbitrators are selected and trained, to the ethical problems they may face in their work, and to the kind of ongoing evaluations of performance that are appropriate to insure competent performance.

Little systematic evidence bears on these issues as yet, but much of the mediation and arbitration literature makes at least passing reference to them (see especially McGillis and Mullen 1977).

Conclusion

The recent proliferation of alternatives to court has been accompanied by a rapidly accumulating body of research evaluating such programs. In this chapter we have summarized findings from these studies relevant to the three major policy goals said to be advanced by arbitration and mediation: (1) reduction of the burden of case load and cost on courts, (2) increase in the accessibility of justice to disputants, and (3) improvement of the quality of justice.

The case for alternatives to court as means of reducing costs to the state must receive a Scotch verdict: not proven. No clear evidence exists to support the assertion that costs are lower for either mediation or arbitration than for adjudication. However, since policymakers currently seem more willing to provide funds for innovative dispute-resolution programs than for conventional court expenses, mediation and arbitration may offer one of the few ways in an age of diminishing resources to increase judicial budgets. Thus the cost-reduction argument, though empirically weak, is likely to remain a popular one among proponents of alternatives to court.

The data on the issue of access to justice are only slightly more compelling. While mediation and arbitration do not increase access in any objective sense, there is evidence that mediation, at least, is seen by disputants as less intimidating than adjudication—after the experience, however, rather than before it. These alternatives to court thus far do not really open the doors to justice; they simply make litigants feel more comfortable and satisfied once they have already entered.

Improving the quality of justice is the policy goal most elusive of objective measurement but the one that shows the most striking advantage for mediation. When quality is operationalized as the participants' sense of a fair outcome and, in civil cases, their willingness to abide by it, mediation is a considerable improvement over adjudication. However, if the question is whether alternatives to court have enhanced, or could enhance, social justice more broadly, the answer is less clear and less subject to empirical than philosophical inquiry.

As a final caveat, remember that mediation and arbitration are not, in fact, interchangeable alternatives to adjudication; in fact, they are not even very similar except insofar as they both differ from adjudication. Moreover, they may not be equally appropriate means to the policy ends discussed here. Efficiency and responsiveness are not synonymous. The jurisdiction that adopts compulsory arbitration as a way of reducing case loads may be creating a speedier but more-impersonal process. Conversely, mediation may be so attentive to the myriad of issues underlying a seemingly simple dispute that other cases cannot be heard. The policy goals addressed here are separable and, indeed, must be viewed independently by policymakers interested in studying critically the claims of the alternatives-to-court movement.

Neither arbitration nor mediation programs live up to their advocates' more-extravagant claims and unrealistic hopes. However, the empirical evidence about their implementation and consequences provides modest support for the contention that mediation and arbitration—in their distinctive ways—can at least help to reduce some of the longstanding problems in the administration of justice.

Note

1. Researchers who examine arbitration appear content to discover whether or not the litigants and attorneys experiencing arbitration are simply as satisfied as those experiencing adjudication. No improvement in perceived fairness is expected in arbitration, but the hoped-for gains in speed and efficiency should not come at the cost of reduced fairness (Lind and Shapard 1981).

References

Abel, Richard. 1981. "Conservative Conflict and the Reproduction of Capitalism: The Role of Informal Justice" 9 *International Journal of the Sociology of Law*.

Alper, Benedict S., and Lawrence T. Nichols. 1981. *Beyond the Court-
    room: Programs in Community Justice and Conflict Resolution.*
    Lexington, Mass.: Lexington Books, D.C. Heath and Company.
Bierbrauer, Gunter, Josef Falke, and Klause-Friedrich Koch. 1978.
    "Conflict and Its Settlement: An Interdisciplinary Study Concern-
    ing the Legal Basis, Function and Performance of the Institution
    of the Schiedsmann." In M. Cappelletti and J. Weisner (eds.).
    Access to Justice: Promising Institutions, vol. 2. Alpen aan den
    Rijn, Netherlands: Sijthoff and Noordhoff.
Cappelletti, Mauro, and Bryant Garth, eds. 1978. *Access to Justice:
    A World Survey, vol. I.* Alpen aan den Rijn, Netherlands: Sijthoff
    and Noordhoff.
Church, Thomas W., Jr., Alan Carleson, Jo-Lynne Lee, and Teresa
    Tan. 1978. *Justice Delayed: The Pace of Litigation in Urban Trial
    Courts.* Williamsburg, Va.: National Center for State Courts.
Cohen, Jerome A. 1966. "Chinese Mediation on the Eve of Modern-
    ization." 54 *California Law Review:* 1201.
Conner, Ross, and Ray Surette. 1977. *The Citizen Dispute Settlement
    Program: Resolving Disputes Outside the Courts—Orlando, Flor-
    ida.* Washington, D.C.: American Bar Association.
Cook, Royer F., Janice A. Roehl, and David I. Sheppard. 1980. *Neigh-
    borhood Justice Centers Field Test: Final Evaluation Report.*
    Washington, D.C.: Government Printing Office.
Cratsley, John C. 1978. "Community Courts: Offering Alternative
    Dispute Resolution Within the Judicial System." 3 *Vermont Law
    Review* 1.
Danzig, Richard, and Michael J. Lowy. 1975. "Everyday Disputes
    and Mediation in the United States: A Reply to Professor Felsti-
    ner." 9 *Law and Society Review* 675.
Davis, Robert C., Martha Tichane, and Deborah Grayson. 1980. *Me-
    diation and Arbitration as Alternatives to Prosecution in Felony
    Arrest Cases: An Evaluation of the Brooklyn Dispute Resolution
    Center (First Year).* New York: Vera Institute of Justice.
Ehrhardt, Charles W. 1980. "One Thousand Seven Hundred Days: A
    History of Medical Malpractice Mediation Panels in Florida." 8
    Florida State University Law Review 165.
Felstiner, William. 1974. "Influences of Social Organization on Dis-
    pute Processing." 9 *Law and Society Review* 63.
Felstiner, William, and Lynn Willams. 1980. *Community Mediation
    in Dorchester, Massachusetts.* Washington, D.C.: Government
    Printing Office.

Ford Foundation. 1978. *Mediating Social Conflict: A Ford Foundation Report*. New York.

Fuller, Lon L. 1978. "The Forms and Limits of Adjudication." 92 *Harvard Law Review* 353.

Getman, Julius A. 1979. "Labor Arbitration and Dispute Resolution." 88 *Yale Law Journal* 916.

Gibbs, James. 1963. "The Kpelle Moot: A Therapeutic Model for the Informal Settlement of Disputes." 33 *Africa* 1.

Gulliver, P.H. 1963. *Social Control in an African Society*. London: Routledge & Kegan Paul.

———. 1979. *Disputes and Negotiations: A Cross-Cultural Perspective*. New York: Academic Press.

Harrington, Christine. 1980. "Voluntariness, Consent and Coercion in Adjudicating Minor Disputes." In D. Brown and J. Brigam (eds.). *Policy Implementation*. Beverly Hills, Calif.: Sage.

Heher, R.J. 1978. "Compulsory Judicial Arbitration in California: Reducing the Delay and Expense of Resolving Uncomplicated Civil Disputes." 29 *Hastings Law Journal* 475.

Kojima, T., and Y. Taniguchi. 1978. "Access to Justice in Japan." In M. Cappelletti and B. Garth (eds.). *Access to Justice: A World Survey, vol. I*. Alpen aan den Rijn. Netherlands: Sijthoff and Noordhoff.

Lind, E. Allan, and John E. Shapard. 1981. *Evaluation of Court Annexed Arbitration in Three Federal District Courts*. Washington, D.C.: Federal Judicial Center.

McEwen, Craig A., and Richard J. Maiman. 1981. "Small Claims Mediation in Maine: An Empirical Assessment." 33 *Maine Law Review* 237.

McGillis, Daniel, and Joan Mullen. 1977. *Neighborhood Justice Centers: An Analysis of Potential Models*. Washington: Government Printing Office.

Merry, Sally E. 1981. "Defining 'Success' in the Neighborhood Justice Movement." In M. Feeley and R. Tomasic (eds.). *Neighborhood Justice*. New York: Longman.

Miller, Sheldon L. 1973. "Mediation in Michigan." 56 *Judicature* 290.

Pearson, Jessica. 1981. "Child Custody: Why Not Let the Parents Decide?" 20 *The Judges Journal* 4.

Pound, Roscoe. 1906. "The Causes of Popular Dissatisfaction with the Administration of Justice." 8 *Baylor Law Review* 1.

Rice, P.R. 1979. "Mediation and Arbitration as a Civil Alternative to the Criminal Justice System—An Overview and Legal Analysis." 29 *American University Law Review* 17.

Sander, Frank E.A. 1976a. *Report of the National Conference on Minor Dispute Resolution*. Washington: American Bar Association.

———. 1976b. "Varieties of Dispute Processing." 70 *Federal Rules Decisions* 111.

Sarat, Austin. 1976. "Alternatives in Dispute Processing: Litigation in a Small Claims Courts." 10 *Law and Society Review* 339.

Singer, Linda R. 1979. "Nonjudicial Dispute Resolution Mechanisms: The Effects on Justice for the Poor." 13 *Clearinghouse Review* 569.

Steelman, David C. 1980. "Options for Reducing Civil Volume and Delay: A Review and Analysis for the 1980s." 4 *State Court Journal* 9.

Stulberg, Joseph. 1975. "A Civil Alternative to Criminal Prosecution." 39 *Albany Law Review* 359.

Tegland, K.B., and M.W. Blair. 1980. "Mandatory Arbitration of Civil Claims in Washington." 34 *Washington State Bar News* 11.

Tomasic, Roman. 1980. "Mediation as an Alternative to Adjudication: Rhetoric and Reality in the Neighborhood Justice Movement." Working paper, Disputes Processing Research Program, University of Wisconsin School of Law.

Zeisel, Hans, Harry Kalven, Jr., and B. Buchholz. 1959. *Delay in the Court*. Boston: Little, Brown.

Part II
Improving the Quality and Accountability of the Judiciary

6

The Effects of Judicial-Selection Reform: What We Know and What We Do Not

Mary L. Volcansek

The debate over the most appropriate method for selecting judges in our state courts has persisted for a century and a half. Social scientists have attempted to contribute to the discussion by offering empirical evidence on the actual functioning of the processes of the various selection systems and on the nature of the judges that different systems produce.

Perhaps the primary issue in the judicial-selection debate revolves around the public accountability of judges versus the traditional guarantee of judicial independence. This is an essentially normative question—that is, only the assumptions behind each position are capable of empirical testing. Proponents of the elective system contend that, although some risks are involved, the public should retain the authority to select persons for the bench. Further, elections have both direct and indirect effects on all public officials: Direct in that there is an assumption that voters can participate actively and meaningfully in recruiting their political leaders; indirect in that officeholders are cognizant of public accountability (Dubois 1980a, p. 29). These are the premises that can and should be considered in assessing the desirability of an elective system.

Advocates of judicial independence, conversely, assert that judges are to be insulated from the political process by avoidance of political obligations, from popular critique of essentially technical performance, and from placing judges in the same category as political officials, which presumably the judiciary is not. In essence, as Dubois has concluded, "whether judges should be independent or held accountable for the exercise of their powers is a value laden question that empirical research is ill-equipped to resolve" (1980a, pp. 27–28).

Another theme that persists in the debates is which selection system is most likely to recruit the more-qualified members of the legal profession to the bench. Although apparently more appropriate for empirical

I wish to acknowledge the skillful editorial ability of Philip L. Dubois and the consistent assistance of Judith Sheffield and Christopher Warren.

inquiry, comparing the quality of judicial personnel among the systems is most difficult in the absence of objective, quantifiable attributes of the good judge. Typically, definitions of the good judge rely on subjective factors such as personal integrity, intelligence, legal ability, and judicial temperament. These are difficult characteristics to measure within the current methodological framework of the social sciences.[1]

The accountability versus independence arguments set the parameters for which evidence from empirical research can add to the discussion. Some of the assumptions behind each position can be confirmed or refuted, but the normative positions of each side may not be validated. Further, until some of the methodological barriers can be vaulted, determination of the relative quality of judges produced by each system cannot be verified. With these limitations in mind, our focus can shift to what social scientists have offered as evidence. Table 6–1 lists, in chronological order, the major empirical studies that have been completed since the mid-1960s on the subject of judicial selection.

Elective Systems

Proponents of public accountability of the judiciary typically favor electing judges. However, critics of elective systems counter by noting that the electorate pays little attention to these low-salience races and has limited knowledge of the candidates or their qualifications. That voters know little about the candidates in judicial contests has been empirically verified (Johnson, Schaefer, and McKnight 1978, p. 374; Ladinsky and Silver 1967, p. 161).

If, as the evidence suggests, voters have minimal substantive knowledge about the candidates, what cues do they use in making their choices? Party labels, where used, are the single most significant voter cue. In the absence of a partisan contest, however, voters are inclined to rely on more-specious candidate attributes such as incumbency, name familiarity, name ethnicity, and use of nicknames (Dubois 1979a, p. 757). A sparse minority of voters will rely upon published polls or comments from lawyers (Johnson, Schaefer, and McKnight 1978, p. 374; Goldstein 1980, p. 382).

Another common allegation about the function of elections in insuring accountability is the consistently low voter turnout for judicial elections. The argument follows that accountability is not achieved when few voters exercise their franchise. That there is high voter fatigue in judicial elections is accepted. However, some institutional practices have either discouraged or nurtured voter participation. Non-concurrent election scheduling has consistently been demonstrated to

Table 6–1
Studies Relating to Judicial Selection

Study	System Analyzed	Focus	Conclusions
Henderson and Sinclair (1965)	Texas (partisan election)	Informal and formal processes of initial selection	The majority of judges is appointed to office initially.
Jacob (1966a)	Twelve states representing all systems	Impact of formal processes on social backgrounds of judges	Different procedures recruit judges with different backgrounds.
Jacob (1966b)	Wisconsin (nonpartisan election)	Differences between judicial elections and other elections	Judicial elections do not serve as feedback devices for the judiciary.
Ladinsky and Silver (1967)	Wisconsin Supreme Court (nonpartisan election)	Degree of public awareness of judicial candidates and elections	Judicial elections are low-salience contests.
Watson and Dowing (1969)	Missouri (merit selection/merit retention)	Differences in background characteristics and decisional propensities of judges in different systems	Lawyers rate Missouri Plan judges higher; tenure is much longer under Missouri Plan; background and decisional propensities are not significantly different.
Barber (1971)	Ohio Appellate Judiciary (partisan primary/nonpartisan election)	Patterns of selection, voter turnout, and winners of elections	Supreme Court elections reflect partisan influences; appellate court elections exhibit no consistent patterns.
Canon (1972)	All states' supreme courts	Differences in social and professional background of judges selected under different systems	Regionalism and selection system overlap; neither can explain differences in backgrounds.
Levin (1972)	Pittsburgh (partisan elections) and Minneapolis (nonpartisan elections)	Judicial sentencing behavior and methods of selection	Behavior and attitudes of judges are linked to political system and method of selection.

Table 6–1 (*continued*)

Study	*System Analyzed*	*Focus*	*Conclusions*
Nagel (1973)	All states' supreme courts with mixed benches	Differences in backgrounds, decisional propensities, and esteem of appointed and elected judges	Elected judges are slightly more liberal; no difference in esteem or competence; party and ethnic affiliation influence voters and appointers.
Ashman and Alfini (1974)	Five locations using nominating commissions	Characteristics of and influences on nominating commissions	Commissioners are typically white men, average age of 48; important factors are health (mental and physical) and professional reputation; partisan politics have not been totally eliminated.
Atkins and Glick (1974)	All states' supreme courts	Differences in appellant support scores under different systems	No significant differences appear among the mean appellant support scores.
Berg et al. (1975)	California and Iowa Supreme Courts	Differences in backgrounds under different selection systems	Reforms in selection systems did not affect the anticipated changes in judges selected.
Philip, Nejelski, and Press (1976)	New York Court of Appeals (partisan election)	Voter information, interest, and participation	Education level of voter and political party were most important in information and participation.
Adamany and Dubois (1976)	Wisconsin, Michigan, New York, Ohio, and Pennsylvania (partisan and nonpartisan elections)	Influences on voter turnout and voter choice	Nonconcurrent scheduling and nonpartisan elections diminish judicial accountability through elections.
Sheldon (1977)	Bar associations in all states	Level of effectiveness of bar associations in judicial selection	Bar associations exert most effective influence in Missouri Plan system and least in appointive systems.

Author (year)	Setting	Topic	Findings
Uhlman (1977)	One urban trial bench	Differences in social and professional backgrounds of black and white judges	Differences exist in partisan and community activities; appointment favors black candidates.
Jenkins (1977)	Judicial retention elections in thirteen states	Factors affecting retention elections	Fewer judges are removed through retention elections than through elections with opposition; nonappellate judges are removed through retention elections.
Sheldon (1978)	Oregon (proposed merit selection)	Legal-professional perceptions of judicial nominating commission	Rank-and-file lawyers and bar leaders would limit information on candidates to legal circles and would emphasize legal competence primarily.
Johnson, Schaefer, and McKnight (1978)	Texas (partisan election)	Voter knowledge of judicial candidates	Voters have minimal knowledge of judicial candidates; legal sources make candidates more salient.
Volcansek (1978)	Miami, Florida (nonpartisan election)	Cost/benefit perceptions of potential candidates to the bench	Personal accomplishment and prestige attract attorneys to the bench; financial limitations and campaign requirements deter attorneys.
Griffin and Horan (1979)	Retention elections in seventeen states	Factors affecting voters in retention elections	Voters lack meaningful cues and information in retention elections; participation is lowest in retention elections.
Dubois (1979a)	Twenty-five nonsouthern states using election systems	Partisan versus nonpartisan judicial election	Voters in partisan states follow party lines; more variation exists in nonpartisan and mixed systems.

Table 6–1 (*continued*)

Study	System Analyzed	Focus	Conclusions
Dubois (1979b)	Twenty-five nonsouthern states using election systems	Comparison of voter turnout in judicial elections	Partisan elections and party-column ballot increase voter participation; level of voting is a function of institutional relationships.
Schneider and Maughan (1979)	California (election and gubernatorial appointment)	Level of conservatism in judicial decisions with changes in method of selection	Appointment does not create a more-conservative court than elections.
Dubois (1980a)	Twenty-five nonsouthern states using election systems	Level of voter participation and judicial behavior related to type of judicial election	Partisan elections provide meaningful voter cue and higher voter participation than other elective systems; judicial behavior is more predictable in partisan than nonpartisan systems.
Berg and Flynn (1980)	Los Angeles municipal courts (nonpartisan election)	Timing of elections and level of voter participation	Judicial elections held at general election have higher voter turnout than primaries; judicial elections have lower voter turnout than other municipal elections.
Dubois (1980b)	California trial courts (nonpartisan elections)	Level of voter participation by characteristics of county	Voters in smaller counties participate in greater proportions; participation increases with information.
Goldstein (1980)	Louisville, Kentucky, trial courts (nonpartisan elections)	Influence of bar polls on judicial elections	Bar poll ratings most influence election outcomes.

diminish voter participation. Ballot forms have also been shown to affect the level of participation; use of the party-column ballot encourages more voters to cast their votes than the office-block and hybrid ballots (Dubois 1979b, p. 865; Adamany and Dubois 1976, p. 731). This leads to the additional conclusion that partisan elections draw greater voter turnout than nonpartisan races both because of the presence of the party cue and the more frequently contested nature of partisan contests (Dubois 1980a, p. 244; 1979b, p. 886). Researchers exploring the questions of voter participation note that in judicial races it is no lower than in other low-salience contests (Atkins 1976, p. 152; Dubois 1980a, p. 62; Jenkins 1977, p. 80).

Another charge made against judicial elections is that many judges are initially appointed rather than elected. That this does constitute a norm has been substantiated (Dubois 1980a, p. 109). However, the midterm-appointment phenomenon is more prevalent in states using nonpartisan elections than in states with partisan systems (Dubois 1980a, p. 105). The midterm-appointment practice is of particular concern since incumbent judges are rarely challenged. The result is few competitive elections and lengthy tenure for most judges. In fact, there is little competition in judicial races, which is partly due to the timing of elections or the level of the judicial office (Jacob 1966b, p. 80).

What messages are here for policymakers? Much of the conventional wisdom regarding the problems of elective systems has been confirmed. However, some of the alleged fallacies in the system (low voter participation, absence of competitiveness, and lack of meaningful voter cues) have been exacerbated by attempts at reforms such as nonpartisan ballots and nonconcurrent scheduling. Judicial elections were, after all, instituted to involve the public in another aspect of political decision making.

Additionally, the literature on judicial elections strongly suggests that races for judgeships are not significantly different from other subpresidential elections. Systematic jurisdictional comparisons with state, congressional, and local races in terms of competitiveness, voter awareness, voter information, tenure, visibility, and voter participation might shed light on the viability and desirability of an elective system. Similarly, since most studies thus far have focused on appellate courts, some of the hypotheses generated by that research should be tested at the trial-court level.[2]

Merit Selection

The so-called Missouri Plan, which provides for merit selection and retention elections, has become the most-frequently preferred reform plan for judicial selection. Research into the various elements of that system has been more limited than studies of elections, even though approximately thirty-one states employ a form of merit selection for some levels of courts.

The basic goals of the merit selection/merit retention system, against which its actual operation must be assessed, have been stated as follows:

> The reformers who conceived the idea vest it with two principal purposes: lengthy tenure for judges and public accountability. Because judges would be chosen initially on the basis of professional merit, reformers anticipated very few removals by the electorate, and only in egregious cases. [Carbon 1980, p. 213]

Two critical assumptions are implied: (1) that the use of the nominating commissions will guarantee the professional merit of appointees and (2) that retention elections will assure public accountability.

The first goal, professional merit, is to be accomplished through the use of nominating commissions composed of lawyers and lay members. As noted earlier, comparison of the actual quality of judges selected under various systems is a tricky task that has not been very successfully pursued. Therefore, the alternative approach is to look at the processes of the commissions to determine whether they offer a mechanism for recruiting and screening to obtain the most qualified lawyers available for judicial service. The commissioners themselves have indicated they do not believe that partisan politics have been totally eliminated from the merit nomination process. However, they do claim to emphasize the mental and professional health of applicants, along with their professional reputations, as the most important criteria in making nominations (Ashman and Alfini 1974).

One criticism of the merit nominating process is that the commissions are not representative of the public. Indeed, they are comprised of a relatively homogeneous group of establishment lawyers and laypersons—white men with an average age of 48 (Ashman and Alfini 1974). Such composition does not necessarily foster or deter selection of meritorious individuals. However, the charge is that commissions so constituted will be less inclined to nominate qualified applicants who are women or minorities.[3]

Another criticism of the merit selection system is that it gives the organized bar a disproportionate input into the selection of judges.

Officials of state bar associations have been the first to admit that the merit selection system provides them with the most effective means of influencing the choice of who will serve on the bench (Sheldon 1977, p. 397). Further, bar leaders have indicated that they would rely primarily on sources of information within the legal community to assess qualifications of applicants (Sheldon 1978, p. 378).

The other component feature of the Missouri Plan is public accountability of judges through retention elections. Although research is somewhat sparse on retention elections, the existing evidence does cast a long shadow on the goal of public accountability. Prominent characteristics of retention elections are low voter interest, knowledge, and turnout. The absence of voter cues in retention elections is more striking than in other judicial elections. Voters thus choose to support incumbents, even in the presence of active media campaigns detailing deeds of misconduct or incompetence. Less than one percent of all judges standing for retention elections have been removed through that process (Carbon 1980, p. 213). This is a significantly smaller proportion of removals than is found among incumbent judges in elective systems.[4]

Considering that merit selection/merit retention has been tauted as a panacea for the dilemma of selecting judges, a variety of questions must be addressed. The literature on judicial elections offers several viable directions, frameworks, and hypotheses for studying retention elections. In particular, the types of cues that are followed by voters need to be explored. Also, comparisons of voter turnout, information, and efficacy should be conducted between elective and merit retention systems.

Since nominating commissions have been considered the cornerstone of the system, the social system of the commission nominations and gubernatorial appointments deserves attention. How does one obtain an appointment to the commission? How does the commission screen? Does the commission actually recruit? How have commissions responded to the gubernatorial choice? How is the commission lobbied? Framework and hypotheses for approaching these questions have been suggested in studies of the federal nominating commissions (see Neff 1981a, 1981b).

Comparative Analyses of Systems

Perhaps more-definitive conclusions regarding selection systems would be possible through cross-system analysis. Currently such studies are limited in quantity and in scope. Attempts at comparison of objective characteristics of judges have been made, with findings such as the existence of differences in the social and political backgrounds of judges in various systems. In one instance, the differences were attributed to the institutional method of selection (Jacob 1966a, p. 104), but in another the distinctions were thought to be manifestations of regional variations in political recruitment (Canon 1972, p. 579). Yet a third study failed to isolate any significant differences (Berg et al 1975, p. 263). Further, each of these studies hinges on the crucial but unproved assumption that past experience directly affects current behavior.

Another means of comparing judges across systems is behavior. The methodological difficulty of this undertaking lies in defining what constitutes behavior and how to measure it. When studying appellate judges, the politically relevant behavior typically refers to the political or ideological bent of the judges, measured through their written opinions and votes (Atkins and Glick 1974, p. 427; Nagel 1973). Unfortunately, written opinions and votes do not fully represent all judicial behavior.

The relevant behavior of trial-court judges can be conceptualized in terms of sensitivity to different groups, rights, and values. Sentencing behavior—a small segment of judicial behavior—usually serves as the measuring stick (Levin 1972, p. 216). Unfortunately, not only is sentencing a limited aspect of judicial behavior, but also it presents methodological difficulties in that criminal cases and defendant characteristics are rarely comparable.

Cross-state studies of appellate decision making would appear to be the ideal laboratory for testing the effects of various selection systems. However, formal selection systems tend to hide informal aspects such as gubernatorial appointment in elective states. Further, differences in selection systems per se may be observed by variations in law and legal culture. Judges under a single selection system cannot be treated as a homogeneous group, ignoring other obviously important factors that distinguish them—for example, political party. The methodological difficulties in cross-state research have resulted in a minimal contribution to our knowledge about the different effects of different selection systems.

Conclusion

Undoubtedly our knowledge about merit selection/merit retention systems has large gaps remaining. Because of the virtues this system purportedly offers and because of its popularity among legal- and judicial-reform groups, the absence of objective, methodologically sound information becomes more critical for policymakers. Attention appears to be turning in that direction. All of the systems discussed aim at securing quality judges. Despite the height of the methodological obstacles, social scientists can make a significant policy contribution if those barriers can be scaled, particularly in cross-system comparisons.

Notes

1. Legal training, type of law school attended, age at oath taking, prior judicial experience, and other judicially oriented experience are objective factors that have been employed to define the good judge (Berg and Flynn 1980, pp. 266–67). The esteem with which lawyers hold judges has also been used to measure the quality of judges (Watson and Downing 1969, p. 331; Nagel 1973, p. 26).

2. Some studies are currently moving in this direction. Examples are Berg and Flynn (1980), Dubois (1980b), and Volcansek (1981).

3. This point has been debated regarding federal nominating commissions; see Goldman (1979).

4. In 1976, 353 judges faced retention elections, and only 3 lost (Jenkins 1977, p. 80). Yet, in a single state in the same year, 6 judges, running on a partisan ballot, were defeated (Griffin and Horan 1977, p. 79).

References

Adamany, David, and Philip L. Dubois. 1976. "Electing State Judges." 1976 *Wisconsin Law Review* 731.

Ashman, Allan, and James J. Alfini. 1974. *The Key to Judicial Merit Selection*. Chicago: American Judicature Society.

Atkins, Burton M. 1976. "Judicial Elections: What the Evidence Shows." 50 *Florida Bar Journal* 152.

Atkins, Burton M., and Henry R. Glick. 1974. "Formal Judicial Recruitment and State Supreme Court Decisions." 2 *American Politics Quarterly* 427.

Barber, Kathleen. 1971. "Ohio Judicial Elections—Nonpartisan Premises with Partisan Results." 32 *Ohio State Law Journal* 762.

Berg, Larry L., and Leo Flynn. 1980. "Voter Participation in Municipal Court Elections in Los Angeles County." 2 *Law and Policy Quarterly* 161.

Berg, Larry L., Justin J. Green, John P. Schmidhauser, and Ronald
    S. Schneider. 1975. ''The Consequences of Judicial Reform: A
    Comparative Analysis of the California and Iowa Appellate Sys-
    tems.'' 28 *Western Political Quarterly* 263.
Canon, Bradley C. 1972. ''The Impact of Formal Selection Process
    on the Characteristics of Judges—Reconsidered.'' 6 *Law and So-
    ciety Review* 579.
Carbon, Susan B. 1980. ''Retention Elections in the United States.''
    64 *Judicature* 213.
Dubois, Philip L. 1980a. *From Ballot to Bench: Judicial Elections
    and the Quest for Accountability*. Austin: University of Texas
    Press.
————. 1980b. ''Public Participation in Trial Court Elections.'' 2
    Law and Policy Quarterly 133.
————. 1979a. ''The Significance of Voting Cues in State Supreme
    Court Elections.'' 13 *Law and Society Review* 757.
————. 1979b. ''Voter Turnout in State Judicial Elections: An Anal-
    ysis of the Tail on the Electoral Kite.'' 41 *Journal of Politics* 865.
Goldman, Sheldon. 1979. ''Should There Be Affirmative Action for
    the Judiciary?'' 62 *Judicature* 489.
Goldstein, Joel H. 1980. ''Bar Poll Ratings as the Leading Influence
    on a Non-partisan Judicial Election.'' 63 *Judicature* 377.
Griffin, Kenyon N., and Michael J. Horan. 1979. ''Merit Retention
    Elections: What Influences the Voters?'' 63 *Judicature* 79.
Henderson, Bancroft C., and T.C. Sinclair. 1965. *The Selection of
    Judges in Texas: An Exploratory Study*. Houston: Public Affairs
    Research Center.
Jacob, Herbert. 1966a. ''The Effect of Institutional Differences in the
    Recruitment Process: The Case of State Judges.'' 13 *Journal of
    Public Law* 104.
————. 1966b. ''Judicial Insulation—Direct Participation and Public
    Attention to the Courts in Wisconsin.'' 1966 *Wisconsin Law Re-
    view* 801.
Jenkins, William. 1977. ''Retention Elections: Who Wins When No
    One Loses.'' 61 *Judicature* 79.
Johnson, Charles A., Roger C. Schaefer, and R. Neal McKnight.
    1978.
    ''The Salience of Judicial Candidates and Elections.'' 59 *Social
    Science Quarterly* 371.
Ladinsky, Jack, and Allan Silver. 1967. ''Popular Democracy and
    Judicial Independence.'' 1967 *Wisconsin Law Review* 128.
Levin, Martin A. 1972. ''Urban Politics and Judicial Behavior.'' 1
    Journal of Legal Studies 193.

Nagel, Stuart S. 1973. *Comparing Elected and Appointed Judicial Systems*. Beverly Hills: Sage Publications.

Neff, Alan. 1981a. "Breaking with Tradition: A Study of the U.S. District Judge Nominating Commissions." 64 *Judicature* 257.

————. 1981b. *The United States District Court Nominating Commissions*. Chicago: American Judicature Society.

Philip, Cynthia O., Paul Nejelski, and Aric Press. 1976. *Where Do Judges Come From?* New York: Institute of Judicial Administration.

Schneider, Ronald, and Ralph Maughan. 1979. "Does the Appointment of Judges Lead to a More Conservative Bench?" 5 *Justice System Journal* 45.

Sheldon, Charles H. 1977. "Influencing the Selection of Judges: The Variety and Effectiveness of State Bar Activities." 30 *Western Political Quarterly* 397.

————. 1978. "Searching for Judges in Oregon: Where Would the Bar Look?" 61 *Judicature* 378.

Uhlman, Thomas M. 1977. "Race, Recruitment, Representation: Background Differences between Black and White Trial Court Judges." 30 *Western Political Quarterly* 457.

Volcansek, Mary L. 1981. "Explaining Outcomes of Judicial Elections: An Exploration." 34 *Western Political Quarterly*.

————. 1978. "Why Lawyers Become Judges." 62 *Judicature* 167.

Watson, Richard A., and Rondal G. Downing. 1969. *The Politics of the Bench and the Bar: Judicial Selection under the Missouri Nonpartisan Court Plan*. New York: John Wiley & Sons.

Winters, Glenn R. 1973. *Judicial Selection and Tenure: Selected Readings*. Chicago: American Judicature Society.

7

Judicial Disciplinary Commissions: A New Approach to the Discipline and Removal of State Judges

Jolanta Juszkiewicz Perlstein
and *Nathan Goldman*

To attain an independent judiciary insulated from politics, nine of the original thirteen states and the federal government provided for life tenure to judges and difficult procedures for their discipline and removal (Winters and Schoenbaum 1976, p. 31; Kurland 1969). A need to achieve political accountability, however, prompted gradual shifts to fixed terms and elections of judges. During the era of Jacksonian Democracy, a majority of states adopted legislation to elect judges (Haynes 1944, pp. 99–101). This effort was doomed to fail, however, because low saliency of issues and candidates resulted in incumbents' usually running unopposed (Schoenbaum 1977, pp. 9–10). Long, uninterrupted terms in office without periodic checks on performance, therefore, eventually came to characterize both appointive and elective methods of judicial selection (Atkins 1976; Jacob 1966). Although almost all state constitutions provide for the impeachment of judges, impeachment and other traditional methods of discipline and removal (such as recall and address) have been infrequently invoked. As of 1970, for example, fewer than one-half of the states had used impeachment even once.

The apparent failure of traditional methods to handle all but the most egregious cases of judicial misconduct may be attributed to cumbersome proceedings requiring legislative involvement and the lack of formal mechanisms to review and investigate complaints. The rising public concern over the performance of courts and judges and the accompanying need for suitable ways to deal with problems of judicial

This chapter is based on a study supported by contract number JADAG-79-M-1559, awarded to Nathan Goldman by the Federal Justice Research Program, U.S. Department of Justice. Points of view or opinions stated in this chapter are those of the authors and do not necessarily represent the official position or policies of the U.S. Department of Justice.

misconduct and disability has led to the development during the 1960s
and 1970s of alternative mechanisms of disciplining state judges.

New York and California were in the forefront of establishing
modern procedures for judicial discipline. Today, all fifty states have
some form of judicial-commission plan. The New York Court on the
Judiciary was created by constitutional amendment in 1947. However,
only six cases were actually heard by this Court, resulting in the
removal of two judges, the resignation of four others after the proceedings were instituted, and dismissal of one case in which justification for removal was wanting. Lack of initial confidentiality and a
permanent staff to screen and investigate complaints, as well as the
unavailability of a sanction short of removal, contributed to the rare
use of the Court on the Judiciary. That thirty-five states have modeled
their commission plans on the California Judicial Qualifications Commission established in 1960 is evidence of its popularity. The acceptance
and effectiveness of the California commission can be ascribed to its
heterogeneous composition (of lawyers, laypersons, and judges), a
full-time secretary who is invested with the power to screen complaints,
confidential hearings, and the authority to make public recommendations to the state supreme court to discipline or to remove judges.

Today there are three basic kinds of commissions. In the one-tier
system that thirty-five states have adopted, the investigation of complaints and recommendations to the state supreme court are delegated
to one body. Although perceived as the most efficient system, the one-
tier commission is most susceptible to charges of providing insufficient
due-process safeguards. Eight states have some form of the two- or
multitier system, which is designed to separate procedures for screening and investigating from recommending functions.[1] Four states use
a commission-legislature system, which vests the commission with the
responsibility for recommending discipline short of removal to the
highest court of the state while the removal power remains with the
legislature.[2]

Commissions are composed of some combination of lawyers, laypersons, and judges who are appointed typically by the state bar association, the state executive or legislature, and the state supreme court
respectively. Most commissions also use similar procedures for complaint treatment. Following an initial screening, the complaints that
merit further investigation and that are within the commissions' jurisdiction are forwarded to a panel of commissioners, special masters,
or the entire commission for a formal hearing. The commissions' jurisdiction is confined to dealing with conduct that does not involve or
interfere with judicial discretion and constitute proper matter for appellate review. Due-process procedures and grounds for imposing sanc-

tions are established during this stage of the complaint-handling process.

The states' experience with these mechanisms is now sufficient for an evaluation of whether they have achieved their intended policy goals. The foci of such an evaluation are the purposes or objectives of the commission system, whether and how effectively they are met, and to what extent they impinge or influence the outcome of the complaints. Ostensibly, the commisssions are intended to discipline misconduct, reinforce judicial guidelines, remove unfit judges, protect the image of the judiciary, and make judges more accountable to the administration of justice and the public. The fulfillment of these purposes may be hampered by the statutory and constitutional limitations imposed on the commissions not to infringe upon the independence of judicial proceedings, as well as internal and external factors that influence their decisions and recommendations. This research attempts to provide evidence about the success of the commission system in achieving its intended objectives while maintaining judicial independence.

Evaluation of Commissions

Who Complains?

A study conducted in 1977 revealed that three-quarters of the complaints were brought by disgruntled litigants and concerned citizens. Judges, judicial personnel, and lawyers also brought a considerable proportion (16 percent) of the complaints. One out of every twenty-five complaints was initiated by the commission, and the remaining were brought by public officials, court watchers, and others (Tesitor 1978, pp. 5–6).

The media play an important role in publicizing the existence and work of the commissions. In this capacity the media can exert pressure on the commission. The public likewise can influence the commission, indirectly, through the election of public officials who are instrumental in establishing the commissions and, directly, as complainants.

Table 7–1 is a compilation of disciplinary cases reported by several sources.[3] It is apparent that the overwhelming majority involves either a judge's on-bench behavior or the effect on it of off-bench activities. Cases of offensive on-bench behavior have included rudeness, racist or sexist language, show of favoritism, abuse of power, failure to perform duties, and alteration of court records. Cases involving off-

Table 7–1
Reported Cases of Misconduct Handled by Commissions,
by Nature of Activity

Nature of Activity	Number of Cases	Percentage
In-court conduct	*117*	*56.5*
Failure to perform	35	16.9
Lack of decorum, rudeness	25	12.1
Ticket fixing	21	10.1
Abuse of power, corruption	20	9.7
Ex parte hearing held	16	7.7
Conflicts of interest or appearance thereof	*36*	*17.4*
Direct conflict of interest	12	5.8
Political activities	14	6.8
Practicing law	10	4.8
Incapacity	*6*	*2.9*
Alcoholism	3	1.5
Senility, old age	3	1.5
Off-bench activities	*34*	*16.4*
Criminal cases	22	10.6
Private activities	12	5.8
Miscellaneous	*14*	*6.8*

Data from: Irene A. Tesitor 1978. *Judicial Conduct Organizations*. Chicago: American Judicature Society; New York Commission on Judicial Conduct 1978. *Annual Report*. New York; and mimeographed compilation of North Carolina cases by Dallas Cameron, Jr. (available from authors).

bench activities have dealt with criminal conduct as well as impropriety in business and social dealings.

Complaint Processing

An initial screening by the executive secretary eliminates most of the complaints that are found to be frivolous or not within the commission's jurisdiction. The executive secretary performs these duties in twenty-eight states and the District of Columbia. The next step for the few surviving cases is a hearing before the commission. Commissions may opt to dismiss the case during this stage, order disciplinary action subject to appeal, or more typically, recommend sanctions to the state supreme court, a second tier, or a court on the judiciary. In twenty-seven states, the executive director of a staff member conducts the preliminary investigation (Gillis and Fieldman 1977, pp. 123–125). Sixteen commissions hire an outside investigator or attorney, and another eight bring in government agencies to perform this task. Only ten states thus far conduct open hearings (Appendix 1977, pp. 206–207).

Commission Performance

As with other organizations, it is to be expected that the attitudes and perceptions of the commissioners will influence the commissions' performance in processing complaints. After all, the commissioners represent different constituencies and are appointed by different processes.

To assess commissioner perceptions, we mailed a questionnaire to all executive secretaries and commission members in the states in the continental United States that have judicial-conduct organizations. Respondents returned 148 questionnaires, producing a 35 percent response rate. Commissioners were asked how accurately each of the following five statements describes the role (purpose) of the commission:

1. To reinforce guidelines,
2. To make judges accountable to the administration of justice,
3. To protect the image of the judiciary,
4. To make judges more accountable to the public,
5. To punish misconduct.

Some differences among the groups were noted despite an overall similarity of views held by judges, lawyers, and laypersons. The lay commissioners (67 percent) are most likely to perceive the commission's role as reinforcing guidelines (compared with 52 percent and 56 percent of judges and lawyers respectively), while lawyers (67 percent) most often cited punishing misconduct as most accurately portraying the commission's role (compared with 57 percent of judges and 54 percent of laypersons). Judge members agree with the other groups' perceptions but also found that commissions function to make judges more accountable to the administration of justice (44 percent of judges as opposed to 35 percent of lawyers and 32 percent of laypersons had this perception).

In a follow-up question the commissioners were asked to assess the effectiveness of the commission in influencing judicial behavior in each of seven areas that could or have become subjects of complaints against judges: punctuality, temperance, open-mindedness, courteousness to lawyers and witnesses, professional integrity, knowledge of the law, and susceptibility to influence. The other eight categories of judicial attributes and behaviors such as neat appearance, decisiveness, sense of humor, dignity, common sense, understanding of people, hardworkingness, and controlling cases have not generated complaints. Fewer than one in eight commissioners viewed the commission as having influenced the second set of judicial attributes. At best, only two-fifths of the commissioners found the commission to be very effective in controlling the susceptibility to influence, which potentially constitutes a bases for complaints. The evidence concerning the ability of the commission to influence judicial behavior is pretty weak; what it really shows is that commissioners think that their main function is as a reactive body and not as a deterrent to bad behavior.

In an attempt to determine whether the attitudes of commissioners affect complaint handling, commissioners were asked to make decisions about fourteen hypothetical complaints. These complaints were drawn largely from actual cases involving on- and off-bench conduct. Only one case dealt with a judge's disability rather than misconduct. On-bench behavior was divided into conduct related to specific pending cases and conduct that was not case related.[4] This exercise revealed very few differences in the disciplinary actions recommended by the three groups of commissioners. All commissioners were more willing to recommend removal of a judge for off-bench misconduct (27 percent of judges, 29 percent of lawyers, 28 percent of laypersons) than for on-bench misconduct (4 percent of judges, 5 percent of lawyers, and 10 percent of laypersons).

Although the recommended disciplinary actions were found to be very similar for the three groups of commissioners, it might nevertheless be possible for the composition of the commission to affect the processing of complaints. Judges who serve on panels dominated by judges are possibly influenced by their colleagues to be more lenient on the judge under investigation than other members in order to protect the image of the judiciary in general and their fellow judge specifically. To determine the veracity of this hypothesis, the commissions, grouped according to the nature of their composition, were assessed on the basis of their decisions about the hypothetical cases (see table 7–2).

The composition of the commission had no apparent effect on judges' recommendations in nine of the fourteen hypothetical cases. Table 7–2 includes only the five cases in which differences appeared among the diversely composed commissions. Judges on judge-dominated commissions, defined as those containing at least two more judges than other members, on the one hand were less likely than other members to recommend removal or suspension of a judge for on-bench

Table 7–2

Disciplinary Recommendations of Judges in Hypothetical Cases, by Composition of Commission

Case	Commission Composition	Dismissal or Cannot say		Censure or Reprimand		Removal or Suspension	
		N	Percentage	N	Percentage	N	Percentage
Reference letters for convict to reduce sentence in another court	Judge-dominated	5	29.4	9	52.9	3	17.6
	Other-dominated	4	16.0	16	64.0	5	20.0
Backdated docket entry to appear timely made	Judge-dominated	2	11.1	11	61.1	5	27.8
	Other-dominated	2	7.7	13	50.0	11	42.3
Erratic driving revealed unregistered weapon	Judge-dominated	5	27.8	9	50.0	4	22.2
	Other-dominated	9	37.5	14	58.3	1	4.2
Intoxicated at country club dance	Judge-dominated	6	33.3	12	66.7	—	—
	Other-dominated	15	57.7	11	42.3	—	—
Refused to discipline bailiff arrested at gambling raid	Judge-dominated	9	50.0	9	50.0	—	—
	Other-dominated	20	80.0	5	20.0	—	—

misconduct such as backdating docket entries or attempting to influence a sentencing decision of another court. Judges on judge-dominated commissions were, on the other hand, severer than judges on other commissions with judges charged with off-bench misconduct such as being intoxicated at a country-club dance, driving erratically, or trying to conceal an unregistered weapon.

Judges are probably more likely than others to interpret any on-bench behavior as potentially in the realm of the proper exercise of judicial discretion and not the appropriate subject of outside review. Off-bench misconduct that damages the image of the judiciary should be punished to protect other judges. For the most part, however, the composition of the commission does not substantially influence the nature of the outcome. Judges are influenced to some degree by their peers but only if they constitute a dominant group. Lay and lawyer commissioners do not appear to set their views aside in deference to the judge commissioners.

Judicial Independence

Commissions on judicial discipline are entrusted to respect judicial independence and not to infringe upon areas of judicial discretion. Gray areas inevitably arise between discretionary use and abuse of power. The commissions cannot, of course, exceed their authority to review cases of abuse.

A hypothetical complaint in the realm of judicial discretion was designed to test whether or not commissions on judicial discipline overstep their bounds. The complaint concerned a judge's failure to instruct a jury properly—a matter that should be of appellate and not commission review. The commissioners were expected, therefore, to choose to dismiss the case for lack of jurisdiction. Any other recommended action could be construed as infringement on judicial independence.

An overwhelming majority of respondents (75 percent) recommended that the case be dismissed. Interestingly, lay members were least willing to dismiss the case; whereas nearly 90 percent of the judge and lawyer members recommended dismissal, only a third of the lay commissioners chose this disposition. Two lay commissioners went so far as to recommend that the judge be suspended or removed. More lay members (six compared with one lawyer and one judge commissioner) were less sure of what action the commission should take in this case. On the whole, however, judges need not fear having their judicial independence questioned.

Outcome

State supreme courts have decided, usually on the basis of the American Bar Association approved Standards of Judicial Discipline and Disability, almost 200 cases since 1964 (*Decennial Digests* 1967, 1977–1979; Frankel 1968; Fifth National Conference 1976).[5] In 1977, state commissions received roughly 2,500 complaints (Tesitor 1978, pp. 5–6). Nearly 80 percent were dismissed before an investigation, 7 percent more were dismissed after an investigation, and another 11 percent of the complaints were settled by the commission by private adjustments or a promise by the judge to cease his or her offensive behavior. In addition, almost 2 percent of the complaints terminated in resignations. Less than 1 percent of the complaints resulted in a commission's recommendation to a court or in an order disciplining a judge. These cases do not include an undertermined number of cases from states such as Illinois, Delaware, and New Mexico, which do not report or publish all of their cases, or hundreds of unreported judicial resignations occurring before the cases reach the courts. The dismissal rate is also underestimated because some of the state courts only publish sanctions so as to protect the judges in cases that have been dismissed.

The majority of cases that reach the courts upon the commissions' recommendations involved on-bench conduct. Abusing judicial power by interfering with the lawyer-client relationship or by using offensive language exemplifies the kind of on-bench conduct that was brought to the attention of the commission and subsequently to the courts. According to table 7–3, removals account for 32 percent (60 of 186) of all the actions taken by the courts. Judges are most likely to be removed from office for on-bench misconduct such as showing favoritism and ticket fixing (7 of 13 and 5 of 10 cases respectively resulted in removal rather than less-severe sanctions) and for off-bench misconduct such as committing criminal acts (11 of 22, or 50 percent of the time).

To assess whether the composition of the commissions and the state supreme courts' acceptance of the commissions' recommenda-

Table 7–3
Reported Disciplinary Cases of State Supreme Courts, by Nature of Sanction

	Disciplinary Action									
	Removal		Suspension		Censure		Reprimand		Release	
Nature of Activity	N	Percentage	N	Percentage	N	Percentage	N	Percentage	N	Percentage
On-bench	39	65.0	14	45.2	44	74.6	6	40.0	10	47.6
Failure to perform	5		0		5		1		5	
Ex parte hearing	0		2		12		2		0	
Show of favoritism	7		2		3		1		0	
Ticket fixing	5		2		2		1		0	
Abuse of power	12		8		11		1		3	
Temperament	10		0		11		0		2	
Conflict of interest	8	13.3	4	12.9	2	3.4	4	26.7	4	19.0
Practicing law	3		3		0		3		1	
Political activities	5		1		2		1		3	
Off-bench	13	21.7	13	41.9	13	22.0	5	33.3	7	33.3
Criminal acts	11		3		2		1		5	
Impropriety	1		7		8		4		0	
Other acts	1		3		3		0		2	
Totals	60	32.2	31	16.7	59	31.7	15	8.1	21	11.3
(N = 186)										

tions are related, we coded the cases that reached the courts between 1964 and 1978 on the basis of how the courts received and acted on the commissions' recommendations. The composition of the commissions was defined, as before, in terms of judge- or other-dominated panels.

Table 7–4 shows that recommendations made by judge-dominated commissions are more likely to be affirmed by state supreme courts than those made by other-dominated commissions. There are at least three plausible explanations for the relationship between commission composition and court outcome. It may simply be that judges on the court are deferring to their colleagues on the commission. Alternatively, the predominance of judges in judge-dominated commissions may result in a membership more highly attuned to the views of the high court on disciplinary matters. Finally, judge-dominated commissions may be employing a screening process that more effectively eliminates cases that are unlikely to receive disciplinary action at the high-court level. Whatever the explanation, the findings suggest that commission composition may be related to the ultimate decision rendered by the court.

Summary

The documented cases constitute a tiny percentage of the tens of thousands of complaints brought to the commissions. Between 1964 and 1978, the commissions have removed sixty judges and the courts have imposed formal sanctions against one hundred other judges. The commissions, given these statistics, do not appear to be straying beyond their authority in disciplining judges.

Table 7–4
Effect of Commission Composition on State Supreme Courts'
Disposition of Cases

Commission Type	Recommendation Affirmed by Supreme Court		Recommendation Modified by Supreme Court		Total	
	N	Percentage	N	Percentage	N	Percentage
Judge-dominated	33	84.6	6	15.4	39	41.9
Other-dominated	33	61.1	21	39.9	54	58.1

$X^2 = 6.07$
Degree of freedom $= 1$
Level of significance $= .02$

Conclusions and Recommendations

As a result of the 1980 Judicial Councils Reform and Judicial Conduct and Disability Act (PL #96-458), the question of a federal disciplinary commission is, for the moment, moot. The federal solution incorporates the existing administrative structure of the federal judicial system for processing complaints against federal judges and magistrates. The act stipulates that any person who asserts that a judge's conduct is ''prejudicial to the effective and expeditious administration of the business of the courts'' or that the judge is disabled can file a complaint with the judicial council.

The judicial council, composed of at least a 3 to 1 ratio of appellate and district judges, in the person of the presiding judge, screens complaints and dismisses those that are frivolous, lacking jurisdiction, or directly related to the merits of litigation. A committee of the council actually conducts any investigation and makes recommendations to the full council. The council has several sanctioning options, all short of removal, which still rests with Congress via the impeachment process. Any matter can be referred directly to the Judicial Conference, but the judicial council must refer cases that might constitute grounds for impeachment. The Judicial Conference can also hear, on a certiorari basis, petitions submitted by complainants, judges, or magistrates for review of judicial-council actions.

The state experience provides some insights into the chances of success of the federal plan. On the positive side, that the plan employs judges and retains removal power with the legislature obviates any problems associated with separation of powers and judicial independence. The attitudes of judges concerning discipline are not much different than nonjudges, and commission composition usually does not make a difference in terms of commission action, although there may be some effect in cases involving off-bench behavior.

The act does not, however, address the issue of confidentiality. It is important that the preliminary stages are not publicized to protect the judge. Lack of a permanent staff to handle the initial screening and investigations may, like for the New York Court on the Judiciary, be the downfall of the federal plan. The presiding judge, who must simultaneously discharge other duties, may find it difficult to process complaints.

The state experience suggests that maintaining judicial independence must be balanced with an effective method of processing complaints. This may be accomplished by having a permanent staff composed of judicial or quasi-judicial personnel handle the first few stages of complaint processing instead of an active judge on an ad hoc basis or nonjudicial personnel. Magistrates or retired judges seem to be reasonable condidates for this position. The only true indications of the success of the federal plan will be how future cases of judicial misconduct will be decided.

Notes

1. The eight states are Alabama, Delaware, Hawaii, Illinois, Ohio, Oklahoma, New York, and West Virginia.

2. These four states are Arkansas, Massachusetts, Rhode Island, and South Carolina.

3. These sources include statistics cited in Tesitor (1978), which does not contain figures for New York, the New York Commission on Judicial Conduct's 1978 *Annual Report,* and a mimeographed compilation of North Carolina cases by Dallas Cameron, Jr. (available from the authors).

4. The off-bench complaints include a judge, stopped for erratic driving, who was found to have a concealed revolver, a judge who fenced his yard two feet beyond his neighbor's property line, and a series of complaints involving a judge who ran for Congress without first resigning his judgeship. The on-bench conduct, not involving pending cases, includes writing letters of reference for a convict to get another judge to reduce the sentence, allowing a TV station to film and air an interview with the judge about a pending trial, and refusing to discipline a bailiff arrested in a gambling raid. The hypotheticals concerning on-bench behavior directly connected with pending cases include failing to instruct a jury properly, backdating a docket to appear that a motion was timely made, not reporting an attempt to get a judge to fix a ticket, criticizing and humiliating counsel in the courtroom, and refusing to withdraw from hearing cases involving a conflict of interest.

5. In 1964, the California court decided its first commission case, *Stevens* v. *Commission on Judicial Qualifications,* 393 P.2d. 709 (California 1964). There has been a dramatic increase in the number of disciplinary cases handled by the state courts in the past fifteen years. A 300 percent rise in the number of cases reflects the growth in the number of states with disciplinary commissions from two (New York and California) to fifty-three (fifty states, the District of Columbia, Guam, and Puerto Rico).

References

Appendix. 1977. "Standards Relating to Judicial Discipline and Disability Retirement." 54 *Chicago-Kent Law Review* 206.

Atkins, Burton M. 1976. "Judicial Elections—What the Evidence Shows." 50 *Florida Bar Journal* 152.

Decennial Digests. 1967, 1977–1979. St. Paul, Minn.: West Publishing Co.

Fifth National Conference of Judicial Conduct Organizations. 1976. *Resource Materials*. Chicago: American Judicature Society.

Frankel, Jack E. 1968. "Fitness and Discipline of Judges: The California Plan" 41 *State Government* 120.

Gillis, John H., and Elaine Fieldman. 1977. "Michigan's Unitary System of Judicial Discipline: A Comparison with Illinois' Two-Tier Approach." 54 *Chicago-Kent Law Review* 123.

Haynes, Evan. 1944. *The Selection and Tenure of Judges*. Washington, D.C.: National Conference of Judicial Councils.

Jacob, Herbert. 1966. "Judicial Insulation—Elections, Direct Participation and Public Attention to the Courts in Wisconsin." 1966 *Wisconsin Law Review* 801.

Kurland, Philip. 1969. "The Constitution and the Tenure of Federal Judges: Some Notes from History." 36 *University of Chicago Law Review* 665.

New York Commission on Judicial Conduct. 1978. *Annual Report*. New York.

Schoenbaum, Edward J. 1977. "A Historical Look at Judicial Discipline." 54 *Chicago-Kent Law Review* 1.

Tesitor, Irene A. 1978. *Judicial Conduct Organizations*. Chicago: American Judicature Society.

Winters, Glenn, and Edwrd J. Schoenbaum, eds. 1976. *American Courts in Justice*. Chicago: American Judicature Society.

8

Judicial Discipline at the Federal Level: A New Response to an Old Problem

John H. Culver and
Randal L. Cruikshanks

Interest in the accountability of judges has been rekindled in recent years for a variety of reasons including Watergate, public dissatisfaction with lawyers, the arbitrary manner in which judges all too often resolve cases, and accounts in the popular press on the misdeeds of jurists. Although there is agreement that judges should epitomize the high level of professionalism expected of the U.S. judiciary, the problem remains of how best to deal with the judge who is no longer acting in a professional manner. This problem is all the more troublesome since any disciplinary mechanism has the potential to infringe upon the independence of the bench. The resulting dilemma is this: How can the public be protected from the incompetent judge, and how can the judiciary be protected from the rancor of unjustified public and private attacks occasioned by controversial decisions rather than competency? Incompetence is a difficult concept to define, but prescriptive devices to deal with it can have a chilling effect that could stifle the ability of judges to issue rulings contrary to the opinions of citizens in local, state, and federal jurisdictions.

Since 1960, all fifty states and the District of Columbia have created disciplinary tribunals to receive complaints alleging misconduct on the part of state judges. Although their formal authority varies, these disciplinary bodies can investigate complaints and levy appropriate sanctions. Common grounds for discipline include (1) mental or physical disability that interferes with judicial duties, (2) willful misconduct in office, (3) persistent failure or inability to perform judicial duties, (4) habitual intemperance, and (5) prejudicial conduct that maligns the judicial office (Culver and Cruikshanks 1978, p. 35). When a judge's behavior merits official action, that individual may be admonished, censured, or suspended from the bench. In the most serious instances, judges may be involuntarily retired (usually applicable where mental disability is found) or removed from office.

For over fifty years, Congress has debated the merits of instituting some mechanism for disciplining federal-court judges. Serious constitutional questions arise in such discussions since the Constitution specifies that federal judges may be removed from the bench by impeachment. However, the Constitution is silent on disciplining judges for less-serious breaches of conduct where removal would not be warranted. Though Congress passed legislation creating judicial councils within each of the federal circuits in 1939, and the councils have some authority over the behavior of judges, their primary function is administrative (Wheeler and Levin 1979, pp. 32–36; Snarr and Parker 1977, p. 49). In 1980, Congress passed, and President Carter signed into law PL 96-458, called the Judicial Councils Reform and Judicial Conduct and Disability Act of 1980. This act establishes a procedure for the processing of complaints against federal judges and allows for sanctions short of removal to be applied against errant judges. This chapter reviews the legislative efforts to establish federal judicial disciplinary procedures and evaluates the potential of PL 96-458 to correct judicial misconduct.

Federal Action: The Limits of Impeachment

Clearly, the framers of the Constitution sought to cloak the members of the judiciary with as much insulation from political harassment as possible. Life tenure is necessary, Hamilton argued in *Federalist,* no. 78, because the judiciary would be the weakest branch of government; thus, ''all possible care is requisite to enable it to defend itself against their attacks.'' Life tenure during good behavior is specified in Article III §1 of the Constitution. Moreover, Article III §4 states that federal judges can only be removed from the bench by impeachment ''for, and conviction of, treason, bribery, or other high crimes and misdemeanors.'' In an impeachment proceeding, the House of Representatives votes to impeach, and the trial takes place before the Senate.

In the almost 200 years since the passage of the Judiciary Act of 1789, formal impeachment proceedings have been instituted an average of once every twenty-two years. Of the nine judges who were impeached, four were acquitted, one resigned the day the Senate trial commenced, and four were convicted, the last in 1936 (Berkson and Tesitor 1978; Rosenbaum and Lee 1978). Additionally, as Professor Henry Abraham has noted, nine other judges have resigned from the bench before formal impeachment charges were filed (1980, p. 45). Judges who were impeached and removed from the bench include District Judge John Pickering (1804), who was considered to be insane and because he was habitually intoxicated and followed irregular judicial procedures; District Judge West Humphreys (1862), who held office in the Confederacy during the Civil War; Commerce Court Judge Robert W. Archbald (1913), who took favors from litigants; and District Judge Halsted L. Ritter (1936), whose impeachment for misbe- havior resulted from numerous charges of improprieties. District Judge George W. English (1926) was impeached on the grounds of partiality and oppression but resigned before Senate action. The four judges who were impeached but acquitted are Supreme Court Justice Samuel Chase (1805) for misconduct; District Judge James H. Peck (1830) for misuse of contempt powers; District Judge Charles H. Swayne (1905) for financial irregularities and misuse of contempt powers; and District Judge Harold Louderback (1933) for appointing incompetent receivers. There was Senate support for the impeachment of District Court Judge Mark H. Delahay in 1873, but he resigned before House action commenced (Abraham 1980, p. 46).

More recently, formal action was taken against three federal-court judges to lessen their influence on the bench. In late 1965, the judicial council for the Tenth Circuit Court reassigned the cases of Judge Steven Chandler of the Western Oklahoma District on the grounds that he was ''unable or unwilling to discharge efficiently the duties of his office.'' Chandler appealed to the Supreme Court but an accord between him and the council was reached, leaving unresolved the question of the council's authority to discipline a judge by reassigning cases (Gallo 1966; Davis 1967). In a second action, the late Supreme Court Justice William O. Douglas was the subject of several impeachment attempts during his long and controversial tenure on the Court. The first occurred as a result of his stay of execution for convicted spies Julius and Ethel Rosenburg in 1953. The Supreme Court overturned the stay order, the Rosenburgs were executed, and the move against Douglas lost momentum (Abraham 1980, p. 48). Two resolutions for his impeachment for ''high crimes and misdemeanors'' were introduced in 1970 and subsequently voted down in a special House Judiciary Subcommittee vote. At the time the resolutions were introduced, then Representative Gerald R. Ford gave a legally confusing response to the specific grounds for action against Douglas: ''An impeachable offense is whatever a majority of the House of Representatives considers it to be at a given moment in history; conviction results from whatever offense or offenses two-thirds of the other body considers to be sufficiently serious to require removal of the accused from office'' (*Congressional Quarterly* 1974, p. 6).

Last, Utah Federal District Judge Willis Ritter was the subject of two suits brought by the Justice Department and the Utah attorney general in 1978. The judge was charged with ignoring correct judicial procedure, insulting U.S. attorneys, rendering decisions with ''arbitrary and erratic authority,'' and essentially bringing the federal courts into disrepute (Johnson 1978, p. 37). The suits were not intended to remove him but to prohibit Ritter from hearing certain cases. Ritter's death at age 79 rendered the suits moot.

These three examples illustrate several additional dilemmas of judicial discipline at the federal level. First, impeachment was not perceived as an appropriate means of dealing with Judges Chandler and Ritter. Their conduct presumably reflected negatively upon their ability to judge but was not severe enough to institute formal, lengthy impeachment proceedings in the House. Second, the abortive attempt to impeach Douglas in 1970 and Ford's lack of specificity regarding grounds for his impeachment exemplifies the potential misuse of impeachment. The rancor directed at Douglas probably had more to do with his outspokenness, marriages to young women, and the Senate's refusal to confirm the Nixon nominations of Carswell and Haynesworth to the Supreme Court than with his suitability for the bench. Third, the issue of whether sanctions can be employed by internal mechanisms such as the judicial councils when a judge's good behavior is questioned has not been determined. Fourth, the time factor in all three examples mitigates against the notion of a timely resolution of disputes. The action against Chandler began in late December 1965, and the Supreme Court denied him a rehearing in 1970. He eventually retired from the bench in October 1975. The debate over the possible impeachment of Douglas lasted not quite a year. The suits against Ritter were filed some six months prior to his death and surely would have drawn on for many more months, or years, since no hearings had been held at the time of his death.

There are a number of objections to the impeachment process. It is a cumbersome, lengthy, and partisan procedure. The Senate must abandon its other duties while the trial takes place. Votes for impeachment follow party lines (TenBroek 1939). The average impeachment proceeding consumes some sixteen days although some have lasted as long as six weeks. Moreover, there are no real procedural safeguards for the accused. During the 1936 impeachment trial of Halsted Ritter (no relation to Willis Ritter), as few as five senators were present while evidence was presented against him. Although conviction requires a two-thirds vote in the Senate, the members of the upper house are not required to attend the proceeding. Perhaps most damaging, impeachment is a mechanism of last resort for dealing with the most unfit judges; there is no provision for correcting minor improprieties. Finally, impeachment is directed at criminal offenses, thus ignoring the physical or mental disabilities that may bring a judge's suitability for the bench into question.

Raoul Berger, one of the foremost authorities on impeachment, poses three questions regarding the constitutional interpretation of impeachment (Berger 1973, pp. 122–180). In brief, Berger's contention is that (1) impeachment is not the only means available for disciplining judges, (2) "high crimes and misdemeanors" are not inclusive of all infractions of "good·behavior," and (3) Congress has the authority by means of its "necessary and proper" power to devise an alternative disciplinary mechanism to impeachment. As Berger acknowledges, his position is countered by the arguments of others who stand convinced that impeachment presently is the only constitutionally permissible means, unless the Constitution is amended, to deal with the unfit judge (Kurland 1969).

The emphasis on the formal process of impeachment overshadows the subtler informal devices that can be employed to correct or to entice a judge to retire before improper behavior is publicized (Berkson and Tesitor 1978, pp. 447–451). What these informal devices suggest is that some judges should not be on the bench because of their conduct or temperament and that alternatives to impeachment are necessary to deal with these individuals. The difficulty with these alternatives is to cull out the incompetents without undermining the rights of fit judges.

Congressional Efforts to Establish Disciplinary Mechanisms

The first statutory attempt to permit federal judges to remove unfit colleagues from the bench came in the Sumners and McAdoo bills in 1936–1937. Their legislation would have created a High Court for the Trial of Judicial Officers that could initiate a hearing on the lack of good behavior of a judge on a resolution by the House. The bills (first McAdoo's, then Sumner's) were passed in the House but died in the Senate in 1938, 1941, and several successive sessions (Holloman 1970, pp. 130–133). A lapse of more than twenty years occurred before Senator Tydings (D-Maryland) reinitiated congressional efforts to create federal disciplinary mechanisms after his appointment as Chairman of the Subcommittee on Improvements in Judicial Machinery.

The Judicial Reform Act introduced by Tydings in 1969 proposed a Commission on Judicial Disabilities and Tenure, composed of five federal judges, that would have the power to investigate charges of judicial misconduct and to recommend removal, if needed, to the U.S. Judicial Conference, a body headed by the chief justice and composed of thirty-two other federal-court judges. The Tydings bill, summarized with other efforts in table 8–1, was never voted on in the Senate. As with earlier legislation aimed at removal, the constitutionality of the act was open to serious question since it would allow the Judicial Conference to do what the Constitution specified only Congress could do by impeachment.

Senator Sam Nunn (D-Georgia) followed the Tydings bill with his own proposal for a Judicial Tenure Act that would have created a Judicial Conduct and Disability Commission (Berkson and Tesitor 1978, pp. 455–457). Nunn's plan called for censuring judges when necessary and recommending inpeachment action to the House in the most serious cases. As with the Tydings legislation, the proposed commission would be staffed by federal-court judges (see table 8–1). Tydings's bill died in the Senate, Nunn's in the House. What emerged from Nunn's proposal has been incorporated into the Judicial Conduct and Disability Act ot 1980 and represents a modified version of Nunn's proposal as amended by Senators Birch Bayh (D-Indiana), Edward Kennedy (D-Massachusetts), and Dennis DeConcini (D-Arizona), Chair of the Subcommittee on Improvements in Judicial Machinery. In essence, the act (S1873) is a supplement, not an alternative, to impeachment and purposely avoids the constitutional question of removal by any means other than impeachment by the House. After a year of debate, Congress approved the act in early October 1980, to become effective a year later.

According to S1873, "each judicial council shall make all necessary and appropriate orders for the effective and expeditious administration of justice within its circuit" [§2 (d)(1)]. The processing of complaints is a three-step procedure. In the first step, complaints alleging misconduct are filed with the clerk of the court of appeals for that district. The clerk gives the complaint to the chief judge of the circuit or to the next senior person if the complaint is against the chief judge. The complainant and judge whose behavior has been questioned also receive copies of the complaint. The chief judge may, by written order, (1) dismiss the complaint if it is directed at the judge's decision rather than at the judge's behavior, or if it is frivolous; (2) conclude the proceeding if he feels the action has been corrected or, beginning step two, appoint himself and an equal number of circuit and district judges of the circuit to a Court on Judicial Conduct and Disability to investigate the allegations. The special court conducts appropriate inquiry into the charges and submits its report to the judicial council. In the third step, the judicial council can conduct an additional investigation or take the following actions: (1) direct the chief judge of the district of the magistrate whose conduct is deficient to take appropriate action, (2) certify the disability of the judge, (3) request the judge to

Table 8–1
Provisions of Three Congressional Judicial Disciplinary Bills

	Tydings Bill (S1506) Judicial Reform Act	Nunn Bill (S1423) Judicial Tenure Act	The Judicial Conduct and Disability Act of 1980 (S1873)
Tribunal	Commission on Judical Disabilities and Tenure	Judicial Conduct and Disability Commission	Court on Judicial Conduct and Disability
Staffing	5 federal judges, including at least 2 district and 2 circuit court judges, appointed by the chief justice	12 members; 1 elected from each circuit and 1 elected by the judges of the three special federal courts	5 judges, including at least 1 district court judge, appointed by the chief judge of the appellate district
Ancillary support	None	3-judge panel for each circuit and for specialized courts	Judicial councils for each circuit
Process	Commission would investigate, try, and recommend removal of judges; if removal action, this would be reviewed by the Judicial Conference, which has sole removal power; review by Supreme Court on writ of certiorari.	Executive director would screen complaints and refer them to appropriate 3-judge panel; panel would recommend investigation by the Commission or dismissal of complaints; if panel recommends sanctions, a hearing would be held before the Commission; removal action by the House.	Judicial councils would receive and investigate complaints; councils would recommend santions to the Court, which could accept, modify, or reject recommendations.
Sanctions	Removal by the Commission	Censure; removal by the House	Certification of disability, request for voluntary retirement, temporary or permanent suspension of cases, private or public censure, reprimand, recommendation of impeachment to the House
Grounds	Willful misconduct in office or willful and persistent failure to perform official duties or intentional failure to file reports required by this act	Willful misconduct in office, willful and persistent failure to perform duties, habitual intemperance, or prejudicial conduct that brings the office into disrepute	Conduct "inconsistent with the effective and expeditious administration of the courts;" mental or physical disability that interferes with judicial duties
Status	Never voted on in the Senate	Passed Senate and died in the House, 1978; reintroduced in 1979 as modified into S1873	Passed Senate, 1979; passed House, 1980; signed into law, 1980, to be effective October 1981

retire, (4) issue a private censure or reprimand, (5) issue a public censure or reprimand, or (6) order other appropriate sanctions except removal. In the most serious of circumstances for which removal appears warranted, the judicial council will file its report with the Judicial Conference of the United States, which then presents this information to the House of Representatives for action. Further, the Judicial Conference may be requested by the judicial councils to handle other special problems that the councils can not successfully resolve. Last, the judicial councils are responsible for formulating provisions requiring that the judge against whom the complaint is filed has adequate opportunity to defend his or her actions and that the complainant has an opportunity to appear before the special investigating panel to answer questions about the complaint.

It is premature to assess the impact of S1873 on the behavior of the more than 850 judges sitting on the federal bench today. By 1990, the number of judges is expected to increase to over 1,200 (Senate Report 1979, p. 7). There is neither solid evidence to suggest that the disciplinary sanctions now provided will be used frequently nor a demonstrated need that they be employed in more than a few isolated instances. When members of the Senate Judiciary Committee debated the merits of the Judicial Conduct and Disability Act in 1979, they acknowledged that the act was designed to give the appearance of accountability, not to address an urgent need to resolve judicial misconduct:

> The Committee recognizes that the great majority of our existing federal judges performs their duties in a dedicated and capable manner. *In a very real sense the problem addressed in the Act is more of perception than actuality—the need to assure the public that procedures are in place to deal with the rare instance justifying an inquiry related to the condition or conduct of a member of the Judiciary. Stated another way, the growing public demand for the accountability of public officials should extend to the judicial branch.* [Senate Report 1979, p. 26]

Under the 1980 act, complaints alleging misconduct will be for "conduct prejudicial to the effective and expeditious administration of the business of the courts" and for mental or physical disability, rendering the judge incapable of conducting the court's business. Most likely, a judge who is found to be unable to discharge the duties of the office because of physical or mental disability will be persuaded to retire without the initiation of congressional impeachment proceedings. This was the case recently on the trial bench in the ninth circuit where the judicial council for that circuit certified one judge's disability because of a physical problem and where a second judge certified his own disability for psychological reasons. Both judges were replaced (Browning 1981, p. 4). As Flanders and McDermott have noted, the judicial councils have had much success, although little publicity, in dealing with behavior problems of district- and circuit-court judges. They found excessive drinking to be the most common problem and the council's informal actions effective in pressuring judges to take senior status or to seek medical treatment (1978, pp. 26–35).

If the experience of the California Commission on Judicial Performance, one of the most closely scrutinized, is an indication of the types of complaints that may be directed against federal judges, then most prejudicial conduct allegations will be on the grounds of attitude, intemperate remarks, and tardiness. For example, U.S. District Court Judge A. Andrew Hauk has been criticized by a number of Los Angeles attorneys, several Los Angeles City Council members, and two superior-court judges for his eccentric behavior and outspokenness. In a deportation case he referred to the immigration of "faggots from Cuba," and in a sex-discrimination suit he spoke of the differences between male and female temperaments, noting that women "have a monthly problem, which upsets them emotionally, and we all know that" (Jones 1980, p. 1).

When attitude complaints about state judges are received by the California Commission on Judicial Performance, the executive secretary routinely sends a letter to the judge notifying him or her of the complaint and asking for a response to it. Typically, in reply, the judge denies the basis for the complaint and promises it will not happen again (Culver and Cruikshanks 1978, p. 6). This action-response experience may resolve the majority of complaints against federal judges as well.

Performance of the Disciplinary Mechanism

While the functional specifics of judicial disciplinary mechanisms vary among the states and within the federal circuits, they must operate in such a way as to provide both the public and the judiciary with appropriate safeguards. However, the public's need to be free from the actions of an oppressive or incompetent judge must not be construed as a license to hound unpopular judges from the bench or to threaten the independence of the judiciary at any level.

The following eight criteria for evaluating the effectiveness of disciplinary mechanisms are extracted from recent analyses of such tribunals at the state and federal level (Culver and Cruikshanks 1978, pp. 6, 30–36; Davis 1967, pp. 448–467; Russo 1979, p. 1082; Wheeler and Levin 1979, pp. 49–68). First, the scope of grounds for discipline must be specific enough to relate offensive behavior to the judge's professional duties. The troublesome issue here concerns on-bench versus off-bench behavior. At what point, or under what circumstances, do the private actions of a judge interfere with judicial duties? For example, Superior Court Judge Robert Stevens was publicly censured by the California Supreme Court upon the recommendation of the state's Commission on Judicial Performance for making obscene phone calls to his former secretary. Also, in 1979, a local NAACP chapter asked for the resignation of the U.S. district-court judge in Texas because of his remarks in a newspaper interview wherein he referred to blacks as "niggers" on two separate occasions. Second, the accused judge needs protection from false attacks. This is recognized in the state mechanisms and in S1873, regarding confidentiality of the proceedings prior to a public sanction if called for. Disciplinary mechanisms for state and federal judges provide for the screening of frivolous, undocumented, and vengeful complaints as well as those that are in response to the judge's decision rather than conduct. Third, disciplinary tribunals require political autonomy to avoid self-serving misuse by politicians or interest groups. The provisions in S1873 leave judicial discipline entirely within the hands of the federal judiciary. This provides federal judges with more insulation from political interference than state judges, but the monopoly of federal judges in the investigating-sanctioning process may protect incompetent judges from valid complaints as well. Fourth, the composition and appointment of tribunal membership should reflect the combined interests of both the judiciary and the public. The absence of lay and bar representation in the federal disciplinary process is obvious and contrary to the makeup of the majority of state disciplinary tribunals. The legislative background to S1873 does not reveal why nonjudge members were excluded. The literature on the state commissions does not suggest any political or procedural defects in having bar and lay interests represented on the disciplinary bodies. Fifth, the ability of a tribunal to act expeditiously is to the advantage of the bench and the public. An accused judge should not have to suffer delays in the resolution of a complaint, and the public should not be expected to tolerate indefinitely a judge whose behavior is inappropriate or one who is unfit. S1873 provides that final action on any complaint will be made within ninety days except in unusual circumstances. The procedures for the processing of complaints against federal judges are more time specific than those in the states. Sixth, to be legitimate, a disciplinary tribunal must be credible as a deterrent to judicial misconduct. Presumably, the fact that procedures for disciplining federal judges now exist should make judges aware that certain improprieties will not go unnoticed. However, this assessment is speculative as there are no data on the deterrent effect of judicial disciplinary mechanisms. Seventh, a disciplinary tribunal needs to be flexible, both in its procedural operations and in the sanctions it can administer or recommend. A judge who is tardy in opening the daily calendar, sometimes but not too often, should not face the same sanction as the judge who berates lawyers, makes racial slurs from the bench, or is inebriated on duty. Given the variety of sanctions that can be employed and the leeway that can be given the judicial councils in formulating rules governing judicial conduct, S1873 procedures appear more flexible than state procedures. Eighth, disciplinary mechanisms must make efficient use of economic and human resources. An overbudgeted, overstaffed agency will justify its existence with trivia if need be, while an unsupported one will be incapable of action upon the complaints that need to be addressed.

Conclusion

This chapter has focused attention on the central problem of judicial discipline at all judicial levels of balancing integrity with independence of the bench, and has illustrated the usual uneven policy response in the face of such dilemmas. It has been shown that the constitutional remedy of impeachment is rarely and ineffectively used. It has also been shown that disciplinary mechanisms supplementary to impeachment have been slow to evolve and, while as yet untested, can be expected to mirror the performance of present state-level mechanisms.

The problem, as the title of this chapter suggests, is an old one. The reasons for the slowness of the emergence of federal disciplinary mechanisms are both old and, in the eyes of many, valid. At the same time, the need for effective supplementary procedures seems equally old and valid, particularly in light of the expected future increase in the number of federal jurists. It is stating the obvious to suggest that numerous categories and instances of judicial conduct exist that neither merit nor are likely to elicit impeachment proceedings but, nonetheless, that are frequent and serious enough to warrant scrutiny by an impartial investigative body. The experiences of the states that have adopted such procedures would suggest that the Judicial Conduct and Disability Act of 1980 is a belated, but probably necessary, step in the right direction. It remains to be seen whether the reality will measure up to expectations.

References

Abraham, Henry. 1980. *The Judicial Process,* 4th ed. New York: Oxford University Press.

Berger, Raoul. 1973. *Impeachment: The Constitutional Problems.* Cambridge: Harvard University Press.

Berkson, Larry C., and Irene A. Tesitor. 1978. "Holding Federal Judges Accountable." 61 *Judicature* 442.

Browning, James R. 1981. "Evaluating Judicial Evaluation Surveys." *Los Angeles Daily Journal* (February 23) 4.

Congressional Quarterly. 1974. *Impeachment and the U.S. Congress.* Washington, D.C.

Culver, John H., and Randal L. Cruikshanks. 1978. "Judicial Misconduct: Bench Behavior and the New Disciplinary Mechanisms." 2 *State Court Journal* 3.

Davis, Robert. 1967. "The Chandler Incident and Problems of Judicial Removal." 19 *Stanford Law Review* 448.

Flanders, Steven, and John T. McDermott. 1978. *Operation of the Federal Judicial Councils.* Washington, D.C.: Federal Judicial Center.

Gallo, Jon J. 1966. "Removal of Federal Judges—New Alternatives to an Old Problem: *Chandler v. Judicial Council of the Tenth District.*" 13 *UCLA Law Review* 1385.

Holloman, John H. III. 1970. "The Judicial Reform Act: History, Analysis, and Comment." 35 *Law and Contemporary Problems* 128.

Johnson, Randy. 1978. "Federal Judge Willis W. Ritter, Who Fought Retirement, Dies at 79." *The New York Times* (March 5) 37.

Jones, Robert A. 1980. "Judge Hauk: Eccentricity in Courtroom." *Los Angeles Times* (December 29) 1.

Kurland, Philip B. 1969. "The Constitution and the Tenure of Federal Judges: Some Notes from History." 36 *University of Chicago Law Review* 665.

Rosenbaum, Judith, and David L. Lee. 1978. "A Constitutional Perspective on Judicial Tenure." 61 *Judicature* 465.

Russo, Anthony. 1979. "The Removal, Involuntary Retirement and Censure of Federal Judges: The Judicial Tenure Act in Context." 12 *Loyola Law Review* 1081.

Senate Report. 1979. "The Judicial Conduct and Disability Act of 1979." 96th Congress, 1st Session.

Snarr, Steven W., and Bradley H. Parker. 1977. "The 'Good Behavior' Alternative to Impeachment: A Proposal for the More Effective Use of Judicial Councils." 4 *Journal of Contemporary Law* 38.

TenBroek, Jacobus. 1939. "Partisan Politics and Federal Judgeship Impeachments Since 1903." 23 *Minnesota Law Review* 185.

Wheeler, Russell R., and A. Leo Levin. 1979. "Judicial Discipline and Removal in the United States." Federal Judicial Center Staff Paper, Washington, D.C.

9 Evaluating Judicial Performance: Problems of Measurement and Politics

John Paul Ryan

A new wave of social accountability, fueled by populists of diverse political viewpoints, has led to unprecedented scrutiny of elite workers. Members of the medical profession are increasingly reviewed by their peers. Teachers now routinely have their performance measured and evaluated by students. Public officials are often subject to new constraints in the arena of ethics and propriety. Thus, it should be expected that judges—once thought to be securely cloaked behind the purple curtain (Becker 1966)—have also been shoved into the glare of accountability. This is particularly true for judges who sit in trial courts, which are confronted with a large volume of work and to which most Americans can relate either by direct personal experience or vicariously.

Furthermore, courts have been subjected to a series of far-reaching changes of formal structure and organization that have rendered their judges more accountable (Ryan et al. 1980, pp. 240–241). Courthouses no longer consist of a few individual fiefdoms but are often a collection of scores of judges welded together into one administrative unit. Increased size had led naturally to the local adoption of management tools, including professional court administrators and more-powerful chief judges. Hierarchical supervisory management of trial courts by state supreme courts has also surfaced. Both the rule-making authority of the supreme courts and the staff of state-court administrative offices serve notice on local trial courts and judges regarding matters such as the speedy disposition of cases.

Before judicial performance is evaluated, however, there is a need to measure that performance in some roughly reliable and valid way. The conceptual and empirical problems in doing so for judges in trial courts are the subject of this chapter. Specifically, I discuss the role of trial courts and the contours of actual judicial work as background for analyzing the contrasting ways in which individual judicial per-

I wish to thank Phil Dubois and Dave Neubauer for their comments on earlier versions of this article.

formance has been and can be measured. Concluding thoughts are offered on the political environment within which judicial performance is debated, measured, and evaluated.

Trial Judges and the Work of Trial Courts

Understanding the work of trial courts and the judges who sit there is an essential prerequisite to evaluating judicial performance. However, the literature on judicial work typically has been impressionistic and, while perhaps insightful into the experiences of a particular judge, lacking a broader perspective. Notable exceptions are Gignoux's (1965) account of the work of federal district judges (only a small percentage of a judge's time is spent on the bench) and DeBruler's (1969) exhortation against the various nonjudicial duties that trial judges are sometimes called upon to perform (in Indiana, for example, the appointment of various board and commission members). These articles reference, in a systematic way, some of the various nonadjudicative tasks that increasingly face trial judges today.

Blumberg (1967) was among the first social scientists to focus on the trial judge through his theme of "judge as bureaucrat." He noted that judges perform administrative work and, from a more-theoretical view, that judges assume a bureaucratic role by diffusing decision-making responsibility in areas such as sentencing among other courtroom actors (for example, probation officers, prosecuting and defense attorneys, and so forth). In an analogous view, Jacob (1965) emphasized the ministerial functions that trial judges often perform, albeit in an atmosphere of decision making that cumulatively leads to policy. More-recent work has focused primarily upon the trial-court process— that is, on the interactions among the several key court actors (see, for example, Eisenstein and Jacob 1977). Some attention has been given to judicial role, but much of this characterizes the trial judge in a highly abstract framework divorced from the reality of day-to-day work (see, for example, Caldeira 1977; Sarat 1977). Still other role studies look to appellate judges for inspiration (see Ungs and Baas 1972), yet the working environment and functions of trial and appellate judges are strikingly different (Sheldon 1974, pp. 85–86).

Only the Federal Judicial Center's (1971) study of the work of federal district-court judges and Ryan et al.'s (1980) study of the work of state trial judges provide an empirical base about the range of judicial tasks. The latter study posits trial judges as adjudicators, administrators, legal researchers, negotiators, and community-relations agents in a mix dependent upon empirical factors such as the size of the community, the availability of courthouse resources, and the skills of the judges themselves. Specifically, we found that judges in the larger courts work longer hours, experience less variety in their daily work, and are more likely both to hear jury trials and to participate in plea negotiations than their fellow judges in smaller courts in the less-urbanized areas. Skills of the judges also helped to define their work. Courts frequently assigned judges skilled at negotiation to a wave of settlement conferences. Judges who viewed themselves as skilled in a given area—especially negotiation or legal research—were likely to spend much more time doing that kind of work (Ryan et al. 1980).

The trial court provides the framework for the role, functions, and actual work or trial judges. But do trial courts hear many trials? This question has been the driving force behind much of the literature on criminal courts over the last fifteen years. Blumberg (1967) first noted the absence of an adversary process, attributing its decline, like many observers, to burgeoning dockets and backlogs.[1] Most scholars who subsequently studied the criminal courts have reached similar, if more-refined, empirical conclusions (see, for example, Eisenstein and Jacob 1977; Rosett and Cressey 1976; Neubauer 1974). As Heumann (1977, p. 1) noted, trial court is seemingly a misnomer; these courts are actually plea-bargaining courts, for most cases are disposed through negotiation and entry of guilty pleas. Much the same can be said for civil courts, which also dispose of most of their cases by settlement (see, for example, Mnookin and Kornhauser 1979; McLauchan 1977; Ross 1970).

Yet the work of a trial court is defined not only by the frequency of particular tasks but also by the duration of those tasks. Ryan et al. (1980, p. 43) report that trial judges in the United States spend a substantial percentage of their time in trial work—both jury and non-jury trials. For example, even if a judge were to hear only one jury trial per month, that could conservatively account for one-quarter of his or her working hours, an estimate that does not include bench trials. The most realistic picture of the work of trial courts seems to be one in which courts spend much of their resources of time and labor on very few cases.[2]

In sum, two myths—perpetuated by two different sets of litera-ture—need to be debunked. First, trial courts are not in the throes of the functional disintegration that some observers have predicted (Barr 1974). Rather, they continue to conduct trials and to display other characteristics of dispute resolution that Shapiro (1981) associates with "courtness." Indeed, these trials, while relatively infrequent in light of the total number of cases disposed, voraciously consume the court's resources, especially the time of its judges and courtroom personnel.

Conversely, trial judges—though they spend considerable time in presiding at trials—also perform a range of other less-visible tasks, including negotiation and administrative work. Thus, neither the work of trial judges nor of the court is as undimensional as has been portrayed. This diversity of work clearly signals the need for breadth in the measurement and evaluation of judicial performance.

Focusing on Judicial Performance

Quantity of Work

The most common attempts at measuring judicial performance empirically have focused on the amount of work performed—that is, a judge's work load. This may reflect a bias toward something that can be measured quantitatively; conversely, it may reflect a belief that the sheer quantity of work is the most important criterion for evaluating trial judges. The latter perspective is not all that implausible if one views volume as the biggest crisis facing trial courts today.[3]

Conceptually, there are at least two faces to the amount of judicial work performed. One is the notion of productivity—how much (of something) is accomplished. The something may vary from the number of jury trials heard to the number of cases disposed or the number of cases still pending. In courts where jury trials are a legitimized mode of disposition in the eyes of courtroom actors, the number of jury trials may be an important measure of productivity.[4] In these courts, judges who avoid jury trials are seen as shirking the tough, time-consuming work that courts ought to be doing.[5] Conversely, in courts that rarely hear jury trials, the number of cases disposed is more likely to be viewed as the appropriate measure of productivity. In these courts, jury trials are seen as aberrations to be avoided. Judges who are foolish enough to hear them instead of encouraging negotiated settlements are viewed as starry-eyed idealists unwilling to pitch in against the court's accumulating backlog of cases.

The use of the number of cases disposed as a measure of productivity is problematic, aside from whether a particular trial court discourages jury trials. For one thing, the measure is all but useless in courts that do not adhere strictly to an individual-case-assignment system. Blumberg's ''workhorses'' on the bench of ''Metropolitan Court,'' for example, were almost certainly formally or informally used as plea judges in that court (1967, pp. 137–142). Their function was to dispose of lots of cases by negotiated plea, whereas other judges on the court were no doubt used to try cases that could not be settled.

For another, the counting of cases disposed is often subject to capricious whim. The definition of a case itself is not straightforward—that is, some courts count a multiple-defendant case as one case, whereas others count cases according to the number of defendants. Conceivably this may vary within the same court. Counting dispositions in a standardized way is no easier. Are defendants who fail to appear ("no-shows") to be considered dispositions or something else? Do they become dispositions when judges individually, and therefore inconsistently, close cases? Experience with working in the case files of the state of Ohio alone, a state that prides itself on the centralization and uniformity of its data by county, is sufficient to lead to a healthy skepticism about the reliability or validity of court-generated data.[6]

A second face to the amount of work performed is the notion of hardworkingness, which implies more emphasis on judicial input and correspondingly less emphasis on tangible outputs. Hardworkingness could be measured by the number of hours worked over a given period of time or on average. This measure, of course, is subject to potential distortion, by both self-reporting methods and random scrutiny (such as by newspaper reporters or court watchers stalking the halls of an apparently empty courthouse). From a conceptual point of view, the measure itself may be too crude. The intensity and pace of work may overwhelm, in significance, the length of time a judge spends inside the courthouse building. In other words, some judges may work much harder than other judges for the same hour's worth of work, discounting entirely any comparison of measurable output. A variety of factors contribute to the differential intensity of work, including the size of the community in which the court is located, the contentiousness of attorneys, and the personality of individual judges (Ryan et al. 1980). These form a complex mix and render comparisons across states or jurisdictions hazardous at best.

Quality of Work

Clearly, the measurement of the amount of judicial work performed introduces a tension between quantity and quality of work. Stott makes this point in his discussion of Colorado's current effort to measure and evaluate judicial performance:

> Many techniques exist to measure judicial activity, but the quantity of matters processed does not provide a qualitative measure . . . Measures of activity are not meaningful measures of productivity and may have no relevance whatever to the quality of a particular judge. [1980, p. 7]

Measuring the quality of judicial work necessarily involves evaluation, an activity that has typically been viewed to be within the domain exclusively of lawyers. Bar polls have been the most visible, and probably the most prevalent, method of ·evaluating judicial performance. These polling results, which are based upon the responses of some segment of lawyers in the community,[7] often provide not only general evaluation (''qualified'' or ''not qualified'') but measures of skill in specific areas of performance (see, for example, Maddi 1977). Guterman and Meidinger (1977, pp. 40–41) found, in their survey of bar-polling formats, that a majority of polls inquired about legal ability, diligence, punctuality, judicial temperament, courtesy, and integrity. Still, these queries do not touch upon all areas of judicial work (for example, negotiation). Furthermore, judicial work is viewed from the not-disinterested perspective of practicing lawyers. Courtesy, punctuality, and judicial temperament are all rather self-serving criteria for judicial performance from the standpoint of lawyers who appear before individual judges who are being evaluated. Members of the public at large, the media, court administrators, or judges themselves might well establish different criteria or rearrange the (unknown) weighting given to each by lawyers making an overall evaluation of judicial performance.

Appellate review of the decisions of trial judges is viewed by some to be an implicit evaluation of the legal ability or soundness of trial judges. One major difficulty with this method is that trial judges are reversed for a variety of reasons. Sometimes, they are reversed for legal errors (for example, blatantly improper instructions to a jury) but at other times for differences in interpretation of statutes or court decisions or even differences of judicial or political philosophy. Furthermore, the predisposition of litigants to appeal varies, at least across jurisdictions, by factors outside of the control of the presiding trial judge (for example, level of attorney adversariness, receptivity of the appellate courts, local and state prison conditions, and so on). Thus, the cases appealed from trial judges are an atypical, rather than a representative, slice of their work. To consider a reversal rate, based upon such a sampling of cases, as a measure of the quality of judicial performance can be quite misleading (see also Howard 1981, p. 51).

Citizens and the media have come to be more significantly involved in evaluating the quality of judicial work. This is most especially the case for criminal-court judges who must often sentence highly visible or unpopular defendants. The media tend to focus on sentencing practices of judges, either in individual cases or across a range of cases. Citizen groups often focus on community-relations aspects of a judge's work—that is, the appearance of fair, impartial, swift, and courteous justice. Such groups are usually looked upon by courtroom actors as intruders who do not understand the necessary processes of case disposition. In some instances this view is entirely accurate (see, for example, A Report of the Illinois Court Watching Project 1976). Court watchers often fail to appreciate how courts operate in either the formal or informal sense. In other instances, professional technical assistance has enabled citizen groups to produce remarkably sophisticated analyses of individual trial courts (see Court Watching Project 1975). Overall, citizen groups and the media are probably better equipped to evaluate stylistic rather than substantive aspects of judicial performance.

In sum, two critical tensions surround the measurement of judicial performance. One is the tension between the quantity and quality of work, and which is the more-appropriate or important measure of a judge's worth. The second tension centers on the diverse institutions and groups that seek, or are routinely accorded, a role in evaluating the quality of judicial work.

Judicial Self-Evaluation: Results from a National Survey

One source, infrequently considered, for evaluating the performance of trial judges is the judges themselves. Though one might initially think the view to be severely biased, Ryan et al. (1980, pp. 162–164) report that trial judges across the nation are only selectively praiseworthy of their skills in the areas inquired about (see table 9–1).

Trial judges as a group distinguish their adjudicative skills from skills in other areas. In adjudication, most judges thought they were above average or excellent. This contrasts significantly with the areas

Table 9–1
Trial Judges' Evaluations of Their Skills in Five Areas of Work
(percentage)

Evaluation	Adjudication	Administration	Community Relations	Legal Research	Negotiation
Excellent	31.0	18.4	21.7	17.1	16.7
Above average	54.1	39.4	35.2	39.1	34.2
Average	14.8	36.5	35.4	38.2	37.9
Below Average	0.1	5.3	6.9	5.2	9.0
Poor	0.0	0.4	0.8	0.4	2.2
N	2,975	2,960	2,941	2,966	2,831

Source: Reprinted with permission of The Free Press, a Division of Macmillan Publishing Co., Inc., from *American Trial Judges: Their Work Styles and Performance* by John Paul Ryan et al. Copyright © 1980 by American Judicature Society.

of administration and negotiation, where a bare majority rated themselves above average or better, and an observable percentage viewed themselves below average or even poor. Trial judges are plainly expected to be good adjudicators for that has been the traditional image or definition of the job. Adjudication is what is emphasized at state and national judicial-education programs, for example. However, skills at negotiation, administration, or community relations have not previously been emphasized for trial judges, and a large percentage feel themselves to be mediocre or worse in these areas.

Trial judges, as individuals, also discriminate among their various skills. The intercorrelations of judges' evaluations of their skills in five areas of work are very small to negligible (see table 9–2). Few judges thought they were excellent in all areas. Much more commonly, individual judges viewed themselves to be excellent, say, in one area outside of adjudication and less stellar in the other areas. The lack of substantial intercorrelations indicates that the patterns were nearly random. Only for adjudication and legal research was there a reasonably widespread perception among trial judges that high (or low) skill in one area went hand in hand with the other area.

In summary, judicial work in trial courts calls upon a very diverse set of skills, and few judges are likely to be highly proficient in all skill areas. The views of judges parallel quite closely recent literature in suggesting that the work of trial judges is heterogeneous. If judicial performance is to be measured meaningfully, this fundamental diversity must serve as the underpinning. Measures pertaining to numbers of cases disposed relate only to the administrative-managerial aspects of a judge's work. Measures of the number of jury or bench trials heard speak only to a judge's adjudicative skills and the frequency with which they are called upon by others. Qualitative modes and measures of judicial performance frequently fail to be adequately ec-

Table 9–2
Interconnectedness of Trial Judges' Evaluations of Their Skills:
Pearson Correlation Matrix

Skill	Adjudication	Administration	Community Relations	Legal Research	Negotiation
Adjudication		.24	.14	.34	.23
Administration			.20	.11	.22
Community relations				.01	.22
Legal research					.11
N = 2,777					

Source: Data from John Paul Ryan, Allan Ashman, Bruce D. Sales, and Sandra Shane-DuBow 1980. *American Trial Judges: Their Work Styles and Performance*. New York: Free Press.

lectic in the criteria on which they seek evaluation. Most bar polls, for example, give short shrift to the trial judge's administrative tasks and even less attention to the judge as negotiator or mediator. Only 25 percent of the bar polls surveyed by Guterman and Meidinger (1977, pp. 40–41) queried lawyers on trial management, only 8 percent on administrative skill, and a mere 16 percent on judges' settlement skills. Organizations seeking to improve judicial performance through continuing education, such as state judicial-education associations, likewise fail to emphasize tasks other than adjudication, especially negotiation (see *Survey of State Judicial Education and Training Programs* 1978). Of course, some judges do cling to a very narrow conception of their work (I am a trial judge; send me cases to try.), but the diversity of tasks and heterogeneity of required skills is likely to increase, not decrease, in the near future. Whether this leads to the trivialization of judicial work or to the proletarianization of judging as a profession (Sheskin and Grau 1981) is open to further question.

The Future Faces of Judicial Evaluation

A number of states and locales are currently developing methods for evaluating the performance of sitting judges, both at the trial and appellate levels. These methods vary sharply and appear to be responsive to the larger political culture within which courts are situated (see Levin 1977). In particular, the methods vary with respect to the form and amount of citizen participation.

In Alaska, the state judicial council conducts surveys of attorneys, police officers, and jurors as the basis for an evaluation report and recommendation for each judge, which is then published in an election handbook distributed to all registered voters. In Colorado, the state's newly formed Committee on Judicial Performance, after extensive planning and public hearings, has adopted an evaluation plan that includes surveys of lawyers who have practiced before a judge and surveys of jurors with similar experience. Results are to be made public prior to Colorado's judicial-retention elections (Stott 1980). The Alaska and Colorado evaluation efforts reflect what I would call a populist, or good-government, model. There is opportunity for citizen input into the evaluation and for feedback to the public prior to upcoming elections. There is the use of outside experts such as the University of Michigan, which processes and analyzes survey responses for the Alaska Judicial Council, in the stages of planning and implementation. There is also recognition (notably in Colorado) of the value of decentralization, reflected in the dispersion of evaluation responsibility to local committees comprised of lawyers and nonlawyers.

In short, these are the values of America's progressive era, which have become institutionalized in state governments throughout the western United States.

New Jersey has recently adopted a quite different evaluation program in which local presiding judges bear the primary responsibility for gathering and interpreting relevant information. The presiding judge may interview knowledgeable attorneys, search the record of cases appealed, and even interview the judge who is being evaluated (Stott 1980). There is minimal, if any, citizen input into the evaluation process as well as a strong determination not to release the results to the public. The stamp of centralization and uniformity appears on this evaluation plan, which reflects its adoption by a state supreme court long viewed as the apex of a hierarchical state-court structure. In essence, the plan resembles a business model based upon an employer-employee relationship. The search for information is restricted (to knowledgeable insiders), and the results—while of little utility to the outside world—bear critically upon the employee's (judge's) future with the company (court). The New Jersey evaluation model reflects the same skepticism toward popular participation as the state's method of judicial selection—appointment by the governor—which is rooted in the values of the colonial (pre-Jackson) United States.

Other states such as Florida, Illinois, Ohio, and Pennsylvania have relied on bar polls to provide a more-informal view of the performance of sitting judges. In these states, no body or council is responsible for judicial evaluation; rather, local bar associations conduct polls of local attorneys regarding judicial qualifications. The public at large does not participate in selecting the form or content of the evaluation but does receive the results, which are widely disseminated by local newspapers before judicial-retention elections. This approach resembles a political model in which a democratic method taps only the opinions of a professional elite for later use by the general public. These large industrial states are themselves typically hotbeds of partisan political activity that spills over into judicial selection and evaluation.

In sum, there are several models of the future of judicial evaluation. The differences among them reflect less upon views of the proper role or functions of judges than upon the political cultures that surround courts in the various states. Which method of judicial evaluation is better may depend upon how one views the import of public participation in the government and the life of the polity. The value of citizen participation, though high in the post-Watergate years, fluctuates both across generations and regions of the country. The future face of judicial evaluation is a collage of political cultures in this country.

Conclusion

The evaluation of judges, like their initial selection, inevitably occurs within a political context. No amount of technical, scientific, or administrative language can cloud this reality. Trial judges are public figures who are sometimes asked to make controversial rulings, decisions, or sentences. In so doing, judges create images—positive or negative—in the minds of those who may be measuring or evaluating their performance. Individual judges become classified or stereotyped as liberal or conservative, soft on criminals, anti-union, underminers of the family structure, or whatever. This, in addition to the usually known political-party affiliation of judges, creates a store of images that can overwhelm the best intentioned efforts at objective evaluation, to say nothing of less-well-intentioned efforts.

These caveats to the likelihood of measuring and evaluating judicial performance in an objective framework should neither be dismissed too readily nor weighed upon too heavily. Political factors cannot be wished away; they are part of the structure of public (and private) life. However, the amount and partisanship of the politics can be controlled. Where judicial positions carry with them little or no patronage in the courthouse, for example, the influence of partisan factors is likely to be reduced.

From the citizen's point of view, it is often unclear whether a good judge is one who makes sound legal decisions or one who makes decisions consonant with the ideology, world view, or specialized beliefs of the beholder. The Republican National Party platform in 1980, with its call for judges sympathetic to human life, is only one bald example. The more difficult it seems to be to decide what a sound legal decision looks like, the more likely that good judging will be defined as broad social and political compatibility. Public participation in the process of judicial evaluation plausibly could either relax or aggravate the tendency to equate quality with compatibility. All in all, such prospects suggest that U.S. judges—in trial and appellate courts[8]—are likely to be thrust from behind the purple curtain into a lion's den of competing views about society and the role of the judiciary in American life.[9]

Notes

1. One should caution that lack of trials cannot automatically be equated with lack of an adversary process. Plea negotiations, for example, can be highly adversarial.

2. Whether the selection of cases to be tried reflects positive choice by judge and/or lawyers or merely random occurrence is a question in need of empirical research; the results of such research would bear significantly upon normative models of court access and usage.

3. A recent survey of public attitudes revealed that "efficiency in the courts" was widely viewed to be an important social problem, more so than the threat of war or racial problems. See Yankelovich, Skelly, and White (1978, p. 34).

4. In few criminal courts are more than 10 percent of indictments or informations ultimately tried before a jury. Some courts hover near the 10 percent figure, whereas others fall near 1–2 percent. Though more difficult to measure, the same is likely to be true in civil courts.

5. See the comments of the then chief judge of the D.C. Superior Court, Harold Greene, in *The Washington Star* (11 November 1977).

6. See *Ohio Courts* (1979) for examples of obvious inconsistencies in the local interpretation of uniform disposition categories across the state's counties.

7. Critics of bar polls charge that the surveys are often unrepresentative because of poor sampling procedures, low response rates, and/or responses from attorneys who have not practiced before the judge who is being evaluated. It should be noted, however, that Guterman and Meidinger (1977) report that most bar associations distribute their polls to universes (of their members or of the legal community) and make some efforts to discourage or prevent respondents who do not have direct contact with a judge from evaluating that judge.

8. The problems in measuring and evaluating the performance of appellate judges are compounded by, among other things, the greater law- (policy-) making role performed by judges in appellate courts. Thus, objective evaluation by groups and individuals who, themselves, have sharply defined views of the law becomes even more difficult.

9. Some would argue that judges are already in the limelight as the clamor for restricting the jurisdiction of the federal courts in sensitive social-issue areas increases.

References

Baar, Carl. 1974. "Will Urban Trial Courts Survive the War on Crime?" In H. Jacob (ed.). *The Potential for Reform of Criminal Justice*. Beverly Hills and London: Sage Publications.

Becker, Theodore. 1966. "Surveys and Judiciaries, or Who's Afraid of the Purple Curtain." 1 *Law and Society Review* 133.

Blumberg, Abraham. 1967. *Criminal Justice*. Chicago: Quadrangle.

Caldeira, Greg A. 1977. "The Incentives of Trial Judges and the Administration of Justice." 3 *Justice System Journal* 163.

Court Watching Project. 1975. *A Citizen's Study of the Franklin County Municipal Court*. Columbus, Ohio.

DeBruler, Roger. 1969. "Non-Judicial Duties of Indiana Trial Judges." 3 *Indiana Legal Forum* 1.

Eisenstein, James, and Herbert Jacob. 1977. *Felony Justice: An Organizational Analysis of Criminal Courts*. Boston: Little, Brown & Co.

Federal Judicial Center. 1971. *The 1969–1970 Federal District Court Time Study*. Washington, D.C.

Gignoux, Edward. 1965. "A Trial Judge's View." 50 *Massachusetts Law Quarterly* 100.

Guterman, James H., and Errol E. Meidinger. 1977. *In the Opinion of the Bar: A National Survey of Bar Polling Practices*. Chicago: American Judicature Society.

Heumann, Milton. 1977. *Plea Bargaining: The Experiences of Prosecutors, Judges, and Defense Attorneys*. Chicago: University of Chicago Press.

Howard, J. Woodford, Jr. 1981. *Courts of Appeal in the Federal Judicial System: A Study of the Second, Fifth, and District of Columbia Circuits*. Princeton, N.J.: Princeton University Press.

Jacob, Herbert 1965. *Justice in America*. Boston: Little, Brown & Co.

Levin, Martin A. 1977. *Urban Politics and the Criminal Courts*. Chicago: University of Chicago Press.

Maddi, Dorothy. 1977. *Judicial Performance Polls*. Chicago: American Bar Foundation.

McLauchlan, William P. 1977. *American Legal Processes*. New York: John Wiley & Sons.

Mnookin, Robert H., and Lewis Kornhauser. 1979. "Bargaining in the Shadow of the Law: The Case of Divorce." 88 *Yale Law Journal* 950.

Neubauer, David W. 1974. *Criminal Justice in Middle America*. Morristown, N.J.: General Learning Press.

Ohio Courts. 1979. Columbus: Supreme Court, Office of the Administrative Director.

Report of the Illinois Court Watching Project. 1976. *Citizens Size Up Their Courts*. Chicago: League of Women Voters of Illinois.

Rosett, Arthur, and Donald R. Cressey. 1976. *Justice by Consent: Bargains in the American Courthouse*. Philadelphia: J.B. Lippincott.

Ross, H. Laurence. 1970. *Settled Out of Court*. Chicago: Aldine.

Ryan, John Paul, Allan Ashman, Bruce D. Sales, and Sandra Shane-DuBow. 1980. *American Trial Judges: Their Work Styles and Performance*. New York: Free Press.

Sarat, Austin. 1977. "Judging in Trial Courts: An Exploratory Study." 39 *Journal of Politics* 368.

Shapiro, Martin. 1981. *Courts: A Comparative and Political Analysis*. Chicago: University of Chicago Press.

Sheldon, Charles H. 1974. *The American Judicial Process*. New York: Dodd, Mead.

Sheskin, Arlene, and Charles W. Grau. 1981. "Judicial Response to Technocratic Reform." In J. Cramer (ed.). *Courts and Judges*. Beverly Hills and London: Sage Publications.

Stott, E. Keith, Jr. 1980. "A Proposal to Evaluate Colorado's Judges." 9 *Colorado Lawyer* 1.

Survey of State Judicial Education and Training Programs. 1978. Washington, D.C.: American University Law Institute.

Ungs, Thomas D., and Larry R. Baas. 1972. "Judicial Role Perceptions: A Q-Technique Study of Ohio Judges." 6 *Law and Society Review* 343.

Yankelovich, Skelly, and White, Inc. 1978. *Highlights of a National Survey of the General Public, Judges, Lawyers, and Community Leaders*. Williamsburg Va.: National Center for State Courts.

Part III
The Effects of Changes in
Court Structure

10 A Tale of Two Reforms: On the Work of the U.S. Supreme Court

Gregory A. Caldeira

Quite a number of scholars, lawyers, and judges have, especially in the last decade and a half, pronounced the existence of a crisis of volume and overload in the Supreme Court of the United States, as well as in the various state and federal appellate and trial courts (for examples, see Casper and Posner 1974; 1976; Freund Committee 1972; Bickel 1973; Brennan 1973). These commentators have argued that the extaordinarily rapid increase of litigation, especially in the 1960s, at both the trial and appellate levels, has lead to a decline in the promptness and quality of the workings of justice in the United States. For instance, the Study Group on the Caseload of the Supreme Court concluded that:

> The statistics of the Court's current workload, both in absolute terms and in the mounting trend, are impressive evidence that the conditions essential for the performance of the Court's mission do not exist. For an ordinary appellate court the burgeoning volume of cases would be a staggering burden; for the Supreme Court the pressures of the docket are incompatible with the appropriate fulfillment of its historic and essential functions. [Freund Committee 1972, p. 5]

Some twelve years earlier, Professor Hart (1959) complained that the deluge of cases had begun to tell its toll on the quality of the Court's products (but compare Douglas 1960; Arnold 1959; and Griswold 1960).

Numerous proposals for resolving the putative overload of the Court have appeared. Professor Freund's group suggested, among other things, the elimination of three-judge district courts and direct review of their decisions in the Court, increased support from staff, and "a nonjudicial body [to] investigate and report on the complaints of prisoners" (Freund Committee 1972, pp. 47–48). That study group's most

I would like to record my debt to Mr. Patrick Kenney, a graduate student in political science at the University of Iowa, who very carefully gathered some of the data that I have used in the research from which this chapter comes. Professor Philip L. Dubois of the University of California at Davis provided very helpful suggestions on an earlier draft of this manuscript.

controversial proposal—a National Court of Appeals—would relieve the Supreme Court of many of its more-"tedious and time-consuming duties" (1972, p. 22).

Crises of volume are nothing new in the development of the Supreme Court and lower federal judiciary (see Frankfurter and Landis 1928; Fairman 1971; and Warren 1923). Twice, at least, in the Court's first two centuries it has found itself overloaded with litigation that outstripped its capacity. Between the Civil War and 1890, the number of cases in the Supreme Court more than tripled, due in part to congressional addition of jurisdiction and expansion of appellate jurisdiction. Congress, through the Circuit Court of Appeals Act of 1891 (hereafter the Circuit Court Act), made certain kinds of cases final in a newly established intermediate court of appeals. The demand for the Court's attention abated for a short time but once again began to increase and multiply until Congress enacted the Judges' Bill of 1925, which made most of the Court's case load discretionary rather than obligatory. These two judicial reforms, or changes in rules, have received a surprisingly small amount of scrutiny (Frankfurter and Landis 1928; Porter 1975; McLauchlan 1979; Halpern and Vines 1977; Bickel 1973), especially considering the sweeping nature of the new policies—for example, moving from almost all obligatory to almost all discretionary jurisdiction. Scholars, lawyers, and judges have usually assumed that these reforms had the desired effect of reducing the pressure of cases. Yet if we know anything about policymaking, we know that a reform will quite often miss its mark and can create all manner of unintended consequences. The studies that have appeared lack the statistical and conceptual sophistication necessary to ferret out the effects of these changes in the jurisdiction of the Court.

The Circuit Court of Appeals Act of 1891

Frankfurter and Landis state that "the conditions under which the Supreme Court labored from 1850 to 1890 show what happens when Congress, the judiciary, and the president are entangled in political passions and represent conflicting perceptions of the role of the federal courts in the national polity (1928, p. 86). "The Supreme Court's docket," these scholars remark, "got beyond all control" in the years between the Civil War and the 1890s (1928, p. 86). Demand for decisions from the Court grew for a number of reasons, including the expansion of commercial activity, economic booms and panics, new problems of admiralty as shipping increased, the creative energy unleashed by the war, and so on. Apparently, however, Congress contributed most to the explosion of filings and appeals in the federal courts because after the Civil War it extended in numerous ways the jurisdiction of the national government and so the federal judicial system (Frankfurter and Landis 1928, pp. 60–65). The Court, too, worsened its situation in construing federal legislation in a fashion that increased the demands made on its docket (Porter 1975, pp. 4–6).

Now, of course, the Supreme Court and the lower federal courts were in no position to process these new cases. Under the law, justices on the Court had to "ride circuit" because Congress had, since 1801, resisted the creation of intermediate courts of appeals (Goebel 1971). Instead, federal district judges, together with the appropriate circuit justice, constituted the circuit courts. This system of circuits wreaked considerable wear and tear on these elderly justices (for example, Frank 1964). Even more important, as the case load of the Supreme Court increased, it often became impossible for the circuit justice to perform his duties.

That Congress procrastinated so long in providing relief for the Court indicates that such changes involved more than mere procedural shifts. Quite simply, Congress could not until 1891 resolve the tensions between the national and state governments, between the South and the North, and between proponents and opponents of judicial power. Here were issues of politics and public policy, not of law. Congress acted only after it became apparent that the Court could no longer function unless the jurisdictional situation changed in a relatively radical fashion. Senator William Evarts lead the fight to establish nine courts of appeals, retain both the district and circuit courts, provide for appeals directly from the district and circuit courts to the Supreme Court in a limited set of cases, and make the remainder of cases from lower courts final in the new courts of appeals (Frankfurter and Landis 1928, pp. 95–100). The Court could review these final decisions at its own discretion through a writ of certiorari. Still, a large portion of its docket remained obligatory in nature.

Did this judicial reform have the intended effect—that is, did it produce a substantial reduction in the press of cases upon the Supreme Court? Two of the most distinguished historians of federal jurisdictional politics believe that it did:

The remedy was decisive. The Supreme Court at once felt its benefits. A flood of litigation had been shut off. While in the October Term,

1887, 482 new cases were docketed; in 1888, 550; in 1889, 489; and in 1890, 623; in 1891 (with the new Act only a few months in operation) new business dropped to 379 cases and in 1892 to 275 cases. [Frankfurter and Landis 1928, pp. 101–102]

Frankfurter and Landis pronounced this law a success in such certain terms that no one has bothered to examine its impact except in the most superficial fashion.

Bickel, in his assessment of current proposals for revising the jurisdiction of the Supreme Court, concurs with Frankfurter and Landis but moves on to state that "the remedy was decisive, but not for long" (1973, p. 3). He argues that relief was short lived because the act "came just as the country was about to enter a period of extensive federal legislative activity, which naturally produced judicial business" (1973, p. 3). From the lower courts, state and federal, cases increased in which the Court, as a matter of law, had to issue a decision. These so-called automatic cases increased, even though Congress continued to make the Court's docket more and more discretionary—for example, through the Judiciary Act of 1916. Porter agrees that "relief . . . proved illusory. While the Court had fewer cases to decide, it was still obliged to settle 'scores' of questions based on wills and contracts and continued to be plagued with routine federal matters arising under postal laws, Indian treaties, immigration regulations," and so on (1975, pp. 6–7).

Figure 10–1 presents the rise of filings in the Supreme Court from 1880 through 1974, and it suggests that the Circuit Court Act had relatively dramatic and immediate effects on the case load of the Court—just as Frankfurter and Landis, Porter, Bickel, and others indicate. However, it seems to me that these data make clear the importance of distinguishing between the short-term and long-term effects of policy changes. Change as a result of a shift in policy comes in a number of forms, but one of the most important sources is a discrete, or near-discrete, historical event—a shock to the system that changes it in some fashion (see Caldeira and McCrone 1981). That shock can appear in the form of something as unplanned as the Civil War or as calculated as the 1891 Circuit Court Act. Under the latter circumstance, one could refer to it as a "policy intervention," in the parlance of econometricians. Such intervention can have a variety of effects on the Court's case load, and figure 10–2 illustrates four that I think merit particular attention (for the mechanics of interrupted-time-series analysis, see Cook and Campbell 1976; Lewis-Beck 1979). In situation 1, the phenomenon under consideration grows in a secular trend toward greater activity; it represents long-term, persistent change, in this case increase, and no abrupt change as a result of an intervention. Situation

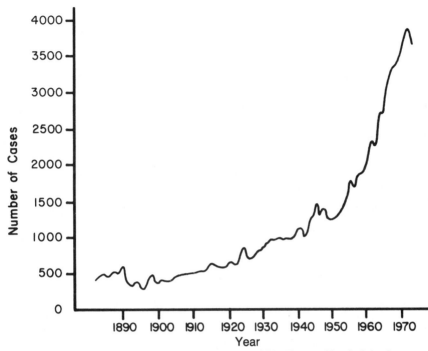

Source: Gerhard P. Casper and Richard N. Posner. 1976. *The Workload of the Supreme Court.* Chicago: American Bar Foundation. Reprinted with permission.

Figure 10–1. Increases in Cases Filed in the Supreme Court, 1880–1974

2 shows a case in which an event introduces a very abrupt change in the overall level of that activity; the shock pushes it to a new level but does not, on a permanent basis, accelerate this activity. Situation 3 shows some historical event or policy that has no short-term effect on the activity but that, over time, increases the level of that activity. Finally, as shown in situation 4, it is possible that an event could induce both short-term and long-term increases in the movement toward greater activity. These four cases by no means exhaust the logical possible outcomes of a reform, but surely they are among the most plausible.

Figure 10–1 suggests the effect represented in situation 2 of figure 10–2: The jurisdictional change produced an abrupt, short-term, but no longer-term, persistent change. In evaluating the impact of a reform, however, one cannot simply look at the pattern before and after the implementation of the policy or policies; numerous outside influences potentially threaten the validity of inferences about the effects of a change. Thus, for instance, if one discovers that filings drop in a

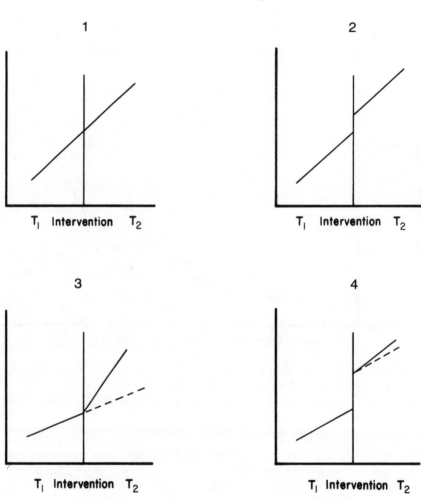

Figure 10–2. Four Results of an Intervention

statistically significant fashion after the imposition of a change in judicial structure, one could quite reasonably conclude that the reform had wrought the decline. If one assumes, however, that filings track with phenomena such as business failures, depression, prosperity, social integration and disintegration, or the expansion of population, then one ought also to entertain the propositions that the decrease in filings could result from perturbations in related social, economic, and political phenomena (Casper and Posner 1976; Schwartz and Miller 1964; Grossman and Sarat 1975). Scholars, lawyers, and judges have over and over again argued for and acted on the presumption that increases in population, greater societal complexity, political mobilization, expansion of commercial activities, enactment of laws that create uncertainty as to people's legal rights, and so on encourage litigation and, by implication, appellate filings in the Supreme Court. To exclude such influences from one's purview is to court the disaster of spuriously concluding that a policy had a certain impact when, in fact, it had no effect at all (McCleary and Hay 1980, pp. 160–201). If one wishes to gain an accurate and precise estimate of the impact of a judicial reform such as the Circuit Court Act, one should specify as part of the model or explanation such macro-level variables as population, economic circumstances, and so on. These influences must be taken account of whether one speaks about the dynamics of the Court's case load in descriptive or impressionistic terms or as part of a rigorous statistical analysis. The use of a statistical model such as interrupted-time-series analysis, for instance, might be advised because it yields such precise and easily interpretable estimates (McCleary and Hay 1980).[1]

The Judges' Bill of 1925

Not even a decade had passed when the potency of the reforms of 1891 began to fade; by 1895, the number of filings in the Court started creeping toward the perilous range that had motivated the policy changes of 1891, and by 1916, the case load had duplicated the apogee of 1890. Congress, having expanded access to the Court by writ of certiorari of decisions from state courts in favor of rights claimed under federal law, contributed to the overload of cases. The Court itself also had done a great deal to make its own situation worse, however. Seemingly besotted with the power of judicial review, the justices of the laissez faire Court made a mockery of deference to legislative judgments and so created further incentives for citizens and corporations to press demands on the Supreme Court. In the period between the enactments of 1891 and 1925, the Court invalidated nearly twice as many federal, state, and municipal statutes as it had in the previous century. Chief Justice Taft in 1925 complained that the Court was about two years behind in its work, but he and his brethren had managed, in the space of three years, to find a bevy of statutes unconstitutional (Porter 1975, p. 7). The Court simply refused to pull in its horns.

Through an extraordinary campaign of lobbying, Chief Justice Taft orchestrated a fundamental change in the nation's judicial politics (Murphy 1964, pp. 135–145). He presented his proposed jurisdictional bill as a means by which the Court could process the overload of cases that had accumulated in the 1920s. Under the bill, the Court would have freedom to pick and choose cases and so, presumably, could more easily manage its docket. Neither Taft nor anyone else involved in the debate addressed the reform's potential impact on the Court's internal procedures or external roles as a policymaker. The Judges' Bill, enacted in 1925, made the Supreme Court a court of discretionary jurisdiction, relieving it of most of its obligatory choices. The bill abolished the right of review in numerous classes of issues, transferred much of the Court's business to the courts of appeals, and in this way, permitted the justices to select a small number of significant questions (for legislative debates, see Frankfurter and Landis 1928, p. 276).

Did this judicial reform have the effect its framers postulated? Did the Judges' Bill make it feasible for the Supreme Court to process its docket? Did the bill have other, probably unintended, effects on the Supreme Court as an institution?

Frankfurter and Landis, in evaluating the effects of the Judges' Bill, argued that the growth of petitions for writs of certiorari would once again push the work load of the Supreme Court to perilous proportions because, even though obligatory cases had nearly disappeared, new discretionary cases had more than taken up the slack (1928, pp. 289–294). In discussing the problems of the overload of the 1960s and 1970s, the Freund Committee said that, although the reforms increasing the discretion of the Court had achieved their goals, "now, however, these solutions have become part of the problem. The courts of appeals have encountered a dramatic rise in their own business, with a proportionate outflow to the Supreme Court; and the task of coping with all the discretionary work on certiorari overhangs all of the Court's work" (1973, pp. 8–9). Furthermore, Frankfurter and Landis recognized, quite correctly, that "the Supreme Court had ceased to be a common law court"; it had evolved, or been transformed into, a "public law" court (1928, p. 307).

Halpern and Vines, in a very important study, have explored the impact of the Judges' Bill on the Court as an institution, but especially on the practice of dissent among its justices. This reform, apparently, had a number of quick and obvious results. First, in the wake of the bill, "cases came to the Court less frequently by right and more often by certiorari" (1977, p. 474). Second, these scholars found about "a 75 percent increase in the rate at which there was dissent in all cases" after the reform (1977, p. 475). The rate of dissent in cases arriving on certiorari remained stable; the rate increased severalfold in obligatory cases because most of the noncontroversial cases had been eliminated. Third, for most of the justices, the rate of dissent increased after the Act. Fourth, dissents in cases arriving on certiorari accounted for much of the increase in the extent of voting cleavages. Even more important than these specific findings, however, is Halpern and Vines's claim, on the basis of historical data, that the "year 1925 stands out . . . as a starting point in the evolution of a new trend in dissenting votes" (1977, pp. 479–480). The Judges' Bill, then, must have afforded the Court the luxury of time to write dissents, together with controversial and weighty issues about which to disagree. Of the studies of jurisdictional reforms of the Court, Halpern and Vines's is by far the finest because it takes into account an unintended consequence and treats the Court as a much more complex institution than, for instance, Casper and Posner's (1976).

The scholarship on the effects of the Judges' Bill of 1925 has a number of obvious and not-so-obvious defects or omissions. To begin with, students of the reform have rather blithely assumed that the legal change caused the temporary decline in the number of cases filed. Of course, the reform is clearly the most plausible account for the drop— as figure 10–2 suggests. Still, scholars should have analyzed and ruled out the numerous threats to the validity of that inference about the reform's effect. Thus Casper and Posner, Bickel, Frankfurter and Landis, and Halpern and Vines should, at the very least, have considered the various social, political, and economic leading indicators in order to be able to state, without equivocation, that declines in economic activity, social mobilization, and the like did not cause the temporary hiatus in case load pressure.

One plausible explanation for Halpern and Vines's results on the Judges' Bill is that huge increases in political mobilization, legal complexity, movement of population, and so forth created the preconditions for insoluble disputes that soon arrived at the Court's doorstep. These disputes, then, translated themselves into more and more dissents on the Supreme Court. If this is so, the Judges' Bill did not have the impact that Halpern and Vines have ascribed to it—that is, these controversies would have landed in the Supreme Court's lap regardless of congressional reforms of jurisdiction. For instance, a scan of figure 10–1 leads one to suspect that World War II accelerated the pattern of growth in filings—above and beyond the underlying trend upward. Indeed, preliminary inquiries encourage this suspicion. Using interrupted time-series analysis (McCleary and Hays 1980, pp. 160–201), I have found that World War II was associated with increased public demand for attention from the Supreme Court—quite apart from the effects of laws such as the Judges' Bill or the Circuit Court Act.[2] Until I have conducted more-comprehensive analyses, of course, one should treat such results with skepticism; but this is surely an avenue worth investigating in a systematic fashion. Thus, if one wishes to make accurate and nonspurious generalizations about the impact of the Judges' Bill, one should control for some of the more-obvious social, political, and economic explanations for the growth of case loads. Had these scholars at the very least made the distinction between long- and short-term effects of a reform—as I have suggested in figure 10–2— we might have now a more-solid evidentiary base on the effects of judicial reforms.

The Court itself might have been responsible for a part of the reduction in filings. "Case load changes may be self-limiting," Clark (1976) suggests. The prospect of a long and probably hopeless wait provides a formidable disincentive to seeking a hearing from the Supreme Court. The more quickly the Court moves its docket along, the more work it will have. "If the case load of a supreme court increases faster than its ability to process its filings . . . , the court will respond either by increasing the backlog or by reducing the fraction of cases it accepts for complete review" (Clark 1976, p. 224). Facing an interminable wait for a hearing from the Supreme Court in the early and middle 1920s, a rational litigant might well have decided to make other plans. That increased delay might have accounted for part of the temporary reduction after the implementation of the reform of 1925; not, of course, all of the decline, but perhaps a measurable amount.

To evaluate the effect, or effects, of the Judges' Bill—or, for that matter, virtually any change in jurisdiction—a proper model would have to encapsulate the social, economic, and political bases of demand for litigation; the lag between the implementation of a new jurisdictional law and its actually taking hold; actions of the Court itself that might encourage or discourage people and organizations to seek a hearing; and new substantive legislation that might create legal rights or legal uncertainty. That one should worry about the impacts of congressional actions—aside from jurisdictional changes—has not much entered into the discussion of the impacts of these reforms, apart from Chief Justice Burger's ruminations about the crisis of the Court. Might not Congress, in the late 1920s, have taken from litigants some cause of action; and might not that same institution have, during the New Deal, added all manner of rights and made knowing one's legal position extremely uncertain? So, again, we have an eminently researchable question, one susceptible to both qualitative and quantitative analysis.

Beyond the proper specification of a model of the effects of this reform of the case load, Halpern and Vines (1977) show the way to a much broader conception of the potential impacts of jurisdictional reforms. The focus of their work is on institutional change. Surely the changing nature of the practice of dissent is one chief candidate for analysis. Judicial activism—that is, the expanding scope of the Court's decisions—could well be another consequence of the Judges' Bill. The courts of the pre-1925 period seldom missed a chance to pursue the path of activism; but it is clear that the Court of the post-New Deal era has become activist in bigger and better ways. If we examine the number of federal and state statutes the Court has invalidated from 1800 to 1973, it does not appear, at least on visual inspection, that the reform of 1925 led directly to an expansion of judicial activism. Indeed it seems evident in figure 10–3 that invalidations of federal laws actually decreased for a time and that nullifications of state statutes increased quite a bit but then declined until the 1950s. Judicial invalidations of state and federal laws are but the crudest form of judicial activism. One might investigate a number of related but much subtler forms of judicial activism in order to determine whether and to what extent the Judges' Bill had an effect on them. For instance, the in-

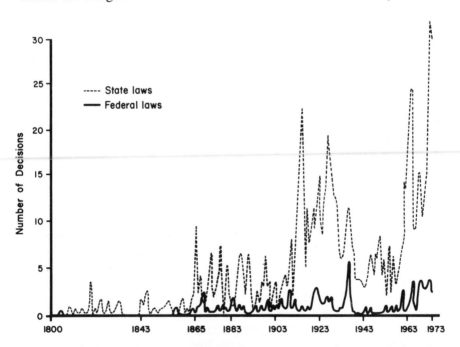

Source: Gregory A. Caldeira and Donald J. McCrone. 1981. "Of Time and Judicial Activism: A Study of the United States Supreme Court, 1800–1973. In Stephen Halpern and Charles Lamb (eds.). *Supreme Court Activism and Restraint*. Lexington, Mass.: D.C. Heath and Company. Reprinted with permission.

Figure 10–3. State and Federal Statutes: The Number of Judicial Decisions Declaring a Law Unconstitutional

creased discretion of the Court could have increased the willingness and propensity of the justices to question established authority, to overrule precedents, and to criticize doctrines—eventualities that I am currently investigating. We should, in any event, cast a jaundiced eye on simple predictions about the effects of judicial reform and on explanations of phenomena such as filings and dissent that do not take into account the Court's social, economic, and political environments. Halpern and Vines (1977) have unearthed solid evidence of radical implications and consequences of a reform billed as a purely procedural change; and I suspect, based upon my preliminary efforts, that we can discover yet other effects.

Conclusion

Is there a lesson to be derived from this review and criticism of scholarship on the effects of the Judges' Bill and the Circuit Court Act? If there is a moral here, it is to beware of substantive judicial reforms cloaked in procedural garb. Changes in jurisdictional boundaries have, in most cases, quite uneven effects on the individuals, corporations, and interest groups involved. The Judges' Bill, together with the Circuit Court Act, has undoubtedly created the preconditions for, and has perhaps even been a major cause of, the great expansion of the Supreme Court's role as a national policymaker. To provide exact estimates of the effects of judicial reforms on the Supreme Court's agenda setting, dissenting practices, and policymaking constitutes an important and urgent task for students of the Court and public policy. This chapter has presented a sample of what I regard as the most pressing considerations in the study of the effects of judicial reforms; in gist, in assessing the impacts of changes in policy, we must provide full specifications of the various possible influences on the growth and decline of phenomena such as case load. Even more important, we should canvass potential impacts that the legislature might not have imagined.

Studies of reforms such as these can shed light on the current debate, now in temporary abeyance, on the case load of the Court and the suggestions for a National Court of Appeals and on the rise of judicial activism and what, if anything, to do about that situation. The most recent barrage of criticism of the Supreme Court for pursuing the path of judicial activism comes at nearly the same time as current proposals for reducing the case load of the Court (Miller 1979; Glazer 1975; Caldeira and McCrone 1981). That the two controversies have materialized simultaneously, I think, is no coincidence. Proponents of schemes such as the National Court of Appeals advertise it as a mere administrative rearrangement. The apostles of judicial restraint claim not to object to liberal policies but, rather, to the judicial methodologies that produce them (for example, Bickel 1970; 1975). Yet further inspection reveals that the apostles of judicial restraint are quite often the proponents of administrative reforms of the Court's jurisdiction. It is imperative to recall, as Professor Ulmer (1973) has warned, that procedural changes are inseparable from substantive changes in public policy. For instance, if the National Court of Appeals accomplishes the purposes its sponsors claim for it, then we should expect, based on extant scholarship, a decline in the Court's discretionary power and so, perhaps, a decline in the extent of its activism. That we have so little knowledge about the effects of controversial and possibly far-reaching judicial reforms such as the National Court of Appeals makes it all the more urgent that social scientists, using sophisticated conceptual schemes and methodological tools, begin work.

Notes

1. Now, of course, the Circuit Court Act might well have had effects on the Supreme Court as an institution—above and beyond the obvious and intended impact of reducing the pressure of filings. Courts with discretionary jurisdiction and relatively light case loads, on the whole, become more intimately involved in making public policy than institutions that face obligatory and heavy loads (Canon and Jaros 1970; Clark 1976; Kagan et al. 1977). Thus, one should be led beyond an evaluation of the reform's impact on the case load to an assessment of its implications for phenomena such as internal procedures, judicial activism, judicial restraint, and agenda building. I have more to say about this later in the next section.

2. That war, apart from the two judicial reforms, has an impact on filings in the Supreme Court is captured in the following formal representation:

$$\text{FILING}_t = B_1 \text{FILING}_{t-1} + B_2 \text{FILING}_{t-2} + B_3 \text{WW2}_t$$
$$- B_4 \text{ST1891}_t - B_5 \text{LT1891}_t - B_6 \text{ST1925}_t$$
$$- B_7 \text{LT1925}_t + e_t,$$

where FILING_t is the number of cases filed in the Supreme Court in a particular year; WW2_t represents the effects of World War II, scored 1 during and 0 otherwise; FILING_{t-1} and FILING_{t-2} represent the autoregressive process that underlies the growth of the Court's case load, much as virtually every public organization seems to have a life of its own regardless of external pressure; ST1891, and ST1925, monitor the short-term impacts of the two reforms; LT1891, and LT1925, assess the long-term effects of the two bills; and e_t is a term for errors. To adjust for the presence of a considerable amount of serial correlation in this series, I have relied upon the use of both the lagged dependent variables and a standard statistical correction, the Cochran-Orcutt procedure (Pindyck and Rubinfeld 1976). This equation yields the following unstandardized regression coefficients (B_1, B_2 . . ., B_7) with the relevant t-statistic appearing in brackets below:

$$\text{FILING}_t = \begin{array}{l} 00.64 \text{ FILING}_{t-1} + 00.37 \text{ FILING}_{t-2} + 177.00\text{WW2}_t \\ \quad [7.24] \qquad\qquad [3.99] \qquad\qquad\quad [2.68] \\ -58.44 \text{ ST1891}_t + 3.40 \text{ LT1891}_t - 119.41 \text{ ST1925}_t \\ \quad [1.40] \qquad\qquad [1.70] \qquad\qquad\quad [2.29] \\ +1.01 \text{ LT1925}_t + e_t. \\ \quad [.35] \end{array}$$

$$R^2 = .99 \quad \text{Durbin-Watson} = 2.06 \quad \text{Rho} = .11$$

The statistical fit is very good, serial correlation drops to trivial levels, some of the coefficients are significant, and none of the parameters takes on a nonsensical sign. These results suggest a number of statements about the growth of the Court's case load but, for present purposes, it is perhaps most impressive that World War II is indeed associated with a substantial increase in appellate filings and that the acts of 1891 and 1925 both damped down filings in the short run but had no impact in the long run.

References

Arnold, Thurman. 1959. "Professor Hart's Theology." 73 *Harvard Law Review* 1298.

Bickel, Alexander M. 1970. *The Supreme Court and the Idea of Progress*. New York: Harper & Row.

———. 1973. *The Caseload of the Supreme Court—and What, If Anything, to Do About It*. Washington, D.C.: American Enterprise Institute for Public Policy Research.

———. 1975. *The Morality of Consent*. New Haven: Yale University Press.

Brennan, William J. 1973. "The National Court of Appeals: Another Dissent." 40 *University of Chicago Law Review* 473.

Caldeira, Gregory A., and Donald J. McCrone. 1981. "Of Time and Judicial Activism: A Study of the United States Supreme Court,

1800–1973." In S. Halpern and C. Lamb (eds.). *Supreme Court Activism and Restraint*. Lexington, Mass.: D.C. Heath and Company.

Canon, Bradley, and Dean Jaros. 1970. "External Variables, Institutional Structure, and Dissent on State Supreme Courts." 3 *Polity* 175.

Casper, Gerhard P., and Richard N. Posner. 1974. "A Study of the Supreme Court's Caseload." 3 *Journal of Legal Studies* 339.

————. 1976. *The Workload of the Supreme Court*. Chicago: American Bar Foundation.

Clark, Davis S. 1976. "American Supreme Court Caseloads: A Preliminary Inquiry." 25 *American Journal of Comparative Law* 217.

Cook, Thomas D., and Donald T. Campbell. 1976. "The Design and Conduct of Quasi-Experiments and True Experiments in Field Settings." In M. Dunnette (ed.). *The Handbook of Industrial and Organizational Psychology*. Chicago: Rand McNally.

Douglas, William O. 1960. "The Supreme Court and Its Caseload." 45 *Cornell Law Quarterly* 401.

Fairman, Charles. 1971. *History of the Supreme Court of the United States: Volume 6, Reconstruction and Reunion 1864–88*. New York: Macmillan.

Frank, John P. 1964. *Justice Daniel Dissenting: A Biography of Peter V. Daniel*. Cambridge: Harvard University Press.

Frankfurter, Felix, and James M. Landis. 1928. *The Business of the Supreme Court: A Study in the Federal Judicial System*. New York: Macmillan.

Freund Committee. 1972. *Report of the Study Group on the Caseload of the Supreme Court*. Washington, D.C.: Federal Judicial Center, Administrative Office of the United States Courts.

Glazer, Nathan. 1975. "Towards an Imperial Judiciary?" 40 *The Public Interest* 104.

Goebel, Julius, Jr. 1971. *History of the Supreme Court of the United States: Volume I, Antecedents and Beginnings to 1801*. New York: Macmillan.

Griswold, Erwin N. 1960. "The Supreme Court, 1959 Term, Foreword: Of Time and Attitudes—Professor Hart and Judge Arnold." 74 *Harvard Law Review* 81.

Grossman, Joel B., and Austin D. Sarat. 1975. "Litigation in the Federal Courts: A Comparative Perspective." 9 *Law and Society Review* 321.

Halpern, Stephen, and Kenneth Vines. 1977. "Institutional Disunity, The Judges' Bill, and the Role of the U.S. Supreme Court." 30 *Western Political Quarterly* 471.

Hart, Henry M., Jr. 1959. "The Supreme Court, 1958 Term: The Time Chart of the Justices." 73 *Harvard Law Review* 84.

Kagan, Robert, Bliss Cartwright, Lawrence S. Friedman, and Stanton Wheeler. 1977. "The Business of State Supreme Courts, 1870–1970." 30 *Stanford Law Review* 121.

Lewis-Beck, Michael S. 1979. "Some Economic Effects of Revolution: Models, Measurement, and the Cuban Experience." 84 *American Journal of Sociology* 1127.

McCleary, Richard, and Richard A. Hay, Jr. 1980. *Applied Time Series Analysis for the Social Sciences*. Beverly Hills: Sage Publications.

McLauchlan, William. 1979. "An Exploratory Analysis of Supreme Court Caseload." Presented at the Annual Meeting of the American Political Science Association, Washington, D.C. (September).

Miller, Arthur S. 1979. "Judicial Activism and American Constitutionalism: Some Notes and Reflections." In J.R. Pennock and J.W. Chapman (eds.). *Nomos XX: Constitutionalism*. New York: New York University Press.

Murphy, Walter F. 1964. *Elements of Judicial Strategy*. Chicago: University of Chicago Press.

Pindyck, Robert S., and Daniel L. Rubinfeld. 1976. *Econometric Models and Economic Forecasts*. New York: McGraw-Hill.

Porter, Mary Cornelia. 1975. "Politics, Ideology, and the Workload of the Supreme Court: Some Historical Perspectives." Presented at the Annual Meeting of the Midwest Political Science Association, Chicago (May).

Schwartz, Richard D., and James C. Miller. 1964. "Legal Evolution and Societal Complexity." 70 *American Journal of Sociology* 159.

Ulmer, S. Sidney. 1973. "Revising the Jurisdiction of the Supreme Court: Mere Administrative Reform or Substantive Policy Change?" 58 *Minnesota Law Review* 121.

Warren, Charles. 1923. *The Supreme Court in United States History*, Vol. 3. Boston: Little, Brown & Co.

11

Creating an Intermediate Court of Appeals: Workload and Policymaking Consequences

John A. Stookey

Judicial reforms are of many types and variously motivated. One of the major motivating factors is the need to cope with the expanding work load of the U.S. court system. This chapter is concerned with the impact of one such work-load-motivated reform: the introduction of an intermediate court of appeals into a state-court system. Two basic types of impact seem to be intended by such a reform. The first and most obvious is to relieve the case pressures on the state supreme court. The creation of an intermediate court is premised on the assumption that, by placing a new court level between the supreme court and the courts of original jurisdiction, the state supreme court's case filings will be substantially reduced.

This impact relates to the second one. It is proposed that the reduction in supreme court case filings accomplished by the creation of the intermediate court will "free the highest court to exercise its primary [policy] making function."[1]

Thus, two hypotheses concerning the impact of creating an intermediate court of appeals emerge:

1. The creation of an intermediate court of appeals will reduce the work load of the supreme court of that system.
2. The reduction in supreme court work load accomplished by the introduction of an intermediate court of appeals will increase the policymaking function of the supreme court in that system.

In the sections that follow, I explicate the theoretical underpinnings of these hypotheses and review the previous attempts to test them. I conclude by trying to synthesize this literature into a proposed comprehensive model of the impact of creating an intermediate court of appeals and testing the explanatory power of that model in a case study of the Arizona court system.

Work-Load Consequences

Closer examination reveals that the first hypothesis, while intuitively plausible, is based on some potentially false assumptions. For example, it appears that the proposed reduction in supreme court work load may be accomplished only if we rule out, or at least limit, double appeals. In other words, while creating an intermediate appellate-court level will relieve the supreme court of much of its duty to hear initial appeals, it will not prevent litigants from appealing further from the intermediate court to the court of last resort. To the extent that such double appeals occur, the impact of an intermediate court on supreme court work load will be reduced.

Recent research by Marvell shows that approximately 40 percent of the cases decided by intermediate courts are appealed to the court of last resort (1979, p. 23). Wasby, Marvell, and Aikman (1979) address the same question with regard to appeal behavior over recent years for twenty-four state courts of last resort.[2] They found that the smallest percentage of intermediate-court cases in which requests to appeal were made was 22 percent in Oregon. Colorado had the greatest percentage of cases in which requests were made, 54 percent. Thus, while considerable variation exists in the level of second appeals, Marvell's 40 percent figure appears to be a good estimate.

Whether a double-appeal rate of 40 percent is large or small need not concern us here. However, this figure does suggest that, if all other things remain constant and if the intermediate court is given jurisdiction over all initial appeals, the creation of such a court should be expected to reduce the number of filings to the supreme court by 60 percent. However, all other things do not appear to remain constant. It has been suggested in the literature that the act of creating an intermediate court of appeals results in an increase in initial appeals, apparently because of the greater ease with which appeals can be filed in the appellate court, particularly if that court has multiple divisions that are regionally located (Zeisel, Kalven, and Buchholz 1959, pp. 115–119). If true, this effect, combined with double appeals, could negate any impact that an intermediate court might have on supreme court filings.

Flango and Blair (1980, p. 761), using an interrupted-time-series design, addressed this question for seven states that created intermediate courts of appeals in the 1960s. They found that in six of the seven there was a substantial increase in the level of initial appeals after the creation of the intermediate court. Similarly, they found that, while there was a decrease in supreme court filings immediately after the creation of the intermediate court, the number returned very quickly to or near the levels that would have been predicted by projecting the preintervention levels. While the states studied were not randomly selected and therefore may not be representative, and while the time series were relatively short, these findings certainly lend credence to the argument that increased initial appeals and double appeals will block any long-term impact of an intermediate court of appeals on supreme court filings.

However, before rejecting the hypothesis out of hand, further evaluation is needed. It must be recalled that, concomitant with the creation of an intermediate court of appeals in most states, there is a modification in the access method of the supreme court—namely, from a predominantly obligatory to a predominantly discretionary procedure. Under the former, the supreme court is required to hear formally all cases brought to it; under the latter, the court has authority to reject some appeals summarily. This shift in access method as a joint reform with the addition of the intermediate court is related to the assumption (usually, but not universally, held) in the U.S. legal system that each litigant has the right to one, and only one, appeal. She or he can, of course, file additional appeals, but it is normally not assumed that they must be formally considered. Therefore, when the supreme court is the sole appellate court in a system, it is required to provide the appeal by right. However, after the addition of the new court level, that court takes on the responsibility to hear the initial appeals and the supreme court, in its position once removed from the courts of original jurisdiction, may now decide to which cases it wishes to grant a second appeal and to which it does not.

The association of the structural change (this term will be used hereafter to refer to the creation of an intermediate court of appeals) and the access-method change requires that we reformulate the first hypothesis since we are now interested in whether these two reforms together will have an impact on supreme court work load.

In order to explicate this potential joint impact, it is first necessary to define more specifically the dependent variable in the first hypothesis and the independent variable in the second hypothesis—namely, work load. This variable has been operationalized here, and in all other literature reviewed, as the number of cases filed. Hence, Flango and Blair (1980) demonstrate that the introduction of a court of appeals has only a temporary impact on supreme court filings. While such an operationalization is certainly reasonable, it may be too limited to measure the total impact of the structural and access-method change.

This point is made when we take into consideration that, as a result of gaining discretionary access control, the supreme court is given two methods by which to dispose of cases: (1) accept and formally review or (2) summarily reject. Clearly the amount of work necessary to dispose of a case is much less if the second option is used. For example, Justice England of the Florida Supreme Court indicates that review of a petition for review (the access decision) takes roughly twenty minutes, which is less than five percent of the time needed to decide a case on its merits (Wasby, Marvell, and Aikman 1979, p. 58).

At the aggregate level, this point can be further demonstrated by the following example. If 1,000 cases are decided in year one and 1,000 in year two, but if in year one all cases were formally decided and in year two half were formally decided and half summarily rejected, we would expect that the work load was less in year two, even though the number of cases considered was the same.[3] Realization of this should, therefore, result in an operationalization of work load other than case filings.

One alternative that immediately comes to mind is to measure work load as the number of formal opinions written each year. While this accounts for the difficulty already mentioned, it is also problematic. It ignores the fact that, while summary rejection takes less work than a full disposition, it nevertheless does take some work; leaving it out of the equation would seem to underestimate work load. One alternative for measuring work load that might be explored is a weighted sum of cases rejected and those formally disposed, along the lines of the following equation:

$$\text{Work load for year } X = \frac{\text{(Number of cases formally decided) } (W_1) +}{\text{(Number of cases summarily rejected) } (W_2)}$$

The work load weight (W) associated with each type of case could be assigned according to the relative amount of work necessary on the average for each type of disposition, which could be determined through interviews with the supreme court justices in question. For illustrative purposes, let us accept Justice England's evaluation that a summary rejection takes 5 percent of the time necessary for a formal disposition. Let us further assume that in year two, the year after the supreme court has been granted discretionary access control, that the court decides 1,000 cases, 200 formally and 800 by rejection of consideration. The work load for year two would therefore be $(200)(1) + (800)(.05) = 240$. If the supreme court formally decided 1,000 cases in year one, it would have experienced a 76 percent $[(1,000 - 240)/1,000]$ reduction in work load from year one to year two, even though the number of cases terminated has not changed.

Thus, it is possible that previous research has not found that creating an intermediate court of appeals has a permanent impact on supreme court workload because the joint reform of granting discretionary access control to the supreme court has not been considered, which in turn led to a too narrow operationalization of workload. This contention will be empirically evaluated later in the chapter.

Policymaking Consequences

The second intended impact of creating an intermediate court of appeals is based on the assumption that the reduction in supreme court work load that would be accomplished by such a structural change and the increased ability to focus on important issues rather than general initial appeals will permit the supreme court to engage in a greater degree of policymaking, rather than merely the correction of lower-court errors.

At least five pieces of research have been conducted that are relevant to this intended impact. Using a cross-sectional design, Canon and Jaros (1970) found that there was a higher dissent rate in state supreme courts when an intermediate court was present than when one was not. They interpreted this data to mean that most of the less-controversial cases, which are decided by the supreme court when it is the only appellate court, are filtered out by the intermediate court when it is present. This leaves the supreme court to concentrate on the more-controversial policy-potential cases that have a higher probability of evoking dissent. Flango and Blair (1980, p. 84) also found support for this conclusion using an interrupted time-series design to study the supreme court of Maryland before and after the introduction of an intermediate court of appeals.

Groot's (1971) before-and-after study of the North Carolina Supreme Court revealed that, not only did the dissent rate of the supreme court increase after the creation of an intermediate court but also that other indicators of supreme court policymaking increased, such as rates of overruling previous decisions, pages per opinion, and reexamination of existing law.

Atkins and Glick (1976) found that significant differences existed between the formal dockets of supreme courts in states with an intermediate court when compared to supreme courts that were the only appellate court in the state. The primary difference was that the courts in states with intermediate courts had a considerably larger proportion of their formal decisions devoted to criminal cases. However, the authors suggest that this may be due to the fact that states with intermediate courts tend to have higher crime rates than states without them. Therefore, there is no convincing evidence to suggest that the higher level of criminal cases is the result of these supreme courts' conscious use of their discretionary access power to decide primarily criminal cases.

The most comprehensive study of the impact of creating an intermediate court of appeals was conducted by Kagan et al. (1978) in the context of a larger study of the evolving role of state supreme courts.[4] The study deals with the evolution of state supreme court behavior and work load over the century 1870–1970, using a sample of opinions from each of sixteen state supreme courts in each of twenty-one sample years (1870, 1875, 1880, . . . 1970). The authors divided their sixteen states into three types:

Type 1. Low-population states with no supreme court case-selecting discretion, no lower appeals court, and relatively light case loads;

Type 2. Medium-sized and large states with little or no supreme court case-selecting discretion and heavy case loads (usually no intermediate court of appeals);

Type 3. Medium-sized or large states with substantial controls over supreme court case loads and relatively light case loads (court of appeals handles most initial appeals).

Kagan and his associates were interested in the different ways in which these three types of courts dealt with their case loads over the past one hundred years. Specifically, they evaluated whether type 3 courts would, because of an intermediate court and discretionary access control, be characterized by greater policymaking than either type 1 or type 2 courts. Their findings were that the supreme courts with high discretion (type 3) wrote fewer but longer opinions, reversed lower courts more frequently, issued more dissents and concurrences, decided more constitutional issues, and invalidated statutes more frequently than the low discretion courts. They concluded:

> Our rough indicators point in the same direction; changes in court organization seemed to make some differences in the agendas, opinion styles, and decisions of the state supreme court. [1978, p. 999]

Thus, it is clear that Kagan et al. have found substantial support for the proposition that the joint reforms of granting discretionary access control to a supreme court and creating an intermediate court of appeals increased the supreme court policymaking function, relative to its simple error-correction function. This conclusion, along with those of Canon and Jaros, Atkins and Glick, and Groot, suggests validity of the proposed linkage between the creation of an intermediate court and increased supreme court policymaking.

Discussion

The central concept in assessing the impact on a state supreme court of creating an intermediate court of appeals is clearly work load. Its centrality is demonstrated in the following diagram of the logical sequence of intended consequences:

Creation of an intermediate court of appeals	$\longrightarrow$	Reduction in supreme court work load	$\longrightarrow$	Increase in supreme court policymaking

However, the literature just reviewed does not present a totally consistent picture of how these linkages theoretically and empirically operate. For example, we have seen that the linkage between the creation of a new intermediate court and the reduction in supreme court work load is only very temporary, if work load is measured in its traditional form—namely, case filings. Nevertheless, the research does demonstrate that supreme courts in systems with an intermediate court of appeals and discretionary access control seem to behave in a more-policy-oriented way than supreme courts not so characterized. In the remainder of this chapter, I try to explain these inconsistencies by suggesting a model of the impact of creating an intermediate court that takes into consideration that such a structural change is usually a joint reform along with granting the supreme court discretionary access control. Following from this model is a definition of work load that may provide the basis for a clearer understanding of this joint reform. Finally, the approach suggested is demonstrated in a case study of Arizona's experience with creating an intermediate court of appeals.

In order to accomplish these goals, it will be helpful to decompose a supreme court's work load into the component parts suggested before: number of cases filed and disposition method of those cases. The relationship between these components can be demonstrated in terms of the cross tabulation shown in figure 11–1. I have made some simplifying assumptions in the figure for illustrative purposes. First, I have dichotomized level of filings into the categories high and low. What these categories mean in terms of real numbers is not significant here; I am only trying to demonstrate a difference in magnitude. Similarly, for simplicity, access method has been labeled as either totally

LEVELS OF FILINGS

	Low	High
OBLIGATORY	(A) 2	(B) 4
DISCRETIONARY	(C) 1	(D) 2

ACCESS METHOD

Figure 11–1. Level of Supreme Court Filings and Type of Access Method as Determinants of Supreme Court Work Load

obligatory or toally discretionary, even though there are variations in degree of access control.

The numerical entries indicate the ranking of the cell in terms of work load. Hence, cell C, representing a low number of filings and the ability to reject cases summarily, is number 1, signifying that this cross tabulation constitutes the smallest work load. Similary, the combination of a large number of filings with obligatory access (cell B) is the largest work load. The other two cells clearly fall somewhere between these low and high work loads, but their relative rankings are ambiguous so they have both been numbered 2. This figure reinforces the point made earlier that whenever there is an intermediate court created and the supreme court is granted discretionary access control, there should be a decrease in work load. Depending upon the original number of filings to the court and whether the level of filings decreases after the creation of the intermediate court, the work load of the supreme court will move in one of the following three manners after the creation of an intermediate court: (1) cell A to cell C, (2) cell B to cell C, or (3) cell B to cell D. Because it is unlikely that an intermediate court of appeals would be created if the supreme court filings were already low (cell A), and because there will most likely be no permanent decrease in supreme court filings associated with the creation of the intermediate court (cell C), the hypothesized consequence of creating an intermediate court would be the movement from cell B to cell D. It is most important to note, however, that this impact on work load is a result of the court's being granted discretionary access control, not the result of merely creating an intermediate court.

The second intended impact of creating an intermediate court of appeals (the linkage between a reduced supreme court work load and increased supreme court policymaking) can also be conveniently explained by referring to figure 11–1. While the cell rankings in that figure represent the level of work load, they also can represent, according to the second intended impact, the ranking of policymaking potential. Therefore, cell C has the highest policy potential because it combines few cases to review with the discretion to focus upon particular policy-potential cases. Similarly, a court represented by cell B would have such a large number of cases to be formally reviewed that significant policymaking would be precluded.

Thus, the cross tabulation of supreme court filings and disposition method demonstrates the expectation that the creation of an intermediate court and the granting of discretionary access control to the supreme court will increase that court's policymaking potential. It is again, however, important to note that, because case filings cannot be expected to decrease permanently after the structural change (Flango and Blair 1980), it is the change in access method that accounts for the increased policymaking potential. Before going on, it should be pointed out that I have been talking about the potential for policymaking, not actual policymaking. I do this because access method and level of case filings seem only to provide the potential for policymaking, not to mandate or prevent it. Other factors such as the political attitudes and values of the justices, their role perceptions, and the local political and legal cultures will also shape the extent to which that potential is realized.

The major contention here is that the granting of discretionary access control, not the creation of an intermediate court of appeals, results in reduced supreme court work load and increased policymaking. While these two reforms are usually combined, a complete understanding requires that we differentiate between their individual and joint impacts. This can be accomplished by studying those instances in which the two reforms are not linked (Wasby, Marvell, and Aikman 1979, pp. 51–58). For example, some states have an intermediate court of appeals but minimal supreme court access control. Conversely, some states, such as West Virginia, have a supreme court with discretionary access control, but no immediate appellate court. If the model just presented is valid, we should expect that the mere creation of an intermediate court, without the granting of discretionary access control to the supreme court, will not permanently affect supreme court work load or policymaking. Similarly, the granting of a discretionary access control should be sufficient to modify supreme court work load and policymaking.

The Arizona case provides an interesting opportunity to explore these expectations empirically. The Arizona Intermediate Court of Appeals was created in 1965 and granted what appeared to be almost total discretionary access control. The only limit to the supreme court's docket control was a statute stating:

The court of appeals shall have: appellate jurisdiction in all actions and proceedings originating in or permitted by law to be appealed from the superior court, except criminal actions involving crimes punishable by death or life imprisonment. [*Arizona Revised Statutes* §12–120.21(A)(1)]

While this limitation on supreme court access control seems minimal, a 1965 court opinion interpreted the statute as requiring the supreme court to hear formally all criminal convictions carrying a possible sentence of death or life imprisonment [*State* v. *Mileham,* 1 Ariz. App. 67 (1965)]. Thus, all convictions for the following offenses had to be reviewed by the supreme court, whether or not the death penalty or life imprisonment was actually given: assault with a deadly weapon by a prisoner, kidnapping, murder (first and second degree), sodomy with a child, child molestation, derailing a train. This limitation resulted in about 20 percent of the supreme court's filings being criminal cases that had to be formally reviewed. This in turn resulted in approximately 50 percent of the court's formal opinions being devoted to such criminal cases.

Legislative change in 1974 modified the court's obligatory jurisdiction in criminal matters to only those in which the death penalty or life imprisonment were actually ajudged. This resulted in the number of obligatory criminal filings being cut by 65 percent from 1974–1975. Thus, we have a quasi-experimental situation where the intermediate court was created in 1965 but where the supreme court still maintained a large measure of obligatory jurisdiction until 1974 when the major portion of that jurisdiction was changed to discretionary. If our analysis and model are correct, we should expect that the Arizona supreme court's work load and level of policymaking will not have significantly changed in 1965 but that the work load will have decreased, and policymaking increased, in 1974.

In order to evaluate these expectations, the author has gathered time-series data concerning supreme court filings (1952–1979), court work load (1952–1980), and frequency of dissent.[5]

Figure 11–2 demonstrates that, as we expected, a temporary drop in filings occurred in 1965, but they soon returned to a growth rate much like that before the court of appeals was created. Similarly, we see that the increases in discretionary access control in 1974 did not have an impact on filings.

The time-series observations for work load in figure 11–3 were calculated on the basis of the formula introduced at the beginning of the chapter[6]:

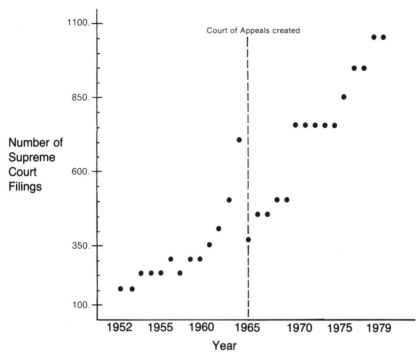

Figure 11–2. Case Filings to the Arizona State Supreme Court, 1952–1979

Work load for year X = (Number of cases formally decided in year X)
   + (Number of cases summarily rejected in year X) (.05)

The .05 weight for cases summarily rejected is based upon Justice England's evaluation that a denial of review takes no more than 5 percent of the time necessary for a formal review. Clearly, in future analyses this figure should be more carefully evaluated through interviews to determine if it significantly varies from court to court and/or justice to justice.

Given these assumptions, we can see in figure 11–3 that there was not a significant drop in supreme court work load in 1965 but that there appears to be a fundamental change in 1974. This is consistent with our expectation that it is the granting of discretionary access control, not the creation of an intermediate court, that affects supreme court work load. It should be emphasized, however, that this single case study is only for illustrative purposes and that the period after the 1974 change is not sufficient to conclude that there has been a per-

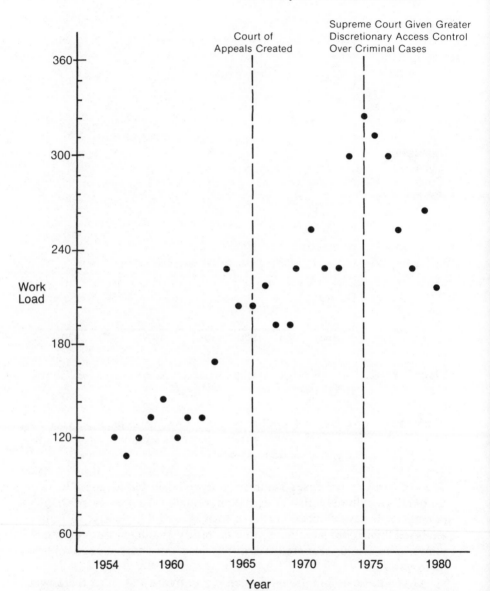

Figure 11-3. Work Load of the Arizona State Supreme Court, 1954–1980

manent change. However, the findings are certainly consistent with our discussion.

Finally, figure 11–4 shows the dissent-rate time series for the supreme court. While data are not presented for an extended period

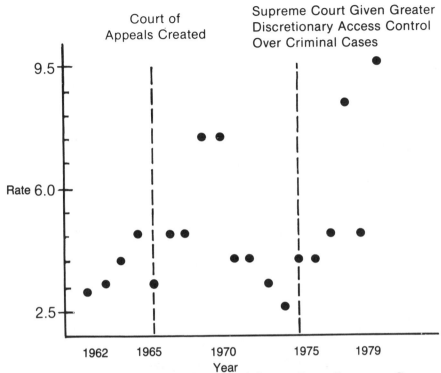

Figure 11–4. Dissent Rate for the Arizona State Supreme Court, 1962–1979

before the 1965 change, it is clear that, if anything, the dissent rate decreased after the creation of the intermediate court. This is consistent with the fact that, although an intermediate court was created, work load continued to rise, and therefore the dissent rate, as an indicator of policymaking orientation, decreased. However, as we would expect, in 1974, when the work load significantly turned downward, there is also a noticeable increase in dissent rate that has persisted since. This would suggest that the proposed linkage between work load and policymaking, at least as measured by dissent rate, is valid for Arizona.

Conclusion

This chapter has explored the impact of creating an intermediate court of appeals on a state supreme court's work load and policymaking. By reviewing the literature, I have constructed a model of the process that suggests that it is not the creation of the intermediate court that has an impact on supreme court work load and policymaking but rather the granting of discretionary access control to that court. This model was supported with data from Arizona. However, clearly, much additional work is necessary in other states to further evaluate the model.

Notes

1. This discussion is taken from Flango and Blair (1980, p. 76). Their article has been a great help in clarifying my ideas, and my debt to it is throughout.

2. Wasby, Marvell, and Aikman (1979) provided an excellent overview of the whole issue of work load at the state appellate-court level. This piece has been very helpful to me in assessing the current understanding of work load and methods of coping with it.

3. For the purpose here, time required to decide a case and work required to decide a case are considered interchangeable.

4. The Kagan et al. article (1978) should be read by individuals interested in the model herein presented. Their analysis is in many ways very similar to mine. The intellectual history, however, seems to be quite different. For example, see Stookey (1975) and Ulmer and Stookey (1975).

5. Data on filings and disposition methods were obtained from reports of the Administrative Director of the Arizona Supreme Court. Dissent rate was calculated by the author from all cases formally decided with more than a one-page opinion as contained in the *Arizona Reports*.

6. Another potential variable that may need to be taken into consideration is backlog. My two measures of work load only deal with cases that are disposed of. However, if there is an ever-increasing backlog, my measure of work load would be an underestimate. In the Arizona case, the backlog has held or been reduced over the period since the creation of the intermediate court. Where this is not true, a third term, reflecting the number of cases filed but not decided during the year, could be added to the equation.

References

Atkins, Burton, and Henry Glick. 1976. "Environmental and Structural Variables as Determinants of Issues in State Courts of Last Resort." 20 *American Journal of Political Science* 97.

Canon, Bradley, and Dean Jaros. 1970. "External Variables, Institutional Structure, and Dissent on State Supreme Courts.'' 4 *Polity* 185.

Flango, Victor, and Nora Blair. 1980. ''Creating an Intermediate Appellate Court: Does It Reduce the Caseload of a State's Highest Court?'' 64 *Judicature* 76.

Groot, Roger. 1971. ''The Effects of an Intermediate Appellate Court on the Supreme Court Work Product: The North Carolina Experience.'' 7 *Wake Forest Law Review* 548.

Kagan, Robert, Bliss Cartwright, Lawrence Friedman, and Stanton Wheeler. 1978. ''The Evolution of State Supreme Courts.'' 76 *Michigan Law Review* 990.

Marvell, Thomas. 1979. ''The Problem of Double Appeals.'' 2 *Appellate Court Administration Review* 23.

Stookey, John. 1975. ''Possible Linkages Between Jurisdictional Change and Policy Output in the Supreme Court.'' Paper presented at the Annual Meeting of the Midwest Political Science Association, Chicago (May).

Ulmer, S. Sidney, and John Stookey. 1975. ''How is the Ox Being Gored: Toward a Theory of Docket Size and Innovation in the United States Supreme Court.'' 7 *University of Toledo Law Review* 1.

Wasby, Stephen, Thomas Marvell, and Alexander Aikman. 1979. *Volume and Delay in State Appellate Courts: Problems and Responses*. Williamsburg, Virginia: National Center for State Courts.

Zeisel, Hans, Harry Kalven, and Bernard Buchholz. 1959. *Delay in the Court*. Boston: Little Brown & Co.

Part IV
Theoretical and Empirical Perspectives on Court Administration

12 Justice-Impact Statements and Court Management: And Never the Twain Shall Meet

Cornelius M. Kerwin

Until recently, one would be safe in assuming that judicial-impact analysis was the study of the effects court decisions and policies have on the larger economic, social, and political systems. This important and difficult undertaking is no less pertinent today, but impact analysis has assumed a new meaning. In 1972, Chief Justice Burger proposed that an impact statement accompany "every piece of legislation that would create new cases for the federal courts" (Davis and Nejelski 1978, p. 180; Boyum and Krislov 1980). Burger's hope was that such statements would provide courts and their administrators with "the ability to rationally plan for the future with regard to the burdens of the courts" (Burger 1972, p. 1050). The chief justice was expressing concern for an alarming increase in federal-court cases, many of which were directly attributable to new or altered rights of action established by congressional act. Judicial-impact statements could inform policymakers of the likely consequences of their actions for court operations and provide the capacity for court managers to deploy resources in ways that offset demands created by new legislation. If such objectives were in fact achieved, judicial-impact statements would constitute one of the most important reforms in the history of the federal-court system.

The good intentions of impact analysis are difficult to fault. Yet efforts to develop techniques that achieve accurate projections of impact and resource needs are beset with serious methodological problems. A panel of distinguished scholars and practitioners worked recently under the sponsorship of the National Academy of Sciences on the subject of forecasting legislative impact. Their report (Boyum and Krislov 1980) is the most comprehensive treatment to date of the obstacles that confront such exercises. The panel recommended against the imposition of impact-analysis requirements for new legislations and suggests instead support for, and continuation of, basic research on adaptive processes in courts, types and behaviors of litigants, and quality of judicial services leading to construction of theories of impact. They also recommend careful study of access to justice and resolution of the basic questions of whether priorities should be imposed on courts in their handling of litigation. The National Academy of Sciences effort and existing examples of impact statements have already led to important observations regarding the relationship between courts and the public policies that produce their work. One essential link has not received adequate attention, however. The recognized deficiencies in the techniques used to project potential impacts also carry with them serious implications for court management. If uncertainty regarding future demands on courts effectively prevents planning for optimal use of judicial and support resources, it is difficult to imagine how the activities usually associated with court management, such as budgeting and resource allocation, can be carried out in a rational, prospective manner.

The purpose of this chapter is to review briefly the methodological difficulties associated with impact statements and to discuss the serious management issues they raise. Many of the research problems mentioned here are handled in greater detail in the National Academy of Sciences report or in other studies. Some such as variation in court administrative practices and the particular problems of projecting impact at the level of the local court deserve more-explicit treatment. This chapter also argues that structural and political features of legislative decision making may obviate even the most dramatic theoretical and methodological breakthroughs in impact research.

Any methodology supporting justice-impact statements is, of necessity, an amalgamation of techniques drawn from various strains in court research. Both case loads and case processing may be affected by proposed legislation and methods to capture these impacts are drawn from forecasting, operations research and formal modeling, studies of judicial and litigant behavior, and analyses of court administration.

Forecasting

The size of changes in court case loads is a fundamental element in any estimate of policy impact. Forecasting techniques rely on the past for assumptions about the future. Two approaches to national-level case load forecasting have been developed for the federal-court system: autoregressive and indicator-based forecasting (Federal Judicial Center 1975, p. 2). Autoregressive forecasting simply extends past trends in data into the future. Indicator-based forecasting treats case load as a dependent variable whose value is related to a variety of elements, or independent variables, such as socioeconomic and demographic conditions. Both forms assume that the dynamics of case load change remain stable over time, meaning most forecasting models are not capable of projecting effects caused by events or indicators that are not associated with current case load content. These so-called surprise events must be handled with subjective estimation based on the opinions of experts, regarding the likelihood of a given phenomenon occurring at some point in the future (Federal Judicial Center 1975, pp. 16–31). The Federal Judicial Center has reported considerable success with indicator-based forecasts of case load changes in specific categories of litigation at the national, circuit, and district levels (Leavitt 1975). The examples are isolated, however, and each type of case requires its own package of indicators. The technical capability to project, with some confidence, increases or decreases in case loads of specific types are available but, as noted in the next section, forecasting remains a limited tool because of the complex nature of legislative impact.

Operations Research and Formal Modeling

Assuming that the volume of case load increases attributable to proposed legislation can be projected, it still remains for analysts to determine how cases will be processed once they reach the courts. Case processing brings the judicial and support resources of any court into contact with its work load; it is the key to estimating the material effects of legislative change. The movement of a case from filing to disposition is affected by general and specific procedural provisions of legislation, the formal rules of civil and criminal procedure, and discretionary case-management practices of judges and, in certain cases, administrative personnel. The field of operations research suggests that these routes can be simulated in a model of case-processing operations for a given type of case (Nagle, Neef, and Munshaw 1978). Where formal rules link case characteristics to specific processing options, the formal methodology of operations research can achieve accurate predictions of how a new work load will be handled.

The applications of management-science principles and techniques to court operations are characterized by heavy emphasis on the development of prototypical models. Unfortunately, there has been very little testing under actual court conditions. Examples of theoretical work on criminal-court processes abound (Chaiken 1975), and special attention is often paid to strategic use of court resources to reduce delay. While proponents are confident that operations research, formal modeling, and related techniques hold great promise, the eventual yield remains a matter of some controversy. Flanders (1979) has argued recently that these tools are ill suited to the complexities and idiosyncracies of courts. Citing the inability of research yet to resolve the problem of delay in a real court, he contends that the multiplicity of case-processing options and routes, combined with the vitally important (and difficult to predict) behaviors of judges and litigants, make the prospects for ''useable results at a reasonable cost'' doubtful (1979, p. 4). The simplifying assumptions of the field carry ''the danger of obscuring the bases of decision making'' (1979, p. 4). Like forecasting, the theoretical possibilities of operations-research and other management-science techniques are considerable, but the magnitude of data-collection efforts and the task of developing of a truly comprehensive research design are formidable indeed.

Judicial Behavior and Litigant Behavior

Many of the obstacles to full use of operations-research techniques would be removed if analysts could better predict the behavior of judges, litigants, and support personnel during case processing. The National Academy of Sciences report outlines the various types of behaviors one must be able to predict in order to project the case load effects of legislation. Obviously the management of these cases, when they arrive, is likewise affected by variable behavior. Management of case loads is an important dimension of actual impact. The literature devoted to the judge's role in case management is often prescriptive in nature and confined to the development of archetypes (Neubauer 1978, p. 223; Cunningham 1978; Rubin 1978). Judge Will's trenchant observation that case management more closely resembles a ''job shop than an assembly line'' (Flanders 1979, p. 5) strikes at the heart of the problem. Each case presents a unique set of participants and circumstances. To these disputes the judge may bring an active or passive approach to case management, but most studies of judicial role indicate that judges infrequently adopt rigid, extreme approaches to the substantive elements of their job (Flanders 1978, pp. 147–150; Wheeler and Whitcomb 1977, pp. 161–181). Pragmatism appears to be a widely shared value. Although a judge may have a distinctive case-management style, the individual characteristics of disputes largely determine the application of available techniques.

Since a dispute is initiated, developed, and sustained by litigants, their behaviors are also key elements in the analysis. The scholarly literature of law and economics posits several important hypotheses regarding litigant behavior in common-law-based judicial proceedings (Posner 1977). A common-law dispute is based exclusively on rights of action based in case law and judicial decisions and has not been codified by a legislature into statute. Operating from basic assumptions of rational behavior, these hypotheses carry the implication that economic calculations establish the demand for judicial case management.

Unfortunately, private litigation is the least complicated to model from an economic perspective because common law affords the principals the greatest flexibility. The federal courts are far more likely to hear cases involving either the government or litigants whose representation is subsidized by the public through a legal-aid program or through a suit brought on behalf of the public by an agency. These types of litigation are based on statutes that frame the substantive dispute and clearly affect the presentation of litigant preferences. A full understanding of these forces is not possible using an exclusively economic approach. Modeling such case-management situations is problematic because public litigation and the interaction between statute and individual preference add complicating dimensions to the expected behavior of judges and litigants (Priest 1977, p. 65; Rubin 1977; Rubin 1980).

Court Administration

The federal courts appear at first glance to be a highly unified system of courts with uniformly available support services, consistent personnel classifications and policies, and established patterns of work load management and supervision across the ninety-five federal district courts. Official reports and manuals of the Administrative Office of United States Courts describe such a system. In practice, however, the administrative infrastructure of the federal courts is not uniform, and diversity in the organization of support services appears to be the rule rather than the exception. Allen (1981) has studied the organization patterns in district-court clerk's offices in an attempt to apply formal organization theory to the administrative component of courts. Based on the work of prominent theorists, Allen, positing relationships between office size and organizational complexity, tests hypotheses that have been tested successfully in other organizational settings. Allen's results indicate that such relationships do not exist in courts as they do in other forms of organization. Further, few consistent patterns of administration and management exist across federal courts (Allen 1981).

The implications of these results for concepts of court management are discussed shortly, but apparently the range of administrative relationships supporting case processing is quite broad. This adds yet another complicating factor to the task of estimating the future effects of proposed legislation. Support structures and activities are organized differently in the various courts of the system and will respond differently to new case load demands.

The Utility of Justice-Impact Statements

This review of methodological complications and obstacles points to a pessimistic conclusion regarding the likely yield of further investment in judicial-impact statements. Pessimism is certainly justified if proponents expect a panacea for the perceived ills of the federal-court system. Nevertheless, expectations regarding the role of impact statements are the critical elements in their further development. As vehicles for basic research, judicial-impact statements can serve to synthesize efforts in case load forecasting, management science, and studies of judicial behavior and administration and to enhance understanding of how federal courts process their work loads. As Nejelski has observed, this knowledge will lead to "enriched policy debates" (1980, p. 9). Embedded in the procedural and structural foundations of institutions that make and administer public policy, however, are characteristics that virtually prohibit the use of impact statements as definitive bases for policymaking or as reliable guides to court management.

If the intent is to prepare impact statements for all congressional actions likely to affect the court system, then all legislation must be analyzed (Boyum and Krislov 1980, pp. 1–5). Because they are called on to resolve disputes regarding the interpretation and application of public policy, federal courts are affected by any piece of legislation over which conflict occurs during implementation or ongoing administration.

Political science has elevated to the status of axiom the observation that public policy is formed and administered in subsystems. As these subsystems grow in number and deal with increasingly narrow issues involving specialized expertise, the implications for courts are obvious. Components of subsystems, particularly regulatory and administrative agencies, fail to resolve disputes that arise incident to their activities. Therefore, filings in federal district courts increase (Kerwin, Koehler, and Dawson 1980).

The growing role of regulatory and administrative institutions as primary policymakers has been accompanied by an easily documented increase and diversification in federal district-court case loads. (This also suggests that those concerned with policy impacts on courts should be looking beyond legislation for potential sources of work load.) When one considers the annual policy output of these specialized subsystems, be they legislative, regulatory, or administrative, with direct or indirect effects on the courts, it is difficult to conceive of a methodology that would comprehend this enormous range of activity. It also calls into question the wisdom of more-narrowly based impact efforts since actions taken in one subsystem could easily be exacerbated or ameliorated by those taken by other, unobserved subsystems. For example, the Speedy Trial Act, passed in 1974, had documented effects on programs established by the Criminal Justice Act of 1964 by increasing administrative demands on assigned-counsel systems (Kerwin 1979, p. 438).

A far more-dramatic example of unanticipated effects arises from the deregulation and regulatory-reform proposals of the Reagan administration. Interests that have benefited over time from regulatory processes that are eliminated or curtailed will take their arguments to the federal courts. Such litigation has already begun in the areas of equal employment opportunity, environmental policy, and workplace safety. Rarely, if ever, do these implications for the federal judiciary enter debates on the wisdom of specific reform strategies, but it is inevitable that courts will be called upon to resolve the numerous and complex issues that surround this major element of domestic public policy. The actual nature, volume, and location of such litigation is virtually impossible to predict.

When considering the effects of uncoordinated subsystems on the entire federal-court system, it is easy to chart the historical increases in case-load size. It is more difficult to chart the actual degree of diversification in case loads since existing categories used in official statistical reports most certainly underestimate the spread of statutes and provisions under which actions are taken. More important, at the local court level, one confronts a crazy quilt of changes in case load volume and composition. Tables 12–1 and 12–2 show the changes in case load volume and composition of these large categories from 1963 to 1978.

These tables demonstrate clearly that the political and social forces that produce litigation do not have uniform effects on the size and composition of individual court case loads, regardless of the aggregate national effects. While most of these courts, selected at random, predictably follow the overall national trend of increases in all categories, it is apparent that the degree of change and the resultant mix of cases in a court's work load differ markedly. As noted in the discussion of

Table 12–1

Percentage Change in Filings in Selected Districts, 1963–1978

District	Civil/U.S.	Civil/Private	Criminal	Total
All districts	+119	+117	+22	+82
Maine	+152	+135	+109	+132
Connecticut	−133	+365	−24	+148
Delaware	+79	+153	+12	+93
Maryland	+145	+168	+89	+124
Alabama (North)	+99	+250	+68	+133
Kentucky (East)	+267	+119	−40	+63
Illinois (North)	+33	+158	−16	+80
Arkansas (East)	+111	+250	+6	+101
Arizona	+4	+168	+45	−180
Colorado	+66	+252	+53	+124
D.C.	+39	−82	−28	−58

Source: Administrative Office of the U.S. Courts, 1963, 1978. *Report of the Director.* Washington, D.C.

Table 12–2

Change in Case-Load Composition in Selected Districts, 1963–1978

	Civil/U.S.		Civil/Private		Criminal	
District	1963	1978	1963	1978	1963	1978
All districts	21	22	42	52	37	26
Maine	28	31	40	40	32	28
Connecticut	25	24	34	63	41	12
Delaware	20	18	49	63	31	19
Maryland	18	20	51	43	30	37
Alabama (North)	24	20	32	48	44	32
Kentucky (East)	24	54	18	25	58	21
Illinois (North)	20	14	50	72	30	13
Arkansas (East)	23	24	29	50	48	25
Arizona	30	20	18	31	52	49
Colorado	25	18	34	53	41	28
D.C.	13	44	70	27	16	28

Source: Administrative Office of the U.S. Courts, 1963, 1978. *Report of the Director,* Washington, D.C.
Note: Figures are percentage of total case load comprised of each category of cases.

forecasting, the level of effort required to develop indicators for each change in each district is awesome.

Such information is critical to any mangement effort since there is reason to believe that the composition of a court's case load has a greater effect on its performance than mere volume. The weighted case load system is the federal courts' implicit recognition of the differential effects of various case types. Serial arrivals of new types of cases bring unpredictable demands on judges for interpretations of new and unfamiliar statutes, regulations, or administrative procedures, and similarly unpredictable options for litigants. This is the situation federal courts face, and the trend is very likely to continue in the future. This presents a greater challenge to court management than fluctuations in the volume of a case load whose composition is stable.

Assuming, for the sake of argument, that these numerous, simultaneous, and interactive effects of legislation, regulation, and administration could be projected accurately, and the even more unlikely prospect that policy decisions will be based on these studies of impact, there remains the task of establishing criteria for what our court system ought to be doing. Whether the objective of a given proposal is to alleviate the oft-proclaimed crisis in the courts, or to provide access for interests deserving relief, or to protect society from criminal activity, Congress lacks the general criteria to evaluate the benefits of proposed legislation, reasonableness, or costs. Lacking an operational definition of justice, Congress has behaved as if the quality and quantity dimensions of federal-court work were entirely compatible. It essentially ignores the simple fact that if demands on courts increase without commensurate increases in resources needed to dispose of cases, justice, however it is defined, will be rationed.

Congress, of course, bases its policy decisions on political considerations. There is nothing in justice-impact methodologies to cure the structural and procedural obstacles to a fully coordinated process for making policy for the courts. They cannot achieve a truly comprehensive view of policy effects either. Impact statements will neither create a new, powerful constituency that will argue persuasively for interests of the courts in the multiplicity of subsystems that produce new work for the judiciary; nor will they provide an unequivocal, consistent statement of ultimate goals that the court system should pursue and that policymakers should serve in their deliberations. As basic research, impact statements will make the trade-offs between quality and quantity, between various objectives, and even between classes of litigants more visible and explicit.

Conclusions and Implications

The implications of these patterns of policymaking for court management are profound. An important by-product of prior impact research is the observation that legislation that alters the processing of cases, such as the Speedy Trial Act, is more likely to lead to significant consequences for the courts than legislation that merely alters the volume of work (Kerwin, Koehler, and Dawson 1980, p. 1076). This statement is also supported by research on the experience of the federal courts in implementing legislation that altered some aspect of their operations (Kerwin 1979). Reference to the nature of work in the federal courts confirms the logic of this finding and, consequently, the limited prospects for management of courts at any level beyond that of the individual case.

It is evident that case management drives court management. In the federal system a multiplicity of administrative forms and rules serves to emphasize the critical position of the individual judge (Flanders 1977). Case management is best understood as a series of decision points, the time and results of which depend on strategies of attorneys and use of judicial prerogatives. Judges distribute their resources, expertise, and time according to the dictates of short-term, often momentary considerations relating to dozens, if not hundreds, of cases. The activist judge may develop case-management practices that become routine aspects of dispute resolution in his court, but characteristics of case load and litigant behavior guarantee that case processing consists of symbiotic, dynamic relationships.

Judicial resources are essentially undifferentiated, and their application to increasingly diverse case loads is dominated by discretion. The preservation of this discretion allows judges, for better or for worse, to assess the needs of their entire case loads and to provide to each case the attention deemed essential. When this discretion is threatened by mandatory case-processing elements such as recent attempts to reform federal class-action litigation, or deadlines, as in original provisions of the Speedy Trial Act, the consequence is removal of the flexibility that forms the basis of our utilitarian system of justice. Impact analysis teaches us that a proper strategy for those concerned with policy effects on courts is to seek more judicial resources and to resist proposals that would mandate case-processing practices. Given the historical patterns of resource constraint and a work load whose arrival is essentially uncontrollable, it is hard to conceive of an alternative strategy.

What can court management achieve in a system whose major characteristics are variation and unpredictability? Much depends on the definition of management but, at the very least, it can assure that support services are available to judges when needed and to litigants to facilitate case processing. Beyond this assistance to the core technology of the courts, management usually entails the distribution of judicial work, administration of support activities, and record keeping of various sorts and levels of sophistication. Case assignment in the federal courts aims for a rough equivalence of work load among the judges, but experience indicates that this effort is hostage to existing case loads and the discretionary use of available processing techniques and options. Record keeping is certainly essential to effective case processing, but aggregation of data to demonstrate some characteristic of performance is usually more important in making a case for more resources than for centralized-management efforts. Court management, as a regulator of court performance, is severely constrained by unpredictable forces that produce case loads. Court management follows rather than leads dispositive processes, and these are notoriously resistant to efforts that would make them regular and predictable.

So the twain have met. The political and social forces that limit the efficacy of justice-impact statements exert similar influence on court management. A better understanding of these forces is the great current challenge, and the magnitude of the research task assures it will be with us for some time to come.

References

Administrative Office of United States Courts. 1963–1978. *Reports of the Director of Administrative Office of United States Courts*. Washington, D.C.: Government Printing Office.

Allen, John. 1981. "Organizational Dimensions of the Office of Clerk in United States District Courts." Ph.D. dissertation, School of Government and Public Administration, The American University.

Boyum, Keith, and Sam Krislov, eds. 1980. *Forecasting the Effects of Legislation on Courts*. Washington, D.C.: National Academy Press.

Burger, Warren. 1972. "State of the Federal Judiciary—1972." *American Bar Association Journal*, p. 1050.

Chaiken, Jan. 1975. *Criminal Justice Models: An Overview*. New York: RAND.

Cunningham, H. Stuart. 1978. "Some Organizational Aspects of Calender Management." 4 *Justice System Journal* 233.

Davis, Robert, and Paul Nejelski. 1978. "Justice Impact Statements: Determining How New Laws Will Affect the Courts." 62 *Judicature* 18.

Federal Judicial Center. 1975. *District Court Caseload Forecasting: An Executive Summary*. Washington, D.C.

Flanders, Steven. 1977. *Case and Court Management in United States District Courts*. Washington, D.C.: Federal Judicial Center.

———. 1978. "Case Management in Federal Courts: Some Controversies, Some Results." 4 *Justice System Journal* 147.

———. 1979. "Models of Judicial Efficiency and Delays." Presented at Annual Meeting of Midwest Political Science Association. Chicago (April).

Kerwin, Cornelius. 1979. "Judicial Implementation of Public Policy:

Judges and Legislation for the Courts.'' 16 *Harvard Journal on Legislation* 438.

Kerwin, Cornelius, David Koehler, and John Dawson. 1980. ''Resource Estimation, Implementation and Policy Optimization.'' 8 *Policy Studies Journal* 1070.

Leavitt, Michael. 1975. ''A Short-Range Forecast of Federal Caseloads.'' Washington, D.C.: Federal Judicial Center.

Nagel, Stuart, Marian Neef, and Nancy Munshaw. 1978. ''Bringing Management Science to the Courts to Reduce Delay.'' 62 *Judicature* 128.

Nejelski, Paul. 1980. ''The Judicial Impact Statement: Better Servant Than Master.'' Testimony before Subcommittee on Jurisprudence and Governmental Relations, Committee of the Judiciary, U.S. Senate, 96th Congress, 2d Session (September 24).

Neubauer, David. 1978. ''Judicial Role and Case Management.'' 4 *Justice System Journal* 223.

Posner, Richard. 1977. *Economic Analysis of the Law*. Boston: Little, Brown & Co.

Priest, George. 1977. ''Common Law Processes and the Selection of Efficient Rules.'' 6 *Journal of Legal Studies* 65.

Rubin, Albin B. 1978. ''The Managed Calendar: Some Pragmatic Suggestions About Achieving the Just, Speedy and Inexpensive Determination of Civil Cases in Federal Courts.'' 4 *Justice System Journal* 135.

Rubin, Paul. 1977. ''Why is the Common Law Efficient?'' 6 *Journal of Legal Studies* 51.

―――. 1980. ''Common Law and Statute Law.'' Unpublished paper, University of Georgia.

Wheeler, Russell, and Howard Whitcomb. 1977. ''Processing Cases: How a Case Gets From Here to There.'' In R. Wheeler and H. Whitcomb (eds.). *Judicial Administration: Text and Readings*. Englewood Cliffs, N.J.: Prentice-Hall, Inc.

13 Alternative Models for the Organization of State-Court Systems

Carl Baar and
Thomas A. Henderson

A new generation of judicial research has conceptualized the trial court—or, more precisely, the trial courtroom—as an organizational unit. This conception has allowed students of judicial behavior to adapt the diverse work of organization theory to the study of court processes. Yet for decades, those interested in the reform of trial courts and court systems have implicitly adopted theories of organization in an effort to modernize court organization and to increase the efficiency of court management. The shortcoming of the court-reform literature, according to its critics, has been the unsophisticated acceptance of premises from classical theories of organization (Saari 1976; Gallas 1976). The conceptual problems are even more serious, however. As reform of court organization, under the rubric of unification, has taken hold, its advocates have lost sight of crucial assumptions underlying reform efforts. As a result, a richer variety of organizational models have not been considered. This chapter therefore develops three models of court organization—franchise, corporate, and federal—that contrast with the prevailing models of unified and nonunified court systems.

Unified and Nonunified Courts

Larry Berkson and Susan Carbon's extensive study of court unification spells out five elements that comprise a unified court system: (1) consolidation and simplification of court structure, (2) centralized management, (3) centralized rule making, (4) centralized budgeting, and (5) state financing (1978, chapter 1). The unified court system thus becomes the ideal (or extreme) type of a highly centralized court organization. At the opposite end of the continuum is the nonunified, or fragmented, court system. The nonunified system, in its pure form,

This chapter is a revised version of a paper prepared for delivery at the Annual Meeting of the Law and Society Association, Madison, Wisconsin, 6 June 1980. It was prepared with financial assistance from a grant for Comparative Research on the Organization of State Court systems, awarded by the National Institute of Justice.

would consist of a dispersed set of local courts, each with a specialized jurisdiction and perhaps only a single judge, all locally funded and managed. There would be no central state-court administrator's office, no reassignment power at any point in the system, no rule-making authority outside the case-by-case process of appellate review of trial-court decisions, and no concept that the chief judge of the state supreme court has any general responsibility for any court beyond his or her own.

Because the unified and nonunified models are at opposite ends of a continuum, the reality of actual practices in any state-court system would fall somewhere between. Court-reform efforts, then, become pragmatic attempts to move the courts of any particular state closer to the unified end of the continuum. However, while early reform advocates equated court unification with court integration, and praised any move to coordinate fragmented judicial units (Parker 1941, p. 38), the unification model increasingly emphasized vertical control rather than horizontal integration. Thus, four of Berkson and Carbon's five elements of unification stress centralization (vertical control) and only one emphasizes consolidation. The hierarchical aspects of the unification concept have thus come to dominate the collegial. Why? Because unification advocates, in seeking to create an organization (a judicial branch of government) have been largely unaware of the rich array of organizational designs that provide a different mix of central versus local authority and responsibility. The only alternative to the old fragmented system was one emphasizing central authority and responsibility. A different way of looking at the problem, however, would consider whether one dimension of court organization and management is best centralized, while another is best left under local control. Current organization theory emphasizes the need to develop alternative designs, sensitive to different elements of an organization's environment and technology. From this perspective, unification—with its emphasis on centralization and accountability—is only one of a number of ways to transform a collectivity of local-court units into a single organization. The three models that follow attempt to define other paths in the evolution of a judicial branch of government.

The Franchise Model: Kentucky-Fried Courts?

One of the most common organizational models in the private sector today is the franchise. Franchising allows goods and services to be provided to the public in a highly dispersed fashion but with a high degree of uniformity. It is premised on maximizing accessibility, both by the dispersion of local units and the replacement of particularities by standarization. At the same time, franchising has some attributes we would label centralized and others we would consider highly decentralized. Thus, precise standards are centrally established for the core activity of the local units, and quality control is emphasized. At the same time, funding comes entirely from local revenue, and local units are encouraged to adapt to local circumstances so long as the core activity is performed. The local McDonald's hamburger franchise, for example, can sponsor a local charity or softball team of its choice, but the amount and quality of beef in the hamburger cannot vary. The local Holiday Inn can include a restaurant whose menu reflects the region in which it is located, but the rooms and beds must meet standards established by the corporation headquarters. The local unit can add to, but not detract from, established levels and modes of service.

If the franchise model were applied to state-court systems, it would lead to an increased emphasis on centralized rule making to establish uniform standards. However, the functions and power of central management would vary from the prescription of the unified model. No assignment power would rest in the central headquarters since each local unit would determine its manpower needs. Funding would be entirely local since the central authority is concerned only with uniform standards and not with obtaining resources. Budget and personnel decisions would be made locally. The state-court administrator's office would be primarily involved in quality control—that is, monitoring the degree to which the procedural standards are followed at the local level.

How appropriate is the franchise model? Under some assumptions, it fits the courts surprisingly well. James Thompson's discussion of technology (1967, chapter 2) suggests three techniques to produce the products of an organization: (1) long-linked technology, in which one part of the production process is dependent upon a previous step for completion (for example, an assembly line); (2) mediating technology, in which the primary activity is linking individuals who wish to be interdependent (for example, a commercial bank linking depositors and borrowers); and (3) intensive technology, in which a variety of techniques are used to produce a change in the object but the selection of the techniques depends upon feedback from the object itself (for example, a hospital and its patients). Adjudication in trial courts has traditionally used a mediating technology, and the characteristic method of coordinating units in an organization whose core technology is mediating is through standardization rather than planning or mutual adjustment. Thus the franchise model's emphasis on standardization would be consistent with traditional trial-court operations. Standardization in the franchise model would not emphasize central management but would only standardize rules of procedure for adjudication—that is, the core activity. Thus the organization could expand—more-dispersed units could be created—to achieve the goal of accessibility, without overloading central-headquarters management, because procedural rules would already be known and local management would be permitted to adapt to demands from the local environment.

The emphasis on uniformity is also consistent with a basic concern throughout the history of court reform. From Roscoe Pound through the advocacy of later generations of judges and lawyers, court reform has been valued because it would eliminate the procedural technicalities and variations that make it impossible to move from one court to another. While some lawyers could benefit from their special knowledge of the idiosyncracies of local judges, lawyers committed to court reform emphasize the importance of being able to enter a court in a strange community, or to go before a judge who is a stranger, and to know that a common set of procedures will be followed. To quote the slogan of a current franchise, "the best surprise is no surprise."

The Corporate Model: Buffering Voluntary Associations

The corporate model is in key respects directly opposite to the franchise model. Here, financing is entirely a central responsibility, but there is no demand for uniformity through the imposition of centralized rule making. In one respect, the franchise and corporate models are identical: Both reject the high degree of centralized management set forth in the unification model.

The corporate model was developed by the National Foundation for Infantile Paralysis and described in David Sills's classic case study (1957). The Foundation's fund raising and research were centralized, while numerous local field offices (with no authority to raise their own funds) were responsible for client services such as treatment and referral. The local client services were not subject to any central procedural rules or supervision, but centralized funding meant that the Foundation as a whole would not be threatened by goal displacement—that is, the immediate need to serve waiting clients would not deflect the organization from the research responsibilities that would have long-run benefits for national health.

The corporate model made sense for the Foundation since essential decisions about the distribution of funds between research and client services had to be made centrally to prevent goal displacement, but the intensive technology required for both research and client services would make either central management or uniform standards detrimental to effectiveness. An intensive technology requires the exercise of discretion within a task environment that assures that discretionary judgment does not yield to external pressures.

Does the corporate model make sense for the courts? In many respects it does. Important aspects of modern adjudication use intensive technology, whether in sentencing offenders or drafting opinions. The goal of state financing then becomes a way to stabilize the task environment of the local court by minimizing local funding pressures. To the extent that the court environment has been stabilized, collegial control can work effectively (the need for vertical control is greater when the environment is more turbulent). Judicial discretion would be exercised on the basis of informed legal judgment. Therefore, central management and rule making would not be as essential to ensure that consolidated local courts operate fairly and expeditiously. Thus, the centralization of one dimension (funding) would allow the decentralization of precisely those operations that students of trial courts are increasingly wary of confining within a bureaucratic framework.

The Federal Model: Muddling Through

The federal model differs from the franchise, corporate, and unified models by rejecting the establishment of a single focus of final authority. As in a federal system of government, final authority is not located in any single place, and central/local relations evolve over time in response to operational and policy problems. The goal of the federal model is to encourage interaction among those who share authority as part of a process of solving mutual problems. The federal model therefore advocates a high degree of local-court consolidation and collegial control, a low degree of central management (vertical control), but expanded participation of central-headquarters personnel through technical assistance and support services for local courts. It deemphasizes the use of centralized rule making and argues for increased state financing of the courts, but through grants and other devices more flexible than central budgeting.

The federal model is premised on the view that any court organizational structure must take into account the fact that there is good reason for the local courts to accommodate themselves to the local legal culture. In addition, the courts by definition must operate with the major figure—the judge—having wide discretion. Therefore, a tightly structured, centralized organization is unlikely to be effective, or to produce the desired results. At the same time, some organizational framework for the judicial branch is appropriate and necessary in order to encourage the identification of court personnel with the core values of the judicial enterprise. The most feasible way to build an organization without falling victim to excessive centralization and overcontrol is to emphasize central-management functions that promote a common identification for the judicial branch without coercing members to accept those functions. A combination of coordinating devices, support services, research and planning, and training programs is likely to be used at this stage to achieve that common identification and understanding.

The federal model has been presented without reference to a specific analogy or theory. However, it reflects many currents in organization theory. One set of ideas emphasizes the development of a sense of commitment by members of an organization so that direct control is replaced by identification with a common enterprise. For example, students of administrative responsibility have distinguished subjective responsibility (the development of a feeling of responsibility or loyalty to the organization) from objective responsibility (the enforcement of explicit organizational rules). Literature on professionalism stresses the internalization of standards as a method of increasing predictability where tasks require a high degree of discretion rather than extensive written rules. The current emphasis on professionalism in both judging and court administration represents an effort to create an organization without extensive direct control.

Comparing the Models

The franchise, corporate, and federal models all share some elements with each other and with the prevailing unification model. At the same time, emphases differ sharply. The unification model stresses responsibility and accountability, while the federal model emphasizes involvement and commitment. The franchise model emphasizes uniformity and accessibility, while the corporate model emphasizes the maintenance of discretion. The unification and franchise models conceive of adjudication as a mediating technology; the corporate and federal models are designed to realize the needs of an intensive technology. All four models attempt to structure environmental relations at the local level, either by reducing the number and variety of contacts beween local courts and their political environment (the unification and corporate models) or by developing the abilities or guidelines necessary for local courts to handle their task environments (the federal and franchise models). In one sense, the unification and federal models represent an earlier stage in organization or institution building. The unification model stresses the use of downward communication to define organizational boundaries, while the federal model uses techniques of involvement and commitment to build a shared identity among members of the judicial branch. The franchise and corporate models place less emphasis on creating an organization and more emphasis on the redistribution of functions within the organization consistent with their contrasting views of environmental and technological contingencies

Each of the four models assumes that an unorganized set of judicial units will have boundaries so ill defined and permeable as to threaten court persistence. The nonunified system is seen to lack the essential characteristics of impartiality and independence necessary for a court to function on the basis of either a mediating or an intensive technology and is more likely to operate as a component in a long-linked technology dominated by external political, social, and economic interests. Again, each model emphasizes different techniques for defining those boundaries. The unified model traditionally emphasized the shifting of rule-making and managerial functions away from legislative and executive officials. The franchise model assumes that uniform standards of quality can be a basis for local courts to resist pressures to alter their character. The corporate model assumes that, if local courts are not dependent on local sources of funding, the central-court administrative headquarters can buffer those courts from pressures that would compromise their essential functions. The federal model assumes that a set of judges and court-support personnel that share a sense of loyalty to the essential principles of the judicial branch will increase the likelihood of goal consensus between the court system and its external environment, thus safeguarding the judicial domain.

Finally, the four models differ in their analysis of the sources of goal displacement. The unified model assumes that goal displacement will occur when legislative and executive officials perceive that the courts are behaving irresponsibly in managing their internal affairs and will attempt to impose external standards of conduct. Therefore, the unified model emphasizes the need to vest overall authority and responsibility in a single head of the entire court system so that internal accountability will be high. The franchise model assumes that goal displacement will occur if local courts deviate from a uniform set of adjudicative rules and procedures, so it emphasizes creation of uniformity through centralized rule making. The corporate model assumes that goal displacement will occur if the courts rely on a fragmented system of financing based on an enrollment economy; therefore, the organization's headquarters retains authority over the internal allocation of resources. The federal model assumes that goal displacement will occur if the courts lack an internal consensus about the domain of the court system; therefore, the model emphasizes both involvement in joint activity and commitment to the common enterprise.

New Models, New Difficulties

Like the unification model, these new designs are also open to criticism. Consider first the difficulties facing the franchise model in its present form. It is not equipped to meet one of the key criteria for a model of court organization: the ability to protect the local court from environmental pressures. A franchise can close down one of its outlets if the tastes of the community do not produce sufficient income. In theory, a court would not be necessary in a community in which no judicial business exists. However, the income of modern courts does not come from its customers but from public funding agencies. If the court could support itself on fee revenue and by taxing costs to the parties (a nineteenth-century pattern), the franchise model would fit reality more closely. Since the question of user fees for courts raises fundamental issues of access that go beyond discussion of organizational structure, any model of central/local relations would have to be premised on funding of the courts by public appropriations.

Because the franchise model implies complete local funding, the courts could find themselves subject to local political and economic conditions—even for the salaries of judges with constitutionally secure tenure. Traditionally, local courts have used the doctrine of inherent powers to mandate payment of necessary expenses when local governments have refused to appropriate funds (National Judicial College 1980). However, that approach has been ineffective on a continuing basis. The problem might be more adequately dealt with by some method of costing out the implementation of the standardized procedures and by granting state subsidies to local units. Whatever the solution, the franchise model would require that local spending decisions be in local hands, with a state-court administrative office only monitoring the quality of the local court's core activity.

This criticism suggests the need to explore more fully the implications of the model. The basic framework is the unusual mix of central and local functions: a high emphasis on centralized rule making, a high degree of local funding, and a low degree of central management.

Interestingly, one existing state-court system has combined these three dimensions in recent years—namely, the Ohio court system, especially under the leadership of the late Chief Justice William O'Neill. Ohio has one of the lowest percentages of state funding and a tiny state-court administrative office, given the size of the state (only four professionals) (Nieland and Doan 1979, p. 120). At the same time, the rule-making authority of the state supreme court has been used with great publicity and zeal.

What are the difficulties of a corporate model for state-court systems? The first difficulty is its high degree of local autonomy. Critics of autonomy have argued that uniform rules are necessary for fairness and accessibility (Heflin 1979) and that individualized decision making, while valuable, must be anchored in a strong framework of substantive and procedural law. Their concern is reinforced by the perceived difference in core technologies between the courts and the March of Dimes—the former is a mediating technology and the latter is an intensive technology. The advocates of unification premise their arguments on a mediating technology and the resulting appropriateness of uniform rules (what Thompson termed standardization).

In fact, the assumption that the core technology of the courts is mediating misses the richness of the adjudication process. An increasing emphasis on intensive technology is apparent in trial courts—particularly in criminal sentencing and in family and juvenile matters. Furthermore, deliberations in an appellate court may involve an intensive process of interaction between and among judges and lawyers attempting to mold new principles of law. Thus, the goal displacement that the National Foundation for Infantile Paralysis avoided by centralized fund raising would also be a concern of the courts if local funding were more responsive to the processing of large numbers of routine cases than the more-time-consuming deliberations that use an intensive technology. Research, whether for presentence reports or appellate opinions, would give way to service.

A second difficulty of the corporate model attends the centralized funding of court systems. Complete state funding of the courts would place authority in the hands of a single external agency—the state legislature—creating a monopoly of power that could threaten the independence of the judicial branch (Baar 1979). The March of Dimes sought to increase its ability to raise funds by combining its national effort with a network of local support. While it has been argued (Baar and Baar 1977) that this would be a more-effective strategy for state-court administrative offices to use in securing funds from state legislatures, the monopoly of the central appropriating body would remain. The latest approach to this problem has found state courts advocating federal funding through an independent granting agency. Whatever the solution, the corporate model requires that resource-allocation decisions be centralized within a court system.

The federal model also has its built-in difficulties. While it attempts to build a common identification with the judicial branch as a device for buffering the court's core technology, it could be too open to environmental pressures. Harry Lawson (1978) has argued that the absence of a locus of responsibility and accountability within the judicial branch would lead to externally imposed control. For example, if the judicial branch does not control its expenditures, the legislature is likely to intervene. Proponents of the federal model would argue that the development of internal coordinating mechanisms would generate internal controls on spending without having them imposed by a central authority within the court system. Critics would argue further that a mix of state and local funding would diffuse external responsibility so that each funding source would pass the buck to the other. Proponents of the federal model might suggest that overlapping funding of other programs (federal/state or state/local) has not resulted in decreased resources for those programs and that the twin problems of monopoly state legislative power and local pressure—the consequences of other models—are more serious.

Environmental pressures of the local legal culture would also appear to be even more pronounced in a federal model, making innovation and change more difficult. Yet proponents of that model might argue that any change in court operations will be modified by its local setting and that innovation ordered by a central-court administrative office would be less effective than a change that emerged from a process of contention and debate among local actors.

Conclusion

While the court-unification movement has assumed that one best way does exist to organize any court system, this chapter suggests the existence of more than one best way. The appropriateness of these different models is contingent upon different views of the nature of the court's technology and the sources of critical environmental pressures.

References

Baar, Carl. 1979. "Building and Maintaining a Court System." Robert H. Jackson Lecture, National Judicial College, Reno, Nevada (July).

Baar, Ellen, and Carl Baar. 1977. "Judges as Middlemen?" 2 *Justice System Journal* 210.

Berkson, Larry, and Susan Carbon. 1978. *Court Unification: History, Politics and Implementation*. Washington, D.C.: U.S. Department of Justice, Law Enforcement Assistance Administration, National Institute of Law Enforcement and Criminal Justice.

Gallas, Geoff. 1976. "The Conventional Wisdom of State Court Administration: A Critical Assessment and an Alternative Approach." 2 *Justice System Journal* 35.

Heflin, Howell, 1979. Speech before the Annual Meeting of the American Judicature Society, Dallas, Texas (August).

Lawson, Harry O. 1978. Testimony before the Minnesota State Judicial Planning Committee, St. Paul (October).

National Judicial College. 1980. *Inherent Powers of the Courts*. Reno, Nevada: National Judicial College.

Nieland, Robert G., and Rachel N. Doan. 1979. *State Court Administrative Offices*. Chicago: American Judicature Society.

Parker, John J. 1941. "Court Integration Through Voluntary Leadership." 26 *Journal of the American Judicature Society* 38.

Saari, David J. 1976. "Modern Court Management: Trends in Court Organization Concepts—1976." 2 *Justice System Journal* 19.

Sills, David L. 1957. *The Volunteers*. Glencoe, Ill.: Free Press.

Thompson, James D. 1967. *Organizations in Action*. New York: McGraw-Hill.

14

Courts as Discrete Organizations and System Components: The Case of the D.C. Circuit Court of Appeals

Phillip J. Cooper

Some time ago, Ebersole (1973) warned persons interested in studying courts to be more self-conscious about just what they meant by court study. From an analytic standpoint, such an awareness is needed since problems and opportunities will be noticed or missed depending upon the particular perceptual blinders that the investigator is wearing. There are, of course, any number of possible motives for launching a court study, ranging from a purely analytical effort to find and implement new management techniques to justifying a court reorganization for any number of purposes (Ebersole 1973, pp. 19–20; see also Seidman 1976; Rourke 1969). In recent years, the focus of court studies has been on state and local, rather than federal, courts, with a particular emphasis on trial courts (see Berkson, Hays, and Carbon 1977; Friesen, Gallas, and Gallas 1971; Gazell 1978; Wheeler and Whitcomb 1977). That emphasis is not surprising given the fact that the federal courts are often perceived to be more advanced in the process of management modernization than state and local courts and the fact that much of the impetus for the court reform movement in the late 1960s and early 1970s grew out of the belief that swift justice would be effective justice (Bazelon 1971, p. 653). It was believed, with considerable justification, that the causes of delay in the judicial system could be found in the trial courts. This chapter looks to the U.S. Circuit Court of Appeals for quite a different approach to the subject of court reform. The tendency of the judicial-reform literature and actions of policymakers who allocate resources for the judiciary to view courts as components of a larger judicial system rather than as discrete organizations is the focus of this inquiry.

This chapter argues that, while the view of the federal courts as a system is important for some purposes, it must also be supplemented with a perspective of courts as individual discrete organizations in addition to system components. If it can be shown that: (1) there are significant factors in court operation in one circuit that can be shown to be ignored or undifferentiated in system-level analyses used by the national judicial administrators or the Congress; and (2) that these differences can be understood through the use of a conceptual framework drawn from the organizational theory and behavior literature, then organizational perspectives on courts should be considered important for the theoretical development of judicial administration, as well as for pragmatic challenges of resource allocation faced by the legislature and administrators. While this study focuses on the District of Columbia Circuit, the problems of management and resource allocation noted and the conceptual approach developed can be applied to all federal courts.

The Systems Framework

Nature of the Framework

The term *judicial system* has become almost a synonym for the *judiciary* in court studies. However, whether a work is done by court-reform advocates from the legal profession, judicial administrators, or political scientists studying judicial process and behavior, the use of the term *judicial system* to describe research matters a great deal. Judicial system is used to describe court organization and also to describe methods for studying the judiciary. It is useful to clarify the meaning of the system-of-courts concept as it is used in the literature and to suggest why the systems-analysis view is significant in court reform.

That a systemic approach should be taken to court reform according to interested members of the legal profession is clear from an examination of the *ABA Standards Relating to Court Organization:*

> The aims of court organization can be most fully realized in a court system that is unified in structure and administration . . . and that has uniform rules and policies, clear lines of administrative authority, and a uniform budget. . . . The direction of effort, however, should be consistently toward unification of court structure and management. Rendition of equal justice throughout a court system is possible only if the system as a whole applies equal standards through rationally allocated effort. [1974, pp. 2, 4–5]

Similar interest in systemwide reform and a systems analysis as method approach to court study was found in the literature of political science and court administration by Goldman and Jahnige. They found the term *systems analysis* used in two quite different ways. First, there is literature, concerned with explanation, that employs general systems theory adapted to political science. The second systems analysis approach

> . . . might be called the operations research variant. This is used primarily in applied research. It is aimed at indicating weaknesses and insufficiencies in the use of judicial manpower, the processing of cases and court structure. Its main thrust is to indicate areas in need of reform.[1971, p. 336]

This systems and systemic approach can be found in a variety of literature on courts (see, for example, Klein 1977; Commission on Revision of the Federal Appellate Court System 1975; Vanderbilt 1949; Schubert 1974; Goldman and Sarat 1978; Goldman and Jahnige 1976). Above all, the systems perspective is important because it involves a rational approach to the study of courts that avoids the narrowness that comes from concentrating solely on the unique characteristics of one court in favor of a comprehensive understanding. In this approach, individual courts are merely units within the conversion portion of the judicial-system model in which lawsuits are the primary inputs and legal decisions are the primary outputs (Sheldon 1974, pp. 165–168).

Reinforcements for the Framework

A number of factors have reinforced the view that managers and policymakers in the judiciary and in the Congress who deal with the judiciary should use a systems approach. Probably the two most important of these are the attractiveness of rational approaches to management decision making and the pressures of the history of judicial reform. Both are heavily affected by politics within the judiciary and between the judiciary and other levels and branches of government.

Systems analysis is attractive in part because it is based on the idea that government should make decisions in as rational a manner as possible (Rivlin 1971). In general, as Churchman has argued quite effectively, the goal of such systems analyses is the efficient utilization of scarce resources to accomplish important purposes. One establishes a system by organizing the components of the system, seeks methods for allocating resources, and develops techniques for evaluating whether the system is functioning efficiently (1968, p. 44).

The judicial-reform movement was born of the national drive to do business and government efficiently. Its roots are in the progressive movement and the municipal-reform effort. In his classic assessment of the progress of judicial-reform efforts, Vanderbilt observed:

> Whatever the reason may be for our neglect, we cannot escape the inevitable contrast between the streamlined efficiency of the age of the assembly line and of the scientific methods of modern technology and our cumbersome and inefficient methods of utilizing our judicial machinery. [1949, pp. xvii–xviii]

A number of developments in the last two decades have pressured judicial administrators to concern themselves with more than the mere internal management of the judiciary. Congress has become accustomed to receiving arguments in support of requests for funds couched in contemporary analytical forms. As the competition for scarce resources among government units has increased, the judiciary has had to learn to communicate its needs and its accomplishments to policymakers in terms they understand, respect, and will listen to. With the centralization of the budget process in the Judicial Conference, the primary preparation work being done by the Administrative Office of U.S. Courts (AO), and supporting research being accomplished by the Federal Judicial Center (FJC) (Fish 1973), the pressures have been strong to employ the systems approach to support requests for funds.

The history of judicial reform provides a significant amount of inertia favoring the systems focus. The historical development of the federal judiciary is a tale of battles over the centralization of control over resources of the various courts as well as disputes over national versus regional and state influence waged by various political interests (see, for example, Fish 1973; Richardson and Vines 1970; Frankfurter and Landis 1928). In the area of resource management, among others, the state reformers have contemplated with envy the federal Judicial Conference and the AO with their centralized budget preparation, personnel administration, matériel control, and statistical-reporting capabilities.

In sum, the systems perspective on federal courts is based upon the maintenance of the unified federal-court organization with centralized managerial decision making in the Judicial Conference, which relies heavily on the work of the AO and the FJC. The system managers attempt to do analyses and make recommendations for action within the judiciary and by the legislature that will ensure the integrity and efficient operation of the overall system in which particular courts are but component parts. In an effort to deal with the political environment in which the judicial system operates, its managers and advisors seek to present their findings and recommendations in a manner supported by hard case data, analyzed and presented according to accepted management practice.

The results of this effort by system managers and decision makers is, among other things, a unified budget. So completely unified is it that no actual budgets are prepared for individual circuit or district courts for their use, for internal use in the AO, or for submission to Congress.[1] Instead, individual courts submit personnel requests that are evaluated in terms of the principal data used by system managers, the total number of cases filed in the requesting court in the past year and estimates for the upcoming year. For courts of appeals, one staff person is justified for each seventy-five cases filed.[2] Equipment, facilities, space, and in general terms, travel and other expenses are then distributed on the basis of the personnel number produced by the case-filing formula. In general, neither the AO nor the FJC will do studies at the request of individual courts.[3] Instead, they concentrate on systemwide statistical data analysis and in-depth comparative analyses for the entire judicial system.

The Organization-Theory Approach: The Court as Discrete Organization

Courts are discrete organizations as well as system components. It is the individual court that takes a case from filing through coordination of advocates and judges, management and distribution of briefs and case records, scheduling of arguments, and finally, to the decision on and drafting, distribution, and recording of orders and supporting opinions (Meador 1974; Marvell 1978). Clearly such a court is a complete organization that requires more than a mere room full of judges to perform its assigned responsibilities. Yet it is surprising to find that the court-reform literature makes little reference to the organization-theory and behavior literature, which is considered by many to be the heart of public administration.[4]

James D. Thompson's *Organizations in Action* (1967) provides a useful framework for understanding the court as an organization. According to Thompson, organizations have patterns of behavior. Human behavior is important for Thompson to the degree that it influences organizational behavior. Organizations attempt to behave as rational actors. The nature of an organization is primarily determined by its core technology, the kind of work that the organization does. A rational organization attempts to operate its core technology as efficiently as possible. However, the task environment, the environment within which the organization functions, is often unstable. Demands for the organization's services vary over time. These changes and complexities in the environment complicate decision making and work processes within the organization. To protect the organization's core technology from the vagaries of changing conditions, organizations obtain people or units, referred to as boundary spanners, whose task is to mediate the effects of environmental turbulence. They attempt to buffer the fluctuations in demand and smooth the flow of work into, through, and out of the organization. Their task is not so much to do the work of the organization but to facilitate the accomplishment of primary tasks like deciding cases through careful management of the organization's resources by interaction with policymakers and the attempt to meet the ever-changing work load placed on the organization.

In the case of courts, the core technology consists of the types of decision making the particular court normally does, viewed from the perspective of those in the organization. The task environment refers to the persons, conditions, and organizations that significantly affect the operation of the court. This would include the types and numbers of individuals and groups who litigate in the court; the problems of facilities, communication, and geographical diversity faced by the court; the special role placed upon the court by its location; the Supreme Court feedback to the organization; the role of the AO and the Judicial Conference in providing resources for operations; and the number and characteristics of the district courts served and supervised by the circuit court. Organization boundary spanners who seek to resolve conflict and pressures from that environment on the court's work, its core technology, include the chief judge, circuit executive (if any), the clerk's office, and the chief staff counsel or central legal staff, depending upon the particular court involved.

If it can be shown that system-level analyses alone are inadequate to describe and understand the operation of these system components; that there are one or more circuit courts within the system of appellate courts that are, for reasons beyond mere numbers of cases, sufficiently unlike other system subunits so that individual analysis is needed to understand their operation; and if the Thompson core-technology, task-environment, and boundary-spanning organizational analysis, in conjunction with systems analysis, provides a better understanding of the needs and operations of the circuit, then such a multifaceted approach ought to be applied in assessing productivity and also in allocating resources.

Problems of Conceptual Myopia:
Findings from the Data

For reasons of brevity, this chapter can do no more than report findings from several kinds of data that show that the D.C. Circuit is a discrete organization in the Thompson sense and that the system-level decisions and analyses do not reflect those distinctions.

Biographical Data

As Thompson noted, the types and perspectives of the individuals within the organization are the driving forces behind organizational behavior. A brief examination of biographical data shows that the D.C. Circuit has a very unusual bench.[5] It is the only circuit that draws nationally for appointments, with nineteen states having contributed members to the court since the late 1930s. For many of the judges, training was at national, rather than regional or state, law schools. The members have a much greater level of previous federal executive branch and legislative experience than circuit judges usually have. Senate clearance is not a factor, and neither regional nor local political questions play significant roles in most appointments.

Interview Data

An assessment of interview data indicates that the members of the court and the boundary spanners within the court do see the D.C. Circuit as a discrete organization that cannot be understood primarily as a system component and that their perceptions tend to fit the Thompson model.[6] In contrast, system-level interviewees view the courts, including the D.C. Circuit, primarily as system components and not as discrete organizations.

The judges seemed interested in eliminating any suggestion that they felt superior to any other circuit, but they very clearly see the D.C. Circuit as unique. The major distinguishing factors are in the areas of core technology and task environment. Most noted that the D.C. Circuit does not deal with a normal cross section of federal cases. Its cases are predominantly national administrative-law or policy questions of the level of *EPA* v. *Ethyl,* the *Taiwan Treaty* case, or the *Iranian Students* cases. When one adds the administrative-law filings to the U.S. civil cases on the AO docket evaluations, it becomes clear that nearly 90 percent of the court's work is on this scale.[7] Such cases have massive records with many parties requiring oral arguments in almost all cases. Such complex and important cases also require more and longer opinions in support of decisions, according to some of the respondents.

Chief among the task environment's peculiarities are the court's location at the seat of the national government, the frequent litigation by large organizations and associations of large organizations that represent interest groups in Washington, D.C., the presence of the specialized administrative and public-policy bar in the capital, and the nationwide impact of its rulings. They also noted the unique role the court plays in that Congress has placed exclusive jurisdiction for many national-policy-related cases in the D.C. Circuit and has permitted others outside the District to opt for a suit in the D.C. Circuit as opposed to their home circuit. Finally, the judges noted the national draw of judges, the compact nature of operations with all judges in one location, and the lack of problems of a state or local nature. In terms of docket, the judges were very much aware of the massive increase in the level of technical complexity of the cases.

The judges were also sensitive to the need for boundary spanners. They praised the administrative support within the court, particularly the chief staff counsel, and were pleased to have the circuit executive working to communicate the court's needs and effort to policymakers. The judges were well aware of, and unhappy with, the statistical case-processing approach to the assignment of judges and supporting personnel.

Those who Thompson would call boundary spanners clearly perceived the difference between their tasks as boundary spanners and the core technology of the organization operated by the judges.[8] Their perceptions were slightly different from, although not in conflict with, those of the judges concerning the nature of the task environment and problems of boundary spanning. They saw the court as a discrete organization. They reiterated some of the comments about core technology but emphasized those aspects concerned with processing of the large records, which can run to over one hundred thousand pages in a case, and the difficulties of coordinating the large number of litigants and intervenors, often thirty or more, before the court. In the area of boundary spanning, these respondents were pleased that the AO management statistics had improved, but they were clearly frustrated because the classifications used and the case-filing formulas made it almost impossible to communicate the court's needs to system-level decision makers.

System-level administrators who responded indicated primary concern for problems of the judicial system as a whole with relatively little interest in specific courts.[9] There also was little interest in organization theories or perspectives. All recognized case load and case mix as significant concepts but referred to little else that would differentiate courts and their work loads. Most assumed that the circuit executive would deal with organizational problems. There was a common interest in docket data as central to the effort to convince legislators of the needs of the judicial system. General resistance was exhibited toward the organizational perspective, particularly the suggestion of organizational budgets. There was a high level of concern for systemwide improvements and the need to communicate those concerns to Congress.

Statistical Data

Several findings with respect to statistical data examined suggest that an organization perspective is needed in addition to the systemwide approach.[10] Before proceeding to specific examples, it is necessary to clarify the most important statistical problem—the use of gross case processing volume as the fundamental measure of need for resources and the use of terminations as a measure of effectiveness.[11] Whether it is an effort to justify more judges, more personnel, geographic-boundary changes, or system budgets, the primary statistic used is either the total number of cases filed in all circuits or in one particular circuit. That is an inherently dangerous indicator.

The attempts to use case mix (the different types of cases dealt with by a particular court) to supplement case load in work load assessments is also troublesome because it is often used in a general way to refer to large aggregate categories developed by the AO. The counting of total numbers of cases before the courts of the system and the use of the few categories is a top-down view by system-level decision makers that seeks commonalities among courts for purposes of comparison and for aggregation into systemwide totals. This approach is not the same as an organizational perspective.

Consider the following example. Assume one manages several medical clinics and wishes to know how effectively and efficiently the clinics were operating and how newly acquired resources should be allocated. One could determine the number of patient calls, the number of patients actually treated, the number of satisfactory treatments, and the median time of treatment per patient. The figures could be compared among all clinics, but one might recognize the problems of comparability since one clinic may see a great many patients with minor complaints while others have fewer but more-complex patient demands. One might establish a few categories such as surgical versus nonsurgical treatments, but the same problem remains since surgery can vary, even within clinics, from the lancing of a small skin malady to major trauma surgery. As the categories multiply, clinic-system managers see the data as increasingly unwieldy and weak in comparability. At the same time, the administrators and doctors in individual clinics are pleased to see more-sensitive measures, but because the categories are designed from the system-level perspective, they never quite capture what local administrators perceive to be important peculiarities in core technology or task environment. A solution requires two kinds of analysis from two different perspectives to supplement each other—one organizational analysis and one system-level analysis.

In general, an examination of docket data and appropriations materials shows that the statistical data are too general in several respects, that gross case processing volume is not a good measure of need or work load, and that rank ordering among circuits in several AO categories, such as median time to terminate a case, are deceptive. One example demonstrates the point. In 1973, the D.C. Circuit underwent a reorganization in which it was relieved of its local appellate responsibilities for the D.C. local criminal and civil courts, but the loss of criminal cases was replaced virtually one for one by major administrative-law and policy cases. Total case load does not reflect it, but there has been a dramatic increase in actual work load.

Other problems include the fact that, without additional information from an organizational level, one can not really say much about opinion output or median time from completion of record to termination of the case. The statistics give no information about the environment served, such as problems of coordination, scheduling, communications, or the need for oral argument. Termination figures and opinion data without more do not help one to understand the impact of the court's central staff, which is different in every circuit court. Minimal categories used for case-mix comparisons are not sufficiently sensitive to evaluate core technology. The management information system is not as responsive as it could be given the amount of data collected for each case by the AO. The data presented and the format for congressional appropriations presentation of system needs is at much too high a level of generalization. Finally, the formula-based budgetary system that uses gross case filings divided by seventy-five is inadequate.

Documentary Evidence

Several pieces of documentary or historical evidence that have not previously surfaced in the reform literature both support the interview findings concerning the prevalence and problems of the system-level approach and underscore important evaluation problems for those using system perspectives to evaulate the D.C. Circuit. For example, studies in the records of the Commission on Revision of the Federal Appellate Court System by the Business Committee for Court Management and the "Institute for Court Management Intern Study" both criticize the centralized system-level control of the budgetary process and the lack of organizational budgets. In particular, the Business Committee rejected "the rather vague yardstick of court case-load volumes" as the basis for budgetary decisions.[12] Regarding the special problems of the D.C. Circuit, the commission records contain a memorandum, noting that "Judge Leventhal's testimony at our May 21, hearings underscores the difficulty of evaluating the actual burden of administrative appeals to the Court of Appeals. It seems clear that many NLRB [National

Labor Relations Board] cases involve little or no meaningful judge time, while some appeals from the FTC [Federal Trade Commission] or the EPA [Environmental Protection Agency] may be enormously complicated and time consuming.''[13] Several judges who have sat as visiting judges on the D.C. Circuit have noted similar distinctions in letters.[14] The fact that this evidence existed and that a number of diverse parties apparently agreed on the problems of system-level management did not seem to convince national-level policymakers of the need to take action.

Conclusion

Indeed, one or more circuits within the system of federal circuit courts of appeals are sufficiently unlike other system subunits so that individual organizational analysis is needed in order to understand their operations along with the systemwide perspective. In particular, the D.C. Circuit operations, structure, personnel, work load, and relationship to other units of government cannot be adequately understood as exactly like, or comparable to, other courts. There are a variety of ways in which system-level variables alone are inadequate to describe the operations of these different organizations. While case-mix difficulty is a distinguishing characteristic for the D.C. Circuit, task-environment factors may be more important in other courts.

The purpose of this chapter is not merely to suggest that the D.C. Circuit is somehow different from other circuit courts. The D.C. Circuit analysis does, however, demonstrate that different courts are not merely similar squares in an organizational chart of the federal judiciary. They are differing organizations that have qualitatively different management problems and resource needs. The discussion of the D.C. Circuit casts the differences in high relief. The Thompson organization-theory and behavior approach provides a conceptual framework for thinking about the important differences between courts as organizations and the implications of those differences in terms of resource allocation. It suggests the need for sufficient managerial independence and flexibility to deal with those problems.

The study also indicates why some difficulties exist in applying these organizational differences to policy decisions. The interviews and other data suggest two possible reasons. First, the history and lore of judicial administration oppose any decentralization of management, and this is particularly true of judicial-budgeting matters. Unification of court systems has become, in many respects, an end as opposed to a means to an end. Second, the agenda for decision makers at the system level is very different from that of the organization-level personnel. The national policy-level decision makers are concerned with system development, system planning, training of system personnel, and improving the relationship between the judicial system as a whole and the legislative and executive branches.

What next? From a scholarly standpoint, what is needed are more studies of the management problems of individual courts. These should be studies of courts as organizations. The Thompson approach is a useful one. On practitioner levels there are at least two recommendations. First, it is important to develop organizational budgets so that budgeting can be used as a management tool in the judiciary as it is in other organizations, both public and private. The fact that organizational budgets exist does not mean that system-level managers have to decentralize all or most of the decision making. It merely means that the current system is vastly oversimplified and unrealistic. Second, while it is important to continue to collect and employ the type of data developed and analyzed by the AO, it is also necessary to develop information that can be used to assess the performance of courts as organizations in light of their peculiar individual problems and circumstances. Both types of analysis ought to be used to determine where judicial resources are to be used and how effectively current resources are being managed.

Notes

1. In fact, the form in which budgets are submitted to Congress does not separate costs for circuit courts of appeals from federal district courts. Not only do the figures not permit knowledge of the costs for a particular court but also they do not provide information for all district courts or all circuit courts.

2. This formula was communicated by three of the interviewees.

3. If the board directors of the FJC directs, the center will do any research, but several interviewees confirmed that it is rare that studies are done for individual courts.

4. The few notable exceptions include Heydebrand (1977) and Saari (1976).

5. Biographical data is drawn from Chase et al. (1976) and Marquis (1979).

6. This study is based on interviews conducted from June 1979 to February 1980 with eight of ten judges, regular and senior, sitting

on the U.S. Court of Appeals for the D.C. Circuit. One judge responded briefly in writing to the questions; one other judge did not respond personally but made his three law clerks available. Relatively little reliance was placed on the clerks' comments except to confirm comments made by the judges.

7. Figures given by respondents varied between 82 and 92 percent, depending upon the particular period the judge had in mind.

8. Organizational boundary spanners interviewed included the present and past Chief Judge, the Circuit Executive, the present and past Chief Staff Counsel, and an interviewee in the Clerk's Office.

9. System-level administators interviewed included the Director of the FJC, the Administrative Assistant to the Chief Justice of the United States, the Deputy Comptroller of the AO, and the Deputy to the Chief of the Statistical Analysis and Reports Section of the AO.

10. Docket data were drawn from the Administrative Office's *Management Statistics for U.S. Courts* and the *Annual Report of the Director,* Administrative Office of the U.S. Courts, for the period 1 July 1969 through 30 June 1979.

11. The term *gross case processing volume* is taken from the FJC's Appellate Court Caseweight Project. The project gave up its effort to develop a systemwide weighted docket system for work load analysis.

12. "Review of the Federal Judicial Budgeting Process by the Business Committee for Court Administration" (1971, p. 34) is in the records of the Commission on Revision of the Federal Appellate Court System, National Archives, Washington, D.C. The members of the committee were J.W. Ball of ATT, H.M. Goern of ALCOA, and D.H. Ross of Allied Chemical. The other study noted, "Institute for Court Management Intern Study of Federal District Courts and U.S. Courts of Appeal" (1971), is also in the records in the archives collection on the commission. Other documents reaching similar conclusions in the commission records are Memorandum, Robert J. Martineau, circuit executive, to M.C. Matthes, chief judge, 12 April 1973; and Jack B. Weinstein, judge, to Irving Kaufman, chief judge, 11 January 1974.

13. Memorandum, Arthur Hellman to A. Leo Levin, 9 July 1974, in records of the commission. The reference is to the transcript of testimony by Judge Harold Leventhal before the commission on 21 May.

14. William H. Hastie, senior circuit judge, to David L. Bazelon, chief judge, 23 February 1976; Edward Lumbard, judge, to David L. Bazelon, 9 March 1976; and Elbert P. Tuttle to David L. Bazelon, 23 February 1976.

References

ABA Standards Relating to Court Organization. 1974. Chicago: American Bar Association.

Bazelon, David L. 1971. "New Gods for Old: 'Efficient' Courts in a Democratic Society." 46 *New York University Law School* 653.

Berkson, Larry C., Steven W. Hays, and Susan J. Carbon, eds. 1977. *Managing the State Courts*. St. Paul: West Publishing Co.

Chase, Harold et al. 1976. *Biographical Dictionary of the Federal Judiciary*. Detroit: Gale Research Co.

Churchman, C. West. 1968. *The Systems Approach*. New York: Dell Publishing Co.

Commission on Revision of the Federal Appellate Court System. 1975. *Structure and Internal Processes—Recommendations for Change*. Washington, D.C.: Government Printing Office.

————. 1973. *The Geographic Boundaries of the Several Judicial Circuits—Recommendation*. Washington, D.C.

Ebersole, Joseph L. 1973. "Planning and Conducting a Court Study." Unpublished mimeograph, Federal Judicial Center, Washington, D.C.

Fish, Peter G. 1973. *The Politics of Federal Judicial Administration*. Princeton, N.J.: Princeton University Press.

Frankfurter, Felix, and James Landis. 1928. *The Business of the Supreme Court*. New York: Macmillan Co.

Friesen, Ernest, Jr.; Edward C. Gallas; and Nesta M. Gallas. 1971. *Managing the Courts*. Indianapolis: Bobbs-Merrill.

Gazell, James A. 1978. *The Future of State Court Management*. Port Washington, N.Y.: Kennikat Press.

Goldman, Sheldon, and Thomas P. Jahnige. 1971. "Systems Analysis and Judicial System: Potential and Limitations." 3 *Polity* 334.

————. 1976. *The Federal Courts as a Political System, 2d ed*. New York: Harper & Row.

Goldman, Sheldon, and Austin Sarat, eds. 1978. *American Court Systems: Readings in Judicial Process and Behavior*. San Francisco: W.H. Freeman & Co.

Heydebrand, Wolf V. 1977. "The Context of Public Bureaucracies: An Organizational Analysis of Federal District Courts." 11 *Law and Society Review* 759.

Klein, Fannie. 1977. *Federal and State Court Systems: A Guide*. Cambridge, Mass.: Ballinger Publishers.

Marquis. 1979. *Who's Who in American Law, 2d ed*. Chicago: Marguis Who's Who.

Marvell, Thomas P. 1978. *Appellate Courts and Lawyers: Information Gathering in the Adversary System*. Westport, Conn.: Greenwood Press.

Meador, Daniel. 1974. *Appellate Courts: Staff and Process in the Crisis of Volume*. St. Paul: West Publishing Co.

Richardson, Richard, and Kenneth Vines. 1970. *The Politics of Federal Courts: Lower Courts in the United States*. Boston: Little, Brown & Co.

Rivlin, Alice M. 1971. *Systematic Thinking for Social Action*. Washington, D.C.: The Brookings Institution.

Rourke, Francis E. 1969. *Bureaucracy, Politics, and Public Policy*. Boston: Little, Brown & Co.

Saari, David J. 1976. "Modern Court Management: Trends in Court Organization Concepts—1976." 2 *Justice System Journal* 19.

Schubert, Glendon. 1974. *Judicial Policy Making*. Glenview, Ill.: Scott Foresman & Co.

Seidman, Harold. 1976. *Politics, Position and Power: The Dynamics of Federal Organization*, 2d ed. New York: Oxford University Press.

Sheldon, Charles H. 1974. *The American Judicial Process: Models and Approaches*. New York: Harper & Row.

Thompson, James D. 1967. *Organizations in Action*. New York: McGraw-Hill.

Vanderbilt, Arthur T. 1949. *Minimum Standards of Judicial Administration: A Survey of the Extent to Which the Standards of the American Bar Association for Improving the Administration of Justice Have Been Accepted throughout the Country*. New York: Law Center of the University of New York.

Wheeler, Russell R., and Howard R. Whitcomb, eds. 1977. *Judicial Administration: Text and Readings*. Englewood Cliffs, N.J.: Prentice-Hall.

Index

Index

Abraham, Henry, 108
Access (to courts), 18, 61–62, 67–68, 72–73
Adjudication: alternatives to, 21–22, 61–73 passim; decline of adversariness in, 3, 21–26; interest-group activity and, 19–20; and judicial capacity, 4, 34–39, 46–47. *See also* Judicial process; Litigation
Administrative Office of the United States Courts (AO), 175, 198–204, 206–207
Administrative Procedure Act of 1946, 24
Adversariness. *See* Adjudication; Judicial process
Alabama, 104, 178
Alaska, 129
Alaska Judicial Council, 129
Allen, John, 175
Alternatives to court, 5, 21–22, 25, 61–73. *See also* Dispute resolution; Mediation
American Bar Association, 1, 100, 196
American Law Institute, 54
Arbitration. *See* Mediation
Archbald, Robert W., 109
Arizona, 10, 153, 161, 162, 165–166, 178; Intermediate Court of Appeals, 161; State Supreme Court, 163–166
Arkansas, 104, 178
Askin, Frank, 47, 53
Atkins, Burton, 157, 159
Atlanta, Georgia, 64

Baar, Carl, 12
Bar polls, 126, 128–130, 132
Barron, Jerome, 47, 50–51, 54
Bayh, Birch, 112
Berger, Raoul, 111
Bickel, Alexander, 32, 140, 145

Blair, Nora, 154–155, 157
Blumberg, Abraham, 122–124
Bork, Robert, 53
Brandeis, Louis, 5
Brooklyn Dispute Resolution Center, 64, 66
Brooklyn Felony Mediation Project, 69
Brown v. *Board of Education,* 5, 44
Burger, Warren E., 10, 11, 38, 146, 171

Caldiera, Gregory A., 10
California Commission on Judicial Performance, 115–116
California Judicial Qualifications Commission, 94, 104
Canon, Bradley, 157, 159
Cardozo, Benjamin, 54, 57
Carswell, G. Harrold, 110
Carter, Jimmy, 23, 108
Case loads: and calculation of work load, 155–157, 162–163, 166; changes in federal courts, 176–178; forecasting of, 172–174; impact of changes in court structure and jurisdiction, 137–150, 153–166. *See also* Litigation
Casper, Gerhard P., 145
Chandler, Stephen, 109–110
Chase, Samuel, 109
Churchman, C. West, 197
Circuit Court Act of 1891, 10, 138, 140, 143, 145, 148–149
Colorado, 125, 129, 154, 178
Colorado Committee on Judicial Performance, 129
Commission on Judicial Disabilities and Tenure (Tydings Bill, S1506), 111, 113
Commission on Revision of the Federal Appellate Court System, 204

Connecticut, 178
Cooper, Phillip J., 12–13
Court management, 11–13; and
  judicial impact statements, 11–12,
  171–181; organization theory and,
  199–200, 205–206; systems
  analysis and, 196–199, 205–206.
  See also Court organization.
Court on Judicial Conduct and
  Disability (S1873), 112–113
Court organization (models of), 12;
  compared, 188–192; corporate,
  186–187; federal, 187–188;
  franchise, 184–186; nonunified,
  183–184; unified, 183–184
Court unification. See Court
  organization
Courts: access to, 18, 61–62, 67–68,
  72–73; alternatives to, 21–22,
  61–73; capacity of, 4, 31–39,
  46–47, 49; as discrete
  organizations, 195–196, 199–200,
  205–206; functions of, 34–38, 57;
  legitimacy of, 3, 26–27, 31, 37;
  management of, 171–181;
  organization of, 183–192; as
  system components, 195–199,
  205–206. See also Judicial
  process
Criminal Justice Act of 1964, 177
Cruikshanks, Randall L., 8
Culver, John, 8

Daniels, Stephen, 45, 50
Davis, Kenneth, 47, 50–51
D.C. Circuit Court of Appeals. See
  United States Court of Appeals
De Bruler, Roger, 122
De Concini, Dennis, 112
Delahay, Mark H., 109
Delaware, 101, 104, 178
Denver Custody Mediation Project,
  64, 68
Diamond, Bernard, 52
Dispute resolution: adjudication and,
  35–36; nonadversarial judicial
  alternatives, 5–6, 21–22, 61–73;
nonjudicial institutions and, 4,
  18–19. See also Mediation
Dispute Resolution Act of 1980, 22,
  61
Dissent: on state supreme courts,
  157–159, 164–165; on U.S.
  Supreme Court, 144–145, 148
Douglas, William O., 109–110
Dubois, Philip L., 79

Ebersole, Joseph L., 195
Elliott, Ward E.Y., 26
English, George W., 109
Environmental Protection Agency
  (U.S.), 205
Evarts, William, 139

Federal Judicial Center (FJC), 23,
  65, 122, 173, 198–199, 206–207
Federal Rules of Civil Procedure
  (FRCP), 23–24, 54
Federal Trade Commission, 205
Flanders, Steven, 174
Flango, Victor, 154–155, 157
Florida, 62, 130; State Supreme
  Court, 156
Ford, Gerald R., 109–110
Frankfurter, Felix, 138, 140,
  144–145
Freund Committee, 137, 144

Gignoux, Edward, 122
Glick, Henry, 157, 159
Glueck, Sheldon, 52, 54–55
Goldman, Nathan, 7–8
Goldman, Sheldon, 196
Groot, Roger, 157, 159
Guterman, James H., 126, 129, 132

Halpern, Stephen, 144–146
Hamilton, Alexander, 108
Haney, Craig, 5
Hauk, A. Andrew, 115
Hawaii, 104
Haynesworth, Clement F., Jr., 110
Henderson, Thomas A., 12
Heumann, Milton, 123

Holland, Kenneth M., 2–4
Horowitz, Donald, 32–34, 47
Humphreys, West, 108

Illinois, 101, 104, 130, 178
Impeachment (of judges), 8, 93, 108–111, 117. *See also* Judicial discipline and removal
Intermediate court of appeals (state), 10–11; case study of Arizona, 161–166; effect on appeal rate, 154–155; and supreme court dissent rate, 157–159; and supreme court work load, 153–157, 159–166; and supreme court policymaking, 153, 157–166

Jacob, Herbert, 122
Jahnige, Thomas P., 196
Jaros, Dean, 157, 159
Judges: accountability of, 6–7, 79–80, 107, 121, 131; discipline and removal of, 93–104, 107–117; education of, 128–129; evaluation of, 121–132; functions of, 3, 122–124; independence of, 6–8, 79–80, 100, 107–108, 115, 131; nonjudicial duties of, 122–124; selection of, 79–89; skills of, 122–124, 127–129
Judges Bill of 1925, 10, 138, 143–148
Judicial accountability. *See* Judges
Judicial capacity, 31–39; adjudication and, 34–39; criticisms of, 4, 33–35, 46–47; defense of, 4, 35–39, 49; definition of, 33; social-policy cases and, 34–36
Judicial Conduct and Disability Commission (Nunn Bill, S1423), 112–113
Judicial conduct organizations. *See* Judicial disciplinary commissions
Judicial Conference of the United States, 8, 103, 111–112, 114, 198, 200

Judicial councils (federal), 8, 103, 108–109, 112–117
Judicial Councils Reform and Judicial Conduct and Disability Act of 1980 (S1873), 8, 103, 108, 112–114, 116–117
Judicial disciplinary commissions (state), 93–104, 107, 115–116
Judicial discipline and removal: in the federal system, 8, 93, 103–104, 107–117; in the states, 7–8, 93–104
Judicial elections, 5–6, 79–85, 87, 93. *See also* Judicial selection
Judicial impact statements, 11–12, 171–181; purposes of, 171; methodological difficulties of, 172–176; utility of, for court management, 176–181
Judicial independence. *See* Judges
Judicial performance evaluation, 9, 121–132; bar polls and, 126, 128–130, 132; citizens and, 126–127, 129–130; and measurement of work quality, 125–127; and measurement of work quantity, 124–125; need for, 121; new methods of, 129–130; political context of, 131–132
Judicial process: decline of adversariness in, 21–26; inquisitorial model of, 20–21; public support for, 26–27; traditional adversary model of, 17–18. *See also* Adjudication
Judicial Reform Act (Tydings Bill, S1506), 113
Judicial selection, 6–7; debate over, 79–80; elections and, 79–85, 87–93; merit plan of, 86–87; studies of, 81–84, 87–88
Judicial Tenure Act (Nunn Bill, S1423), 112–113
Judiciary Act of 1789, 108
Judiciary Act of 1916, 140

Kagan, Robert, 158

Kansas City, Missouri, 64
Kantrowitz, Arthur, 55
Kennedy, Edward, 112
Kentucky, 178
Kerwin, Cornelius, 11–12

Landis, James M., 138–140,
   144–145
Law Enforcement Assistance
   Administration (LEAA), 22
Lawson, Harry, 192
Lawyers: as arbitrators, 63; behavior
   of, 65–66; as evaluators of
   judicial quality, 126, 128–130,
   132; on judicial disciplinary
   commissions, 94–100; as problem
   solvers, 21; training of, 51
Legal Realists, 43
Levin, Hannah, 47, 53
Litigation: increases in, 18–21,
   137–150 passim; judicial-decisions
   promoting, 139, 143, 146;
   legislation as source of, 11, 19,
   139, 146, 171–172; regulatory
   agencies as sources of, 11–12,
   176–177; social and economic
   factors affecting, 11–12,
   138–139, 142–143, 145–146. *See
   also* Adjudication
Los Angeles County, 18
Louderback, Harold, 109

Macaulay, Stewart, 21
McEwen, Craig A., 5–6
Maiman, Richard J., 5–6
Maine, 178; small-claims mediation
   in, 64, 67, 69–70
March of Dimes, 191
Marvell, Thomas, 154
Maryland, 178; state supreme court
   of, 157
Massachusetts, 18, 104
Mediation (and arbitration), 5–6,
   61–73; coercive pressures in,
   70–71; compared to arbitration,
   62–63, 68, 73; compared to
   courts, 64; current uses of, 63;

costs of, 66–68, 72; due process
   protections in, 71; impact on
   access to justice, 67–68, 72–73;
   impact on court case loads and
   delay, 65–66; impact on quality of
   justice, 68–71, 73;
   implementation of settlements,
   69–70
Meehl, Paul, 45
Meidinger, Errol E., 126, 129, 132
Merit plan (of judicial selection),
   6–7, 86–87
Michigan, 62
Miller, Arthur, 47, 50–51, 54
Missouri Plan. *See* Merit plan;
   Judicial selection
Moynihan, Daniel, 49, 51

National Academy of Sciences, 55,
   171–172, 174
National Association for the
   Advancement of Colored People
   (NAACP), 19, 116
National Center for State Courts, 23
National Court of Appeals, 10, 138,
   148–149
National Foundation for Infantile
   Paralysis, 186, 191
National Labor Relations Board,
   204–205
Neighborhood Justice Centers,
   64–65, 68–69
Nejelski, Paul, 176
New Deal Era, 146–147
New Jersey, 130
New Mexico, 101
New York, 94; Commission on
   Judicial Conduct, 104; Court on
   the Judiciary, 94, 103
Nixon, Richard M., 110
North Carolina Supreme Court, 157
Nunn Bill. *See* Judicial Tenure Act
   (S1423)
Nunn, Sam, 112

Ohio, 104, 125, 130, 191
Oklahoma, 104

O'Neil, William, 191
Oregon, 154

Peck, James H., 109
Pennsylvania, 63, 130
Perlstein, J.J., 7–8
Pettigrew, Thomas, 53
Philadelphia, 62
Pickering, John, 108
Porter, Mary Cornelia, 140
Posner, Richard N., 145
Pound Conference, 2, 61
Pound, Roscoe, 1, 2, 61, 67, 186

Reagan, Ronald, 177
Republican National Party, 131
Retention elections. *See* Judicial
    elections
Rhode Island, 104
Ritter, Halsted L., 109–110
Ritter, Willis, 109–110
Rivlin, Alice, 52
Ryan, John Paul, 9, 122–123, 127

Sarat, Austin, 4
Science Court, 55
Shapiro, Martin, 123
Sills, David, 186
Small-claims court, 23, 64–70
    passim
Social science (court use of), 5;
    advisory juries and, 54; burden of
    proof and, 50–51, 56; court-
    appointed experts and, 52–54;
    criticisms of, 44–48; defense of,
    47–49, 56–57; masters and,
    53–54; procedural safeguards for
    use of, 50, 56; science-court
    proposal for, 55; social-science
    institute, 54–55; training of court
    personnel for, 51–52
South Carolina, 104
Speedy Trial Act of 1974, 177,
    179–180
State supreme courts: effects of
    intermediate appellate courts on,

10–11, 153–166; and judicial
    discipline, 94, 100–102
Stevens, Robert, 116
Stevens v. *Commission on Judicial
    Qualifications,* 104
Stookey, John, 10–11
Stott, E. Keith, Jr., 125
Study Group on the Caseload of the
    Supreme Court. *See* Freund
    Committee
Swayne, Charles H., 109
Systems analysis, 196–199

Taft, William Howard, 143–144
Thompson, James D., 185, 191,
    199–202, 205–206
Tribe, Lawrence, 46
Tydings, Joseph W., 111–112
Tydings Bill. *See* Judicial Reform
    Act (S1506)

United States Court of Appeals, 139,
    195; for the District of Columbia
    Circuit, 12–13, 196; backgrounds
    of judges on, 201; organizational
    analysis of, 200–205; unique role
    of, 201–202; inadequacies of
    statistical data concerning,
    203–204
United States Congress, 8, 10–11,
    22, 61, 103, 107, 109, 111–112,
    138–140, 143, 146–148, 179,
    196–199, 202, 206
United States Supreme Court, 5, 19,
    22, 24, 38, 109–110, 200;
    activism of, 143, 147–149; effect
    of reforms upon caseload of, 10,
    139–150; focus of scholars on,
    31–32; increasing caseload of,
    137–141, 143–146; use of social
    science by, 47, 51, 53–54
United States Constitution, 108,
    111–112
United States Solicitor General, 53
U.S. Senate Judiciary Committee,
    114; Subcommittee on

Improvements in Judicial
  Machinery, 111–112

Vanderbilt, Arthur T., 198
Venice MarVista, California, 64
Vera Institute, 64
Vines, Kenneth, 144–146
Volcansek, Mary L., 6–7

Warren, Earl, 19, 24

Washington, 63
Washington, D.C., 107, 178, 201
Watergate, 107, 130
Wellington, Harry, 32
West Virginia, 104, 161
Will, Hubert L., 174
Work load. *See* Case loads
World War II, 145, 149–150

About the Contributors

Carl Baar received the M.A. and Ph.D. from the University of Chicago and is associate professor of politics at Brock University in Ontario, Canada. He is the author of *Separate but Subservient: Court Budgeting in the American States* (1975) and several articles on court reform and judicial administration. From 1974–1977, Professor Baar served as editor in chief of the *Justice System Journal: A Management Review*.

Gregory A. Caldeira received the Ph.D. from Princeton University, 1978, and is associate professor of political science at the University of Iowa. He has published several articles on judicial politics, the politics of crime, and elections in edited volumes and journals such as the *American Journal of Political Science, Law and Society Review, Political Science Quarterly, Justice System Journal,* and *Judicature.*

Phillip J. Cooper received the M.A. (1975) and Ph.D. (1978) from the Maxwell School, Syracuse University. He is currently assistant professor of political science at Georgia State University in Atlanta. Professor Cooper's teaching and research interests are in the areas of public law and public administration.

Randal L. Cruikshanks received the Ph.D. from the University of Oregon (1968) and is a professor of political science at the California Polytechnic State University, San Luis Obispo. He has coauthored several articles on judicial accountability and is currently doing research in the area of energy policy.

John H. Culver received the Ph.D. from the University of New Mexico (1975) and is an associate professor of political science at the California Polytechnic State University, San Luis Obispo. He is coauthor of *Power and Politics in California* and is currently doing research on the politics in state legal systems.

Nathan Goldman received the M.A. and Ph.D. from Johns Hopkins University and is assistant professor of government at the University of Texas, Austin. His scholarly interests include diverse topics such as judicial discipline and the politics of scientific policymaking. He is also coauthor of a forthcoming book on administrative law.

Craig Haney is an assistant professor of psychology at the University of California, Santa Cruz. Dr. Haney received the M.A. and Ph.D. in psychology from Stanford University and the J.D. from Stanford Law School. He has published widely on the criminal-justice system and is currently preparing a book on the psychological and legal consequences of imprisonment.

Thomas A. Henderson received the Ph.D. from Columbia University (1968) and is vice-president of the Institute for Economic and Policy Studies in Alexandria, Virginia. He is the author or coauthor of three books on the policy process and several articles published in journals such as the *Journal of Politics, American Journal of Political Science, Legislative Studies Quarterly,* and *Urban Affairs Quarterly.*

Kenneth M. Holland is an assistant professor of political science at the University of Vermont. He received the M.A. (1971) and Ph.D. (1978) from the University of Virginia and the University of Chicago respectively. He has contributed articles on judicial administration to journals such as the *Justice System Journal* and *Law and Policy Quarterly.* He previously taught political science at the University of Wisconsin—Madison and the University of Chicago.

Cornelius M. Kerwin is assistant professor and director of doctoral programs in the School of Government and Public Administration of American University. He teaches courses in court systems, regulatory processes, and policy analysis. His articles have appeared in the *Harvard Journal on Legislation, Policy Studies Journal,* and a number of books. He is currently working on a book on the performance and reform of the federal regulatory process.

Richard J. Maiman is associate professor of political science in the Department of Political Science at the University of Southern Maine. He is the recipient, with Craig McEwen, of a National Science Foundation grant to conduct an empirical study of mediation in Maine's small-claims courts. Some of this research has appeared in the *Maine Law Review.*

Craig A. McEwen received the A.M. (1969) and Ph.D. (1975) in sociology from Harvard University. Since 1975, Professor McEwen has been a member of the faculty of Bowdoin College where he is associate professor of sociology and chair of the Department of Sociology. He has contributed to the *Annual Review of Sociology* and has conducted other research on vocational education.

Jolanta Juszkiewicz Perlstein received the M.A. (1975) and Ph.D (1980) in political science from Northwestern University. She has served as a staff assistant in the Office for Improvements in the Administration of Justice (U.S. Department of Justice) and has taught political science at Northwestern University and the University of Illinois, Chicago Circle.

John Paul Ryan is director of research of the American Judicature Society. He received the Ph.D. from Northwestern University in 1972 and then taught at Vassar College before assuming a position as a senior research associate at the Judicature Society in 1975; he was named director of research in 1980. Dr. Ryan has authored or coauthored two books and several articles examining various aspects of the judicial process.

Austin Sarat is associate professor of political science and chairman of the Department of Political Science at Amherst College. He is the author or coauthor of three books and more than two-dozen articles in scholarly journals on topics related to the judicial process and court reform. Professor Sarat received the M.A. (1970) and Ph.D. (1973) from the University of Wisconsin—Madison.

John A. Stookey received the Ph.D. from the University of Kentucky (1977) and is associate professor of political science at Arizona State University. He has published many articles and monographs on a variety of topics including remedies for the victim of crimes, the deinstitutionalization of status offenders, juvenile delinquency, and judicial behavior. His current research project is the creation of a quantitative history of court systems in the United States.

Mary L. Volcansek received the Ph.D. from Texas Tech University (1973) and is associate professor of political science at Florida International University. She has authored several articles on the subjects of judicial selection and recruitment and judicial administration. Her current research includes continuing work on judicial elections and a study of the European Court of Justice.

About the Editor

Philip L. Dubois received the M.A. (1974) and Ph.D. (1978) in political science from the University of Wisconsin—Madison. He is the author of *From Ballot to Bench: Judicial Elections and the Quest for Accountability* (1980) and several articles on state judicial selection that have appeared in journals such as *Law and Society Review,* the *Journal of Politics,* and *Law and Policy Quarterly.* He is currently an assistant professor of political science at the University of California, Davis, where he teaches courses in constitutional law, judicial process, and U.S. government. During 1979 and 1980, Dr. Dubois served as a Judicial Fellow at the Federal Judicial Center.

Date Due

Cat. No. 23 233

Printed in U.S.A.

BRODART, INC.